THIS ORIGINAL AND GROUNDBREAKING BOOK DISPELS MYTHS THAT LEAD TO SPIRITUAL AND FINANCIAL BONDAGE WITH PROFOUND TRUTHS THAT WILL SET YOU FREE.

TESTIMONIALS

"Wise, universal truths beautifully permeate this book—a true illustration of the law of the harvest."

STEPHEN R. COVEY, author of National #1 bestsellers
The 7 Habits of Highly Effective People and
The 8th Habit: From Effectiveness to Greatness

"This book is about proper stewardship of our resources. The guidance provided is based on Biblical principles that, unfortunately, have too often been ignored. The wise reader will embrace this message!"

WILLIAM D. DANKO, Ph.D., co-author of
The Millionaire Next Door

"This book beautifully blends Christian values and the principles of financial success into a fun, entertaining read. You will be glad you read this book."

RICHARD PAUL EVANS, author of the
New York Times #1 bestselling novel *The Christmas Box*

"Many books are skimmed, some are read, and a few are studied. This book is the latter. It is inspirational, motivational, and educational. You will return to it often."

CHARLES T. JONES, author of
Life is Tremendous

"This book combines sound finan............................ord, and great stories of people of intere

SUSAN BLACK, R

"I found the book insightful and a very balanced look at the principles of financial prosperity. I love the emphasis upon seeking first the Kingdom of God. I really think the illustrations are excellent."

NATE FUCHS, Minister

"This is a warm, wonderful book full of timeless truths you can apply to every area of your life."

BRIAN TRACY, author of
The Way To Wealth

"WOW! What a great book. Cameron points out choices that determine success or disaster for you, your family, and our country. Every student should be required to read and study *Does Your Bag Have Holes?*. This book is not just a treasure to be discovered, but ideas on which we should all take action. It's easy to read and I guarantee that you will love and profit from it!"

DANIEL C. FALLER, Founder/President of the
Apartment Owners Association

"The personal application of these 24 timeless truths will enable you to achieve breakthrough financial and spiritual results in your life."

HENRY MARSH, 4-time Olympic runner and author of
The Breakthrough Factor

"This book can help anyone replace damaging myths with Biblical truths that will set them on the right course for not confusing the pursuit of money with true success."

RICH DEVOS, Billionaire, owner of the
Orlando Magic, and *co-Founder of Amway*

"Grab a pen and some paper because as you read this book, ideas on how to improve the way you live and work will come to you. Whether in business or in your personal life this book will help you to be a better person."

ED MCCULLOCH, Photographer

"This book contains analogies and short stories that will touch your heart and mind. After reading this book, I see a new potential for myself and others. It is liberating as a Christian to know that business and religion can work hand in hand and that one can be financially independent and spiritually free. I recommend sharing this message with all your loved ones."

LEE GILLIE, High School Science Teacher

"This book is full of compelling real life stories that have motivated and inspired me to set new goals towards achieving true financial and spiritual wealth. The truths in this work taught by exposing the myths that wait to engulf people in their quest for financial freedom will be a blessing in my life for years to come."

DR. SCOTT LOHNER, Ophthalmologist

"For over 30 years my company has taught tens of thousands of individuals the keys to financial success coupled with the principles of human happiness. After reading *Does Your Bag Have Holes?*, I wish I could have issued it as a core textbook to each and every student of the past three decades."

G. KENT MANGELSON, President of
Wealth of America Training Centers, Ltd.

DOES YOUR BAG HAVE HOLES?

24 Truths That Lead to Financial and Spiritual Freedom

CAMERON C. TAYLOR

MOUNT LANAI
PUBLISHING
2007

Does Your Bag Have Holes? is a registered trademark of the Does Your Bag Have Holes?
Foundation. All images and phrases marked ™ are trademarks or registered trademarks of the
Does Your Bag Have Holes? Foundation.
428 E. Thunderbird Road # 504, Phoenix, AZ 85022
Phone: 1-877-No-Holes (664-6537) Fax: 1-480-393-4432
CustomerService@DoesYourBagHaveHoles.org
http://www.DoesYourBagHaveHoles.org

ISBN-13: 978-0-9796861-0-8
ISBN-10: 0-9796861-0-5

Library of Congress Control Number: 2007904034

Printed in the United States of America

PERMISSIONS
Grateful acknowledgment is made to the following publishers and individuals who granted
permission to reprint the following copyrighted material:

Scripture quotations marked New International Version are taken from the HOLY BIBLE,
NEW INTERNATIONAL VERSION®. NIV®. Copyright © 1973, 1978, 1984 by
International Bible Society. Used by permission of Zondervan. All rights reserved.

Scripture quotations marked English Standard Version are from The Holy Bible, English
Standard Version®, Copyright © 2001 by Crossway Bibles, a publishing ministry of Good
News Publishers. Used by permission. All rights reserved.

Scripture quotations marked New King James Version are taken from the New King James
Version®. Copyright © 1982 by Thomas Nelson, Inc. Used by permission. All rights reserved.

Scripture quotations marked New American Standard Bible taken from the New American
Standard Bible®, Copyright © 1960, 1962, 1963, 1968, 1971, 1972, 1973, 1975, 1977, 1995
by The Lockman Foundation. Used by permission. (www.Lockman.org)

Scripture quotations marked Good News Translation are from the Good News Translation in
Today's English Version- Second Edition Copyright © 1992 by American Bible Society. Used
by permission.

Scripture quotations marked Contemporary English Version are from the Contemporary
English Version Copyright © 1991, 1992, 1995 by American Bible Society, Used by
permission.

Scripture quotations marked New Life Version are from the New Life Version Copyright ©
1969 by Christian Literature International.

PREFACE

Why I wrote this book

I felt inspired by God to write this book: He has directed my thoughts and words. While I was the one to put words on the page, I give all honor and praise for this work to God. I was merely an instrument in the hands of the Almighty. The power of this book comes from the truths it contains and the Holy Spirit teaching and impressing upon you the word of God.

Why I teach myths and truths

There are many false teachings and misunderstandings regarding spirituality and finances circulating in our society. I believe these misunderstandings are the cause of many serious problems such as divorce, bankruptcy, mistrust, and lack of faith. Myths are major tools used by Satan to keep people from building a lasting relationship with God and from experiencing all of God's gifts. To simply teach the correct spiritual and financial principles would be insufficient. Myths must be rejected and bad habits broken in order for truths and good habits to be acquired and established. This is the only way to ensure an ongoing and permanent change of conduct. Your ability to apply the principles of prosperity found in this book will be greatly enhanced as you understand each myth and replace it with truth.

Each chapter of this book begins with a myth and discusses its effects. Throughout the chapter, the myth is proven false and the true principle of prosperity is shared. Truths are taught through the words of the Bible, parables, stories, and illustrations. This book cites hundreds of Biblical scriptures which have a great power to uplift, inspire, and guide us in the way we should go. Those who lay hold upon the word of God will not be deceived by the cunning snares and traps set by the devil. The word of God will be a lamp unto your feet and a light unto your path.[1]

The parables in the book make profound truths simple and easy to understand and create powerful mental imagery and conceptual links to everyday life. Another effective teaching method is the use of stories. Stories have the unique power to carry a great amount of spirit and emotion. The stories shared in this book are designed to inspire you to improve, impress truths upon your mind, and provide examples to emulate. This book also contains dozens of powerful images that are intended to help you understand and remember the concepts. Images have an ability to communicate to our minds and souls in ways words cannot.

Why I use different Bible translations

I have referenced eleven different Bible translations throughout this book. I have done this for two reasons: First, the study of various translations can give further insight to the meaning of the Bible's original text. The original text of the Bible contains 11,280 unique words in Hebrew, Aramaic, and Greek. The English translations of the Bible only contain about 6,000 unique words. For example, in the New Testament there are seven different Greek words with slightly different meanings that are all translated into the single English word "servant." Second, often we think we know what a verse is saying because we have heard it many times. Viewing other translations can help us see a familiar scripture in a new light, revealing a deeper and/or alternative meaning. I hope the various translations will help you better understand God's truth.

The teachings throughout this book focus on principles taught and accepted by all Christian denominations—faith, prayer, humility, integrity, industry, and charity. While all the teachings are founded upon Biblical principles, there is nothing taught in this book unique to a particular denomination.

How to get the most out of this book

One of the best ways to learn something is to teach it to others. To help you internalize the concepts in this book, find friends and family members to join you in the reading of this book. As you read it, share your thoughts and ideas with one another. Also, when there is a concept, parable, or story from the book that impacts you positively, find someone who is not reading the book and teach them the concept. By teaching others, the concept will be solidified in your mind and you will uplift the person you share it with.

"A teacher affects eternity; he can never tell where his influence stops."
–Henry Adams

TABLE OF CONTENTS

OVERVIEW

WHAT IS PROSPERITY?

You can obtain great wealth and financial abundance without obtaining prosperity. For example, both a drug dealer and a prostitute can achieve wealth and financial abundance, but they are not truly prosperous. On the other hand, there are those who keep the Ten Commandments, pay their tithes, and strive to live righteously but have not learned and applied certain financial principles and thus struggle financially and never achieve prosperity. "Thou shalt remember the LORD thy God: for it is He that giveth thee power to get wealth."[1] Financial abundance is the result of work and the application of certain financial laws. People who are truly prosperous are financially independent (not necessarily wealthy) and live in accordance with God's laws. They are able to live the life God desires for them without relying on others financially.

Prosperity cannot be achieved by seeking money directly. As the Dali Lama taught, "Accumulation of wealth for the sake of wealth alone is self-defeating. Only in seeing one's work as a calling, a means to serve a higher purpose, can we find true fulfillment."[2] Those who are truly prosperous do not set their hearts upon riches. They love the Lord and recognize that all they have and are is a gift from Him. The prosperous use their financial resources to build the kingdom of God and care for His children by clothing the naked, feeding the hungry, and nourishing the sick.

THE 4 PRINCIPLES OF PROSPERITY™

How effective would you be if you were driving to an unfamiliar location with an inaccurate map? Chances are, if accurate directions were not obtained, the destination would never be reached. Many of us have been given bad directions to the destination of prosperity. If you desire to achieve prosperity, an accurate map of how to do so is essential. This book will address 24 myths (bad directions) that prevent prosperity. These myths are organized in relation to The Prosperity Model™ (map). The Prosperity Model™ illustrates the principles of prosperity as a tree (see illustration). Here is a brief overview of the model's components.

The roots of the tree represent the principle *Our Creator Gives Us All Good Things*. God is the supreme creator of the earth and the father of mankind. All we have and are is a gift from Him. Our power and growth comes by the hand of God, just as a tree receives its strength and nourishment from its roots.

The trunk of the tree represents the principle *Liberty is Given to All Men by Our Creator*. The Founding Fathers asserted in The Declaration of Independence that all men are endowed by their Creator with the unalienable right of liberty. Just as the tree trunk is an outgrowth of the roots, so is liberty given to us by God. Liberty is the right and power to act, believe, or express oneself in a manner of one's own choosing.

The splitting of the trunk into two branches represents the principle of choice. As a result of our God-given liberty, we have the power to make choices. The two main branches of the tree and the fruit of the tree represent the principle *Consequences Are the Results of Our Choices*. Each time we make a choice we are either moving toward freedom and prosperity or bondage and misery. Just as a tree may produce good or bad fruit, our choices will produce the good fruits of freedom and prosperity or the bad fruits of bondage and misery.

Liberty and freedom are often used as synonyms. In this book they are used to illustrate very different concepts. Liberty is given to all men and is the right to choose. Freedom is a possible result of our choices. For example, two people are looking for a place to swim when they come upon a sign that reads, "Danger! Whirlpool—No Swimming Allowed." Both of these people have the liberty to choose whether to swim here or not. One swimmer chooses to enter the water and is sucked in. As a result of his choice, he is now in bondage to the whirlpool. The other

THE PROSPERITY MODEL™

"And [the righteous] shall be like a tree planted by the rivers of water, that bringeth forth fruit in his season; his leaf shall not wither; and whatsoever he doeth shall prosper." –Psalms 1:3

CONSEQUENCE=
MISERY

CONSEQUENCE=
PROSPERITY

person chooses not to enter the water and as a result has the freedom to find another place to swim. Freedom results when we use our liberty correctly. Bondage results when we use our liberty incorrectly.

The fence surrounding the tree represents the principle *Government is Created by the People to Protect Our God-Given Rights*. The government is not to rule the people—the people are to rule the government. Government is illustrated as a protective fence with an armed soldier, separate from the tree, because the proper role of government is to protect mankind's God-given rights of life, liberty, and the pursuit of happiness. The government is the protector, not the grantor, of our rights. The proper role of government is to protect the right to pursue prosperity, not to grant prosperity.

THE 6 CHOICES OF PROSPERITY™

This book will also discuss 6 choices:

Choice 1:	Blame	or	Responsibility
Choice 2:	Pride	or	Humility
Choice 3:	Hypocrisy	or	Integrity
Choice 4:	Idleness	or	Industry
Choice 5:	Debt	or	Ownership
Choice 6:	Greed	or	Charity

The negative choices of blame, pride, hypocrisy, idleness, debt, and greed lead to bondage and misery. The positive choices of responsibility, humility, integrity, industry, ownership, and charity lead to freedom and prosperity.

The choices are illustrated by The Six Choices Model™ (see illustration). The six negative choices are represented as holes in our bag of prosperity, as taught the prophet Haggai: "Now therefore thus saith the LORD of hosts; Consider your ways. Ye have sown much, and bring in little; ye eat, but ye have not enough; ye drink, but ye are not filled with drink; ye clothe you, but there is none warm; and he

THE 6 CHOICES MODEL™

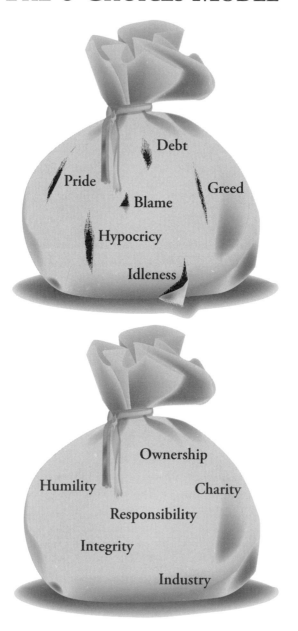

Does Your Bag Have Holes?™
Haggai 1:5–6

that earneth wages earneth wages to put it into a bag with holes."[3] Each portion of this scripture illustrates one of the 6 potential holes in the bag of prosperity.

Choice 1: Blame or Responsibility
Blame—"Consider Your Ways"

The person that is good at making excuses is rarely good at much else. Blame is a tool used by many to avoid taking responsibility. They are too busy considering the ways of others to consider their own ways.

Responsibility

If you kicked the person responsible for most of your troubles, you would not be able to sit for weeks. Everyone is responsible for his or her own actions. The story of your life is not written by what happens to you but by what you choose to make happen. The realization that you are responsible for your fate will produce a sense of power and drive that will lead you to make the choices resulting in the consequences you desire. Those who are responsible realize that living off others is a form of bondage, for if you take from a person the responsibility to care for himself or herself, you also take from him or her the opportunity to be free.

Choice 2: Pride or Humility
Pride—"Ye Clothe You, but There Is None Warm"

In the words of C.S. Lewis, "Pride gets no pleasure out of having something, only out of having more of it than the next man."[4] When clothes are no longer used for warmth but are instead used to build social status or to have finer clothes than others, pride enters our hearts and lives.

Humility

Humility is realizing our total dependence on God and that all we have and are is a gift from Him. A person who is humble is generous, grateful, and teachable. In the words of the Bengali poet Rabindranath Tagore, "We come nearest to the great when we are great in humility."

Choice 3: Hypocrisy or Integrity
Hypocrisy—"Ye Drink, but Ye Are Not Filled with Drink"

Hypocrisy is the result of our outward and inward appearance not coinciding. Haggai taught this with the metaphor of a person outwardly appearing to drink but not being filled with drink inwardly. The Lord condemned the Pharisees for hypocrisy, saying, "Even so ye also outwardly appear righteous unto men, but within ye are full of hypocrisy and iniquity."[5]

Integrity

Integrity is more than our beliefs aligning with our actions. Integrity is the adherence to truth. Surely Satan's actions align with his beliefs, but he is not a person of integrity, because his actions are not in accordance with truth. Integrity is also keeping one's word and commitments. The apostle James taught, "Let your 'yes' be 'yes' and your 'no' be 'no.'"[6]

Choice 4: Idleness or Industry
Idleness—"Ye Have Sown Much, and Bring in Little"

Doing the wrong kind of work is a form of idleness. There are many who work hard but produce little. There is a difference between being productive and being busy. Thus, some do sow much and bring in little.

Industry

Industry is the energetic devotion to a task or endeavor. Thomas Edison taught, "I never did anything worth doing by accident, nor did any of my inventions come by accident; they came by work." In seeking to achieve prosperity, there will be failures along the way. Failure is a part of learning and growing. Benjamin Franklin taught, "The man who does things makes mistakes but he never makes the biggest mistake of all—doing nothing." Prosperity is the result of industry.

Choice 5: Debt or Ownership
Debt—"Earneth Wages to Put It into a Bag with Holes"

When you have debt, it is like putting your money into a bag with holes. The wages that are earned go to the payment of interest instead of toward ownership.

Ownership

Ownership is required to truly be free and prosperous. For example, if you don't own your house, you either pay rent and thus are bound to a landlord, or you have a mortgage and are bound to the bank to pay interest as rent on the money you borrowed.

Choice 6: Greed or Charity
Greed—"Ye Eat, but Ye Have Not Enough"

Greed is an unsatisfiable desire. No matter how much a greedy person has it will never be enough. In the words of Haggai, the greedy "eat, but never have enough."[7]

Charity

Charity is the highest, noblest, strongest kind of love. It will motivate us to care for the needs of our fellow man. "If we will share what we have, many people's lives can be blessed, and what we have left will grow at a geometric rate."[8]

CONCLUSION

Prosperity and misery develop over time and are a result of our choices. Thus, there are varying levels of prosperity and misery. One who is prosperous is responsible, honest, humble, industrious, financially independent, and charitable. One who is miserable is irresponsible, proud, hypocritical, lazy, financially dependant, and greedy.

PRINCIPLE I:

OUR CREATOR GIVES US ALL GOOD THINGS

"Faith is the root of all good works."
–Daniel Wilson

MYTH 1

FAITH IS A CRUTCH FOR THE WEAK

Some people misunderstand faith as a piece of duct tape holding a broken tool together. This is incorrect. Faith is much more than a mending tool; it is a source of power and strength. Faith is to human life what gasoline is to a chainsaw. Gas is the power source for a chainsaw, which makes it productive and useful. If you attempt to cut something using a chainsaw empty of gasoline, the results will be meager. Faith is the fuel that powers the human engine. With faith you can move mountains, heal the sick, do "great wonders and miracles,"[1] and "nothing will be impossible unto you."[2]

5 ELEMENTS OF FAITH

Parable of the Virus Protection Software

Joe was thrilled to have received a brand new laptop for his birthday. His last computer was destroyed by a virus, and he had been hoping for another one for some time. To ensure that his new computer was protected he purchased and installed virus protection software.

A few weeks later, Joe received an e-mail forwarded from a close friend. The e-mail's content stated that it was virus free. When he attempted to open the e-mail the virus protection software flashed a warning stating that the e-mail contained a virus. Joe had two options: he could believe the e-mail's content, ignore the virus protection warning, and open the file, or he could follow the instructions from the software and delete the message. Believing the warning he deleted the e-mail. A few hours later Joe's friend called and reported that this e-mail had infected his computer with a virus and that the virus may have been unintentionally sent to Joe.

To utilize the power of faith, we must understand and apply five elements that make up faith. The parable of the virus protection software will be used to illustrate these elements of faith.

1. Information

The first element of faith is information. In the parable, the virus protection software provided the information warning that the e-mail contained a virus. In life, God has given us information through the Bible. The first step to finding faith in God is to hear His word, for "faith cometh by hearing."[3]

2. Belief

The second element of faith is to believe the information. The opposite of belief is doubt and where doubt is belief cannot be. Doubt and belief cannot exist at the same time. For faith to exist, you must believe the information is true. In the parable, the virus protection software provided Joe with the information that the e-mail contained a virus. The e-mail, on the other hand, contained information that may have caused Joe to doubt since the e-mail was from his friend and the text stated, "This E-mail Contains No Virus."

Which information should be believed—the information from the creator of the virus protection software or the information from the creator of the virus-infected e-mail? The most important step in making this decision is considering the source of the information. What better source could Joe have found than the manufacturer of the software designed to protect and keep his computer running smoothly? Just as the creators of viruses try to entice us to do things that will destroy or hinder the operation of our computers, Satan and the world attempt to persuade us to act in ways that would destroy or hinder the operation of our human machines.

God is the creator of the human machine and the best source of information on how to protect the human machine from infection that will destroy or hinder its operation. God has given us the Bible as the owner's manual for our protection and maintenance. If we believe God is our creator, then we should also believe that His words are the best source for our correct operation.

3. Desire/Hope for an Unseen Result

The third element of faith is a desire or hope for an unseen result. "Now faith is the substance of things hoped for . . ."[4] In the parable, Joe purchased the software with the hope that it would keep his laptop running smoothly.

Likewise, for there to be faith, the result must be unseen as "faith is ... the evidence of things not seen."[5] Once the result is apparent, faith is replaced by knowledge.

4. Action

The fourth element of faith is to act upon the information. In the parable, a choice was offered to Joe. The choice he made was to act upon the information from the virus protection software rather than ignore it. Since Joe trusted the manufacturer, he acted upon the direction it gave him. As the apostle James taught, ". . . I will shew thee my faith by my works."[6]

5. Truth

The fifth element of faith is truth. Information must be true or your faith will be in vain.[7] In the parable, when Joe's friend called to let him know his computer was infected, Joe knew that the information the software provided him was true. The fact that Joe's computer continued to run smoothly showed that the software was able to delete the virus and thus the software's claim that it could delete the virus was true. In relation to God, as we act upon God's word we will know that His word is true. As the apostle John taught, "If any man will do His will, he shall know of the doctrine, whether it be of God, or whether I speak of myself."[8]

One of the challenges of exercising faith is that all five elements are required to create knowledge and power. We may exercise a single element of faith and nothing will happen. For faith to be productive, all its elements are required. In multiplication, if any of the numbers in the equation are zero, the answer to the equation is zero. This is also true of faith. Unless all of the elements of faith are present, there is no faith. Now let's look at a few stories that will illustrate faith.

Gypsum Parable™

Benjamin Franklin discovered that gypsum, a rock similar to limestone, could be pulverized into a powder called land plaster and applied to the field as a fertilizer. Franklin told his neighbors that using gypsum land plaster as a fertilizer would increase their crop yields. They did not believe him and argued that gypsum land plaster was of no use to crops. To prove his point, "Benjamin Franklin [sowed] land plaster in a clover field near one of the main roads in Pennsylvania as to form the sentence, 'This has been plastered with gypsum,' and the letters were detected readily by the height and color of the clover where the gypsum had been sown."[9]

Several studies have compared fields using gypsum land plaster to fields that have not. The studies found that "one bushel of gypsum spread over an acre of land fit for its action may add more than 20 times its own weight to a single crop of clover hay."[10] Franklin's neighbors' lack of faith in gypsum land plaster resulted in their harvests not yielding as much as they could have. Benjamin Franklin in the beginning had faith that gypsum would improve his crops. After testing the idea his faith became knowledge, and thus he fertilized his crops and received higher yields. The harvests of those who lacked faith in gypsum were weak when compared to the strong harvests of those with faith in gypsum.

Franklin's neighbors exercised three of the five elements of faith in relation to using gypsum as fertilizer. First, they received information from Franklin that gypsum could increase their crop yields. Second, they desired or hoped for a greater yield. Third, the information Franklin shared with them was true, as illustrated by the message in the field, as well as the numerous studies on gypsum done since then. However, Franklin's neighbors did not believe him and therefore they did not act on his information. They had no faith in gypsum as a fertilizer because they lacked two elements of faith: belief and action.

If the neighbors would have experimented on Franklin's advice, they would have known his advice was good because their crops would have been improved. If we experiment upon the word of God, we will see that His advice is good and will enlarge our lives.

As we fertilize our lives with faith in God, we will see our lives become stronger and more productive. As gypsum land plaster adds to the harvest at rates of more than 20 times its weight, so will each ounce of faith in God produce pounds of increased productivity in our lives.

Parable of the Gunpowder Harvest™

A trader went to a certain Indian nation to dispose of a stock of goods. Among other things he had a quantity of gunpowder. The Indians traded for his clothes, hats, axes, beads, and other things but would not take the powder saying, "We do not wish for the powder; we have plenty." The trader did not like to carry all the powder back to this camp, so he thought he would play a trick on the Indians, and induce them to buy it. Going to an open piece of ground near the Indian camp he dug up the soft, rich soil; then mixing a quantity of onion seed with his powder he began to plant it.

The Indians were curious to know what he was doing, and stood by greatly interested. "What are you doing?" said one. "Planting gunpowder," replied the trader. "Why do you plant it?" inquired another. "To raise a crop of powder. How could I raise it without planting?" asked the trader. "Do you not plant corn in the ground?" "And will gunpowder grow like corn?" exclaimed half a dozen at once. "Certainly it will," said the trader. "Did you not know it? As you do not want my powder, I thought I would plant it and raise a crop which I could gather and sell to the Crows." Now the Crows were another tribe of Indians which was always at war with this tribe (the Blackfeet). The idea of their enemies having a large supply of powder increased the excitement, and one of the Indians said, "Well, well, if we can raise powder like corn, we will buy your stock and plant it." But some of the Indians thought it best to wait and see if the seed would grow. So the trader agreed to wait a few days.

In about a week the tiny sprouts of the onion seed began to appear above the ground. The trader, calling the Indians to the spot, said, "You see now for yourselves. The powder already begins to grow, just as I told you it would." The fact that some small plants appeared where the trader had put the gunpowder was enough to convince the Indians. Every one of them became anxious to raise a crop of gunpowder. The trader sold them his stock, in which there was a large mixture of onion seeds (which it closely resembles) at a very high price and then left.

From this time the Indians gave no attention to their corn crop. If they could raise gunpowder they would be happy. They took great care of the little plants as they came up out of the ground, and watched every day for the appearance of the gunpowder blossoms. They planned a buffalo hunt which was to take place after the powder harvest. After a while the onions bore a plentiful crop of seeds and the Indians began to gather and thresh it. They believed that threshing the onion seed would produce the powder. But threshing failed to bring it. Then they discovered that they had been cheated.

Of course the swindling trader avoided these Indians and did not make them a second visit. After some time, however, he sent his partner to them for the purpose of trading goods for furs and skins. By chance they found out that this man was the partner of the one who had cheated them. They said nothing to him about the matter; but when he had opened his goods and was ready to trade, they coolly helped themselves to all he had and walked off. The trader did not understand this. He became furiously angry, and went to make his complaint to the chief. "I came here to trade honestly, but your people are thieves; they have stolen all my goods."

The old chief looked at him some time in silence, smoking a meditative pipe. At last he blew a puff of smoke into the air, removed the pipe from his lips, and then said, "My children are all honest. They have not stolen your goods. They will pay you as soon as they gather their gunpowder harvest."[11]

The Indians possessed four of the five elements of faith. They received the information that gunpowder could be planted and grown to produce more gunpowder, and they believed this information. They also had a desire for a gunpowder harvest, and they chose to act upon the information by planting and working the field of planted gunpowder. However, the fifth element of truth was missing. Since it is not true that gunpowder can be planted to yield a harvest, their faith was in vain and produced nothing. Faith will benefit us nothing if it is based on a falsehood. No matter how genuine one's belief may be in a falsity, it will not change that falsity into truth.

FAITH PRECEDES THE MIRACLE

One of my first faith-building experiences happened while I was riding in the car with my older brother. He was listening to a book on tape. As the words were read, the Holy Spirit filled my body, and I knew that the words were true and from God. The book my brother was listening to was the New Testament. Following this experience, I found a copy of the Bible and began reading the New Testament for the first time. The life, ministry, and message of Jesus Christ transformed my life, and I was filled with a great desire to share the message of Christ.

Shortly after this experience, I joined a missionary ministry and served as a volunteer.

I was having some difficulty serving as a missionary due to a back injury. Earlier in my life, I was seriously injured in an accident with a three-wheeler. I was going 50 miles per hour when a truck pulled in front of me and the brakes on the three-wheeler failed. I slammed full speed into the side of the truck. When I woke up a few minutes later, I was lying on the gravel in great pain, surrounded by a large group of people. I looked back to the truck to find I had been thrown an incredible distance from the crash site. I suffered numerous injuries, all of which I recovered from except the one to my back. The accident had jammed two of my vertebrae together. This injury remained very painful and was affecting my work proclaiming the gospel of Jesus Christ. It was impossible for me to kneel for prayer, and at times I needed help getting in and out of the car. As I was experiencing these difficulties, the many stories of healing from the New Testament came into my mind:

"And, behold, they brought to him a man sick of the palsy, lying on a bed: and Jesus seeing their **faith** said unto the sick of the palsy . . . Arise, take up thy bed, and go unto thine house."[12]

"And, behold, a woman, which was diseased with an issue of blood twelve years, came behind him, and touched the hem of his garment: For she said within herself, If I may but touch his garment, I shall be whole. But Jesus turned him about, and when he saw her, he said, Daughter, be of good comfort; thy **faith** hath made thee whole. And the woman was made whole from that hour."[13]

"Two blind men followed him, crying, and saying, Thou Son of David, have mercy on us . . . Jesus saith unto them, Believe ye that I am able to do this? They said unto him, Yea, Lord. Then touched he their eyes, saying, According to your **faith** be it unto you. And their eyes were opened."[14]

These stories greatly increased my faith. I believed that if these people were healed, surely the Lord would heal me so that I could be a more effective messenger for Him. I went to the leader of our ministry and asked him to pray and ask God to heal my back. We found a private room in the church where we could pray. As he prayed and asked the Lord to heal me, I felt the Holy Spirit enter my body and flow to the location of the injury in my back. It was a wonderful feeling of peace, love, and power. The prayer of faith was answered. The pains and restrictions that had plagued me for years were gone in an instant. I had spent years seeking a remedy from various medical professionals with no relief or cure. It wasn't until I sought the Master with a humble prayer of faith that I was made whole, fulfilling the scripture, "Ask, and it shall be given you."[15] Each time I reflect on this story, I am filled with great gratitude for the mercy, love, grace, and healing power of the Savior Jesus Christ.

Faith was not a crutch to assist me with my weak injured back. Faith was the power by which my back was made whole and strong. Faith in God gives us power to do things beyond our physical ability and to do things not possible for man alone. Where there is faith, there will be miracles. Faith allows us to tap into God's power and perform miracles in our lives and the lives of others.

FAITH IS DEVELOPED

Just before being inducted into the Pro Football Hall of Fame, the former San Francisco 49er quarterback Steve Young shared the following faith-building experience.

Being just over six feet tall, Steve is shorter than most NFL quarterbacks. Because of his size, there were many times when he would drop back to make a pass and couldn't see over the huge linemen in front of him. There were numerous occasions when Jerry Rice was open, but since Steve couldn't see Jerry, he wouldn't throw him the ball. Steve recalled one occasion when coach Mike Holmgren yelled at him during a game. "Steve, Jerry was open. Why didn't you throw him the ball?" Steve replied, "I couldn't see him." Mike retorted, "Well, you better start seeing him."

Steve gave Mike's comment a great deal of thought. Was there a way for him to throw the ball to Jerry Rice without seeing him? Steve decided that he could try throwing the ball blind. He knew where Jerry would be going each play, so could he drop back and throw the ball to Jerry in faith, without seeing him? Steve decided to try throwing blind in practice. Not surprisingly, Steve's first attempts at throwing blind were not accurate. Steve was known for being an accurate passer so he felt that he should explain himself to Jerry. Steve approached Jerry and said, "Jerry, I'm going through this metaphysical process of learning

how to throw the ball blind. So while I am learning, the ball may be a little behind you, high, or out in front of you. Please be patient with me while I'm going through this process." In response, Jerry held out his hand and said, "Put it here. Just put it here." It took a great deal of practicing, but eventually Steve got to where he could throw the ball blind right where Jerry wanted it.

One of Steve's favorite memories was during the fourth quarter of a game against the Atlanta Falcons. The game was in Atlanta and the Falcons were winning. The crowd was going crazy. As Steve dropped back to pass, he caught a glimpse of Jerry Rice, but then his sight was blocked by one of the linemen. So Steve threw by faith to where he thought Jerry Rice would be. Just as Steve released the ball, a defensive linemen hit and knocked him to the ground. Steve recalls, "I looked up from the ground at the audience, and suddenly 80,000 fans went silent. As I lay on the ground, covered by a 300-pound defensive lineman, I thought to myself, 'This is the greatest moment of my career. I just threw the ball blind to win the game and silenced 80,000 fans!'"[16]

CONCLUSION

Just as Steve Young developed the skill of throwing the football blind, we also must learn to live by faith. Faith is to be developed by practice. The way to increase our ability to live by faith tomorrow is to practice living by faith today.

TRUTH 1

Faith Is the Moving Cause of All Action in Intelligent Beings and the Process by Which We Gain Power and Knowledge.

MY SUCCESS IS A RESULT OF
MY ENERGIES, LABOR, AND MENTAL CAPACITY

When there is a person with an amazing talent, extraordinary intelligence, or who develops some great invention, the world often attributes these achievements to the individual. The world says, "He has done it," and the individual says, "I have done it." No honor or credit is given to God. The myth that success is a result of an individual's energies, labor, and mental capacity is a common one. The cartoon character Bart Simpson personifies this attitude with the mealtime grace consisting of the words, "Dear God, we pay for all this stuff ourselves, so thanks for nothing."

PARABLE OF THE BASEBALL BAT™

Let's say a major league baseball player hits 74 home runs in a season and breaks the single season homerun record. Does the bat receive the credit? Is the bat somehow better than the other bats and thus entitled to recognition? In the record book, is partial credit given to the bat? Of course not. The bat hits homeruns because of the batter. In our relationship with God, we can be compared to a baseball bat. We can do nothing by ourselves. How many homeruns would a bat hit if it were to enter the batter's box alone? The bat is going to lie in the dirt and do nothing. The bat can do nothing by itself, just as we can do nothing by ourselves.

If a home run is hit, does the crowd honor the bat because it actually made contact with the ball and hit it out of the park? Of course not. However, often in our lives we take credit for our accomplishments or honor others' accomplishments with little or no credit given to God. When people take credit for their accomplishments, it is as foolish as giving praise to a baseball bat for hitting a homerun. When we understand our true relationship with God, we realize He is the source of all our accomplishments and abilities.

In order for a homerun to be hit, both a batter and a bat are required. How many homeruns would a batter hit without a bat? This is where we come in. We must allow Christ to utilize us as instruments in His hands. Our role in bringing to pass righteousness and achieving greatness is submitting to His will. Our role is to become instruments in the Master's hands.

PARABLE OF THE BASEBALL BAT™

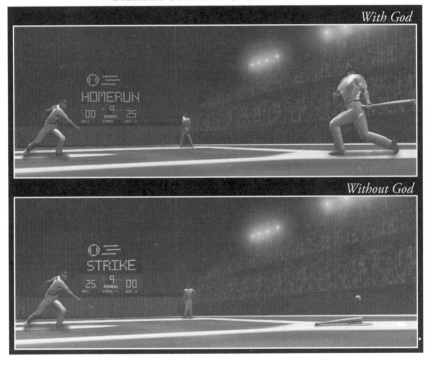

The savior teaches this principle in John 15:4–5 ". . . As the branch cannot bear fruit of itself, except it abide in the vine; no more can ye, except ye abide in me. I am the vine, ye are the branches: He that abideth in me, and I in him, the same bringeth forth much fruit: for without me ye can do nothing."

"Christ does not say, without me ye can do but little, neither does He say, without me ye cannot do any [difficult] thing; nor without me ye can do it with difficulty: But He says, without me ye can do nothing!"[1]

Christopher Columbus—Instrument in the Hands of God

Following Columbus' discovery of the Americas, he wrote a summary account of his voyage for King Ferdinand and Queen Isabella. It reads in part, "The great success of this enterprise is not to be ascribed to my own merits, but to . . . the Lord often granting to men what they never imagine themselves capable of effecting, as he is accustomed to hear the prayers of his servants and those who love his commandments, even in that which appears impossible; in this manner has it happened to me who have succeeded in an undertaking never before accomplished by man. . . And now ought the king, queen, princes, and all their dominions, as well as the whole of Christians, to give thanks to our Saviour Jesus Christ who has granted us such a victory and great success."[2]

"Is it Mine?" or "Is It God's?"

A couple of years ago, my wife and I purchased a home in the mountains. Although we love our home, our backyard was an undeveloped mountainside, a dangerous play area for our children. To solve this problem, we decided to build two rock retaining walls on the mountain to create a large grass playing field below our home. I called a friend in the landscaping business for a bid on the cost of the project. He estimated it would cost $40,000. Our friend agreed to start on the project the following week, so we wrote him a check for $20,000 to cover the expenses of the subcontractors to build the retaining walls.

As it turned out, our friend was experiencing financial difficulties and spent the $20,000 on items other than the renovating of our yard. He hid this from my wife and me for months, continually telling us he would start in a few weeks. Since we loved and trusted him, we never suspected him of dishonesty. When we finally discovered the truth, the summer was over, our yard was still undeveloped, and we were out $20,000. It was frustrating for us, and we were unsure of the most appropriate way to handle the situation.

As I pondered how to respond, the Lord's Prayer came to my mind, "Give us this day our daily bread."[3] Reading this passage helped me realize that everything we have comes from God, so nothing that we have is really ours. God gave me the $20,000 so the money our friend had taken was not mine, but the Lord's.

The prayer continues, "forgive us our debts, as we forgive our debtors... For if ye forgive men their trespasses, your heavenly Father will also forgive you: But if ye forgive not men their trespasses, neither will your Father forgive your trespasses."[4] I also read the parable the Savior taught in answer to Peter's questions about how often he should forgive. In this parable, a servant was forgiven by the king a debt of 10,000 talents (60 million pence, approximately $3 billion in 2006 value).[5] "But the same servant went out, and found one of his fellowservants, which owed him an hundred pence: [approximately $5,000 in 2006 values][5] and he laid hands on him, and took him by the throat, saying, Pay me that thou owest. And his fellowservant fell down at his feet, and besought him, saying, Have patience with me, and I will pay thee all. And he would not: but went and cast him into prison, till he should pay the debt."[6]

As I read these passages, the thought came into my mind that I should forgive this $20,000 debt. I recalled many of my own trespasses the Lord had forgiven. Shouldn't I exercise the same compassion and mercy toward my friend? The Lord had forgiven me of debts far greater than $20,000 and He provided me with the $20,000 in the first place.

I called our friend to discuss the situation. He apologized for his dishonesty and for the pain and frustration he had caused our family. He said that he wanted to return our money and that he didn't have the money currently, but if we were patient with him, he would eventually pay us back. I read him the Lord's Prayer and the Lord's parable on forgiveness and told him that the debt was forgiven. He initially resisted the idea saying, "$20,000 is a lot of money; I must pay you back. I cannot take your money." I explained that the money was not mine, but the Lord's. It was not me, but the Lord, who was forgiving the debt. He thanked me, expressing what a help this was to him and his four children. I showed appreciation for his gratitude, but asked that he direct his thanks not to me, but to the Lord.

We are often caught up in the "mine, mine, mine" mentality, allowing greed and selfishness into our hearts. Once we can say "It is the Lord's" instead of "It is mine" we are freed from the attachment to treasures that can be corrupted by rust or taken by thieves.[7]

THE PRINCIPLE OF INDIRECTION

The principle of indirection is "when the focus and accomplishment of one thing results in the achievement of another." For example, "if you want anyone to laugh you have to provide him with a reason, e.g., you have to tell him a joke. In no way is it possible to evoke real laughter by urging him, or having him urge himself, to laugh."[8] True laughter is the indirect result of the direct action of telling a joke. There are certain things in life that cannot be obtained by direct pursuit. To obtain these things, we must focus on an indirect action, which will cause the result we desire.

Human Needs and the Principle of Indirection

I will contrast two approaches people use to fulfill human needs. One is a direct approach illustrated by Abraham Maslow's Hierarchy of Needs. The other is an indirect approach taught in the New Testament.

Maslow's Hierarchy of Needs is represented as a pyramid, with the larger lower levels representing the basic needs of food, air, water, and shelter, and the upper point representing the need to seek a power greater than oneself and to serve others. One of the fundamental ideas is that there is a specific order in which we seek to fulfill our needs. For example, Maslow's hierarchy teaches that we must fulfill our need for food before we seek to fulfill our need for security, and that we must fill our need for security before we can seek a power greater than ourselves.

While Maslow's theory explains how people driven by fear and selfishness seek to fulfill needs, it does not describe how people of faith seek to fulfill needs. Men of faith seek God before food, security, or friends. Men of faith know that by seeking the will of God first, all their needs will be fulfilled. Matthew 6:33 reads, "But seek ye first the kingdom of God, and his righteousness; and all these things shall be added unto you."

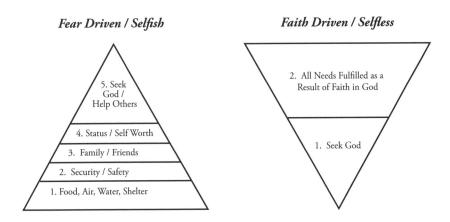

Fear Driven / Selfish

5. Seek God / Help Others
4. Status / Self Worth
3. Family / Friends
2. Security / Safety
1. Food, Air, Water, Shelter

Faith Driven / Selfless

2. All Needs Fulfilled as a Result of Faith in God
1. Seek God

Parable of the Stationary Bike™

Trying to satisfy our human needs without faith in God is like trying to win the Tour de France on a stationary exercise bike. You can peddle as long and hard as those on a racing bike, but at the end of the race you will still be in the same place. The person on the stationary bike can pedal, work, and sweat, but will get nowhere. Truly fulfilling human needs requires application of the principle of indirection. We can't satisfy our human needs by directly seeking them. Instead, we must first seek God and serve others. The Savior taught, "He that findeth his life shall lose it; and he that loseth his life for my sake shall find it."[9] The indirect approach of seeking God is the first step to truly satisfying our needs. Those who are driven by fear and selfishness will attempt to satisfy their needs first, but will find it impossible to truly fulfill their needs.

The more you make the fulfillment of your needs your target, the more you will miss it. True fulfillment of your needs cannot be obtained by direct pursuit. True fulfillment of your needs will come as a result of your personal dedication to God and service of others. If you put God last, you will go nowhere fast.

PARABLE OF THE STATIONARY BIKE™
Put God Last ... Go Nowhere Fast

Parable of Heaven and Hell

A noble Chinese warrior died in battle and arrived at the heavenly portals. He requested that he be allowed to see what hell was like before entering heaven. His request was granted. Much to his surprise, he was taken to a magnificent chamber. In this chamber, there were tables heaped with an abundance of the most desirable foods one could imagine. However, the people in the room were cursing and screaming in anger. The warrior was initially puzzled at their behavior, but he soon understood their plight. They were trying to eat with chopsticks that were three-feet long. They could pick up their food, but because their chopsticks were so long, it was impossible to place the food in

PARABLE OF HEAVEN AND HELL™

Heaven

Hell

their mouths. To his surprise, when the warrior entered heaven he saw a similar scene. He once again saw a magnificent chamber, filled with tables of delicious food and the guests at the table had the same chopsticks that were three-feet long. This room, however, was not filled with frustration, anger, and cursing. It was instead filled with sounds of laughter and joy. The difference was that those in heaven had learned to feed one another. In giving, they received.

Principle of Indirection Applied to Money

Prosperity is elusive to many because they take a money-first approach. They don't realize that prosperity can't be harvested unless they plant the seeds that grow prosperity. The seed of prosperity is service. Service is the approach that creates wealth and prosperity. Businesses that seek to serve others, solve problems, improve the quality of life, satisfy needs, and increase productivity tend to be extremely prosperous. Businesses focused on making money as their top priority may have profits, but the money will be unfulfilling and will not satisfy higher needs of life. The businesspeople may obtain money, but they will not achieve prosperity.

Henry Ford

"Over the course of 1913, the [Ford Motor Company] had to hire 963 workers for every 100 it needed to maintain on the payroll. To keep a workforce of 13,600 employees in the factory, Ford continually spent money on short-term training. . . The rest of the industry reluctantly accepted high turnover as part of the assembly-line system and passed the increasing labor costs into the prices of their cars. Henry Ford, however, did not want anything in the price of a Model T except good value. His solution was a bold stroke that reverberated through the entire nation. On January 5, 1914, Henry Ford announced a new minimum wage of five dollars per eight-hour day, in addition to a profit-sharing plan."[10] The prior wage was $2.38 for a nine-hour day or 26 cents per hour. The new minimum wage of five dollars per eight-hour day was 62 cents per hour—a 138 percent increase. (The Ford employees' wage of 26 cents per hour in 1913 would equal $5.26 per hours in 2006 dollars. The 1914 wage of 62 cents per hour would equal $12.55 per hour in 2006 dollars.)

"It was the talk of towns across the country: Ford was hailed as the friend of the worker, as an outright socialist, or as a madman bent on bankrupting his company. Many businessmen—including most of the remaining stockholders in the Ford Motor Company—regarded his solution as reckless. But he shrugged off all the criticism: 'Well, you know when you pay men well you can talk to them,' he said. Recognizing the human element in mass production, Ford knew that retaining more employees would lower costs, and that a happier workforce would inevitably lead to greater productivity. The numbers bore him out. Between 1914 and 1916, the company profits doubled from $30 million to $60 million [$600 million to $1.2 billion in 2006 dollars]. 'The payment of five dollars a day for an eight-hour day was one of the finest cost-cutting moves we ever made,' he later said. There were other ramifications, as well. A budding effort to unionize the Ford factory dissolved in the face of the Five-Dollar Day. Most cunning of all, Ford's new wage scale turned autoworkers into auto customers. The purchases they made returned at least some of those five dollars to Henry Ford, and helped raise production, which invariably helped to lower per-car costs."[11]

CONCLUSION

A belief that success is a result of a person's energies, labor, and mental capacity will create the vices of pride, selfishness, and ungratefulness. The virtues of humility, generosity, and gratitude will fill our hearts, minds, and souls once we realize our total dependence on God and believe that all we have and are is a gift from Him.

TRUTH 2

If You Put God Last, You Will Go Nowhere Fast.™

MYTH 3

I AM NOT WORTHY OR DESERVING OF PROSPERITY

There is a common cliché: "It is better to give than to receive." Is it better to give than receive? When one thinks about the meaning of this statement, it can be discovered that giving and receiving are actually equals. For every giver there must be an equal receiver, and in order to give, we must have first received. Thus, a more correct statement would be: "It is as good to give as it is to receive." In Jesus' parable of the Good Samaritan, the Samaritan helped a man who was robbed of his money and clothes and left half-dead. The Samaritan bound his wounds, cared for him, and took him to an inn. The Samaritan also paid the host two pence (two days' wages) to take care of the injured man and agreed to repay the host if the cost was higher.[1] The Samaritan had to have first received the financial means before he could give of his means to care for the robbed and injured man. It can be understood, then, that to be good givers, we must also be good receivers.

What makes someone a poor receiver? One of the factors is a belief in the myth "I am not worthy or deserving of prosperity." A belief in this myth prevents us from achieving our full financial potential. God is the ultimate giver. He wants to give us the gifts of prosperity and abundance. Our role is to learn to be a good receiver and accept God's gifts. Many who do not feel worthy or deserving of financial abundance reject God's gifts. What good is a gift if it is not received? A rejected gift hurts both the giver and the receiver because the receiver gives up the joy of the gift and the giver is denied the joy and blessings of giving the gift.

DON'T ROB ME OF MY BLESSINGS
While serving in a missionary ministry in Hawaii, I associated with

many wonderful Christians. The Polynesians regarded representatives of Christ with the same respect and honor as they did their chiefs. As I preached the gospel, people of all denominations would impart to us of their time, food, possessions, and money in support of the Lord's work. They knew the Lord would bless them for their sacrifices.

On one particular occasion, when I was walking along the Kamehameha Highway, a car pulled up right alongside me. As we were both in motion, a man rolled down his window and handed me a $20 bill. At first I didn't realize what he was handing me, but when I found that it was money, I kindly refused and tried to return it. As I ran after the car the man said, "Don't rob me of my blessings." He sped away leaving me with a $20 bill I felt I shouldn't have. Receiving gifts and money became a regular occurrence. Being new to Hawaii and not fully understanding the culture, I tried to refuse gifts and money that were constantly offered me. I quickly learned not to do this. Each time I tried to refuse the gifts, the giver would get upset and say, "Don't rob me of my blessings!" I learned that by humbly accepting gifts, I could in turn, faithfully promise the giver that they would be blessed for their sacrifice.

The Polynesians believed that the more a representative of Christ ate the more blessings they would receive. Joe, a 300-pound Tongan, took me out to eat, and I ate until I couldn't eat another bite. After we finished, Joe went to the cashier to pay for the meals. As Joe began to pay, the cashier said, "Sir, someone has already paid for the meals." Joe looked around the restaurant and called out loudly, "Who robbed me of my blessings?" The restaurant went quiet. Joe was disappointed that he had not been able to pay for the meals and thus was robbed of his blessings. In an attempt to still receive blessings for feeding a representative of Christ, he told the cashier that we were going to eat again and this time not to let anyone else pay for the meals. This experience taught me not only to be a good receiver, but also to be a big eater.

Rejecting Compliments

During the summer I enjoy boating and water skiing. A few friends and I were headed out to the lake one day and as we were in front of my house getting the boat ready, one of them said, "I love your yard, it is beautiful." I replied, "Not really. There are so many weeds and so much trimming that needs to be done." He then said again, "No really, I like your yard." At this point, I realized I had rejected his compliment, and he was trying to give the compliment again to see if I would accept it on the second attempt. I accepted the compliment with a simple "Thank you." As I analyzed why I rejected the first compliment, I realized that it was because I didn't think the yard was worthy or deserving of the compliment. In an attempt to reject the compliment, I came up with reasons why the yard was unworthy and undeserving of the compliment.

An important exchange occurs when compliments are given and received. When you reject a compliment, you also reject the giver of the compliment. This can create awkward exchanges. Imagine, for example, what would occur if someone handed you a beautifully wrapped present and you handed it back and said, "I don't want it."

Some people have learned to be polite by saying thank you to the giver, but in their minds they still reject the compliment with reasons why they are unworthy or undeserving of it. These people have learned how to not reject the giver but are still poor receivers.

Ask and Ye Shall Receive

In one of my first business ventures, I experienced a major set back and was forced to move out of my apartment. My brother had an empty room in his house and agreed to let me stay with him. I knew I could make do with the few possessions I had, but I lacked a bed and dresser. I knelt in prayer and asked the Lord to please provide me with a bed and a small dresser. The next morning, when I went outside, I found in front of the house a bed and a small dresser. I looked at the items with amazement and thankfulness. I moved the items into my room and knelt to thank the Lord for answering my prayer and providing me with these wonderful gifts.

Had I not asked the Lord in prayer for the dresser and bed, slept on the floor, and kept my clothes in a box, the story may have went something like this:

Parable of the Heavenly Warehouse™

Years later I died and went to heaven. When I arrived at the pearly gates, I asked Peter for a tour of heaven. While on the tour, I saw a large warehouse in the distance. I pointed toward it and asked, "Peter, what is that warehouse for?" Peter replied, "We will not be visiting the warehouse on the tour." "Why not?" I asked. Peter replied, "Because the warehouse has to do with your life on earth and will only result in disappointment. We never take new arrivals to their warehouses."

I curiously asked, "What is inside the warehouse?" Peter answered, "Trust me. You do not want to know. You will be much happier in heaven if you don't know what's inside." Peter insisted that I forget about the warehouse and continued the tour. I could not stop thinking about the warehouse and eventually curiosity got the best of me, and I ran toward it. I opened the door and entered. What I saw amazed me. Hundreds of shelves lined the warehouse from wall to wall and floor to ceiling. Each shelf was covered with beautifully wrapped gifts of all shapes and sizes. I approached one shelf and found that each of the gifts had my name on it. By this time, Peter had also entered the warehouse. I turned to him and asked, "What are all these gifts with my name on them?" Peter took me by the arm and led me to a shelf that contained two large presents and asked me to open them. I unwrapped the presents to find a bed and a dresser. Somewhat puzzled I asked, "What are these for?" Peter replied, "Do you remember when you moved in with your brother and needed a bed and a dresser? This is the bed and dresser God wanted to give you." I then hesitantly asked, "What are all the other presents?" Peter answered, "These are all the blessing and gifts God wanted to give to you while you were on earth that you did not receive."

I asked Peter, "God knew I needed and wanted a bed and a dresser, so why didn't He give them to me?" Peter replied, "Let me teach you how the warehouse works." He then took me to an area where all the shelves were empty." I asked, "What was on these shelves?" "On these shelves we kept all the blessing and gifts God gave to you which required no effort or work on your part. Thus, the shelves are all empty, because you received them all while you were on earth," answered Peter.

I anxiously asked, "Well, what about all the other shelves full of gifts, why wasn't I given them?" Peter answered, "Some of the gifts required work or effort on your part before you could obtain them." We walked to a section of the warehouse, and Peter had me look closer at the tags on the gifts. As I looked at the tags, I saw my name and under my name was written what was required of me to receive the gift. The first tag read, "Pray and ask for it." I looked at each tag only to find that they all read, "Pray and ask for it." I said to Peter, "You mean, all I had to do to receive all these gifts in the warehouse was to pray and ask for them?" Peter replied, "You are getting ahead of me. This section of the warehouse contains all the gifts God wanted to give you and all that was required to receive them was to pray and ask for them. Heaven has warehouses full of undelivered gifts because many have not learned that God has countless gifts to give if one will only ask. My fellow apostle James taught, '. . . ye have not, because ye ask not.'²"

"Peter, how was I supposed to ask for these gifts when I didn't even know they existed?" I asked. Peter said, "Here is the next principle of effective prayer. You must pray and ask to know what to pray for." "What do you mean?" I asked. Peter answered, "You need to pray to find out what is in your warehouse. You should pray and ask God to tell you what gifts to pray and ask for. It is a wise man who knows what to pray for, and you can know what to pray for by the spirit, '. . . for we know not what we should pray for as we ought: but the Spirit itself maketh intercession for us with groanings which cannot be uttered.'³"

"This is all very interesting, but there is something I still do not understand. My warehouse is full of gifts, yet there were times on earth when I prayed and asked for things but did not receive them. Can you please explain this?" I inquired. Peter answered, "It could have been one of two reasons. Either you were asking for something that was not in your warehouse,[4] or what you were asking for required more than simply asking to receive."

To demonstrate his point, Peter took me to another section of the warehouse and said, "As I mentioned earlier, God has placed a requirement for the receipt of each of these gifts. When you receive any gift from God it is a result of fulfilling this requirement. Asking in prayer is only one of many possible requirements." I began to look at the tags on the gifts in this section and found the requirements: get married, attend church, start a business, care for the poor, and visit a widow. Some of the gifts contained a long series of requirements to obtain the gift.

As I looked at the many tags, Peter began to relate an experience from his earthly ministry: "One day a man brought his son who was possessed of a devil to me and the other disciples and asked us to cure him, but we were unable to. Then Jesus came and rebuked the devil and the child was cured that very hour. Later the other disciples and I asked Jesus, 'Why were we unable to cast out the devil and cure the child?' To which Jesus replied, 'Howbeit this kind goeth not out but by prayer and fasting.'[5] From this experience, I learned that gifts can require more than asking to receive them."

"Before I leave you to return to the pearly gates, I have one last principle to teach you," Peter said. "Once you understand that God is your Father and you are his child, many of the difficulties of prayer and receiving gifts will disappear. Once you view God as your Father who wants to bless you, prayer and accepting His gifts become natural and instinctive. As taught the Savior, 'Or what man is there of you, whom if his son ask bread, will he give him a stone? Or if he ask a fish, will he give him a serpent? If ye then, being evil, know how to give good gifts unto your children, how much more shall your Father which is in heaven give good things to them that ask him?'[6]"

Whether dealing with God or with our brothers and sisters on earth, it is important to remember that receiving gifts is not always as easy as it may seem. It is important to learn how to become receivers in order to impart of our gifts to others. Remember, "It is as good to give as it is to receive." We need to understand that prayer is a form of work, and is an appointed means for obtaining the greatest of God's gifts. Prayer is not to tell God which blessings and gifts he should give you, but to ask for gifts that God is already willing to give and is simply waiting for you to ask for. "Ask, and it shall be given you; seek, and ye shall find; knock, and it shall be opened unto you."[7]

Truth 3

You Are a Child of God. Your Father in Heaven Wants You to Experience the Joys of Prosperity.

MYTH 4

I CAN ONLY SUCCEED FINANCIALLY AT THE EXPENSE OF OTHERS

THE STORY OF THE FARMER AND THE THIEF[1]

Bobby, a fifteen-year-old, took responsibility for running his family's Arizona farm after his father became ill. Some took unfair advantage of the young man, and crops began disappearing from the fields. Bobby was angry and vowed to catch the thieves and make an example out of them. Vengeance would be his.

As his father was recovering from his illness, Bobby made his rounds through the fields at the end of the day. It was nearly dark. In the distance, he caught sight of someone loading sacks of potatoes into a car. Bobby ran quickly through the field and caught the young thief. His first thought was to take out his frustrations with his fists and then drag the boy to the farmhouse and call the police. He had caught his thief, and he intended to get his just dues.

As Bobby's anger raged, his father pulled up in his pickup. He got out, and placed his weak hand on his son's shoulder and said, "I see you're a bit upset, Bobby. Can I handle this?" He walked over to the young thief and put his arm around his shoulder, looked him in the eye for a moment, and said, "Son, tell me, why are you doing this? Why are you trying to steal these potatoes?"

The young thief replied, "I didn't think you would miss them. You have so very much and I have so very little. Not everyone can be wealthy like you." Then Bobby's father asked the young thief, "Why do you think I have this large farm and comfortable home?" "Because your dad gave it to you," replied the boy. Bobby's father chuckled and put his arm around the young boy. He walked the thief to an area where he could see the undeveloped desert that surrounded the potato farm and said, "Thirty years ago, this is what my potato farm looked like. I originally purchased 10,000 acres of desert land for $27 per acre. Through years of hard work, I transformed the land that was producing very little value into a thriving potato farm which is now worth $3,500 per acre. As a result of years of hard work and industry, I was able to improve this property to the point where now what I purchased for $270,000 is worth $35 million."

The thief's eyes widened and he said in amazement, "Your farm is worth $35 million. Don't you think it is selfish to have so much?" Bobby's father replied, "Selfish, what do you mean?" "Well, if you have so much, that means there is now less for others. Not everyone can be wealthy," stated the young thief.

Bobby's father replied, "When I breathe, does it lessen the amount of oxygen available for you and your family? Is the person who exercises and thus breathes more oxygen selfish because he is taking more than his share of the oxygen?" Perplexed, the young thief replied, "Of course not. There is enough oxygen for everyone to breathe as much as they want." Bobby's father asked, "Why is there plenty of oxygen?" "I don't know. Why?" responded the boy.

Bobby's father explained, "Because oxygen can be created. Since oxygen is created in abundance, we don't have to ration it so we don't run out. Wealth can also be created and thus can be as abundant in our lives as oxygen. We can have as much wealth as we are willing to work to create. To say it is impossible for everyone to be wealthy is as irrational as saying not everyone can breathe as much oxygen as he or she wants. The earth is designed to create, produce, and increase.[2] For example, from a single apple seed you can grow a tree that will produce hundreds of apples each year. Two chickens can be multiplied to feed thousands of people. Once we understand that wealth can be created, we will believe that there is enough in the world for everyone to succeed and, as a result, one does not have to become successful at the expense of others. The success of one does not limit another's ability to succeed.

"If every person produced to his or her potential, everyone's needs would be satisfied with a great abundance. For example, the earth is capable of producing food for a population of at least 80 billion, eight times the 10 billion expected to inhabit the earth by the year 2050. One study estimates that with improved scientific methods the earth could feed as many as 1,000 billion people.[3] In 1930, there were approximately 30 million farmers in the United States, barely producing enough food to feed a population of approximately 100 million people. Technological breakthroughs in agriculture during the next fifty years made farming so efficient that by 1980 approximately 3 million farmers were producing enough food for a population of more than 300 million. This represents a 3,000 percent increase in productivity per farmer."[4]

The young thief then asked, "If the world is capable of feeding hundreds of billions of people, why are people starving?"

"This is a great question," continued Bobby's father. "Remember that I said if every person produced to his or her potential, everyone's needs would be satisfied with a great abundance. There are two problems. First, not everyone is producing. Second, there are those who seek wealth by taking what others have produced rather than creating it themselves. When someone seeks wealth by taking someone else's production, they are stealing. Were you creating or stealing when you attempted to take the potatoes from my farm?"

"I was stealing," replied the young thief. Bobby's father continued, "One of my favorite stories in the Bible is Jesus cleansing the temple. The Lord calls those who use the capitalist system to become takers instead of creators thieves. In New Testament times, there were those outside the temple who used scales of questionable accuracy for exchange and who took advantage of religious pilgrims who traveled to the temple by charging inflated prices. In response to these actions, 'Jesus went into the temple of God, and cast out all them that sold and bought in the temple, and overthrew the tables of the moneychangers, and the seats of them that sold doves, And said unto them, It is written, My house shall be called the house of prayer; but ye have made it a den of thieves.'[5] Many business practices may be legal in the courts of earth but those who steal from their customers with inflated prices or steal from their employees by oppressing them in their wages will be called thieves when judged by the law of God."

Then the young thief asked, "So are businesses and wealth bad things?" In response, Bobby's father continued, "Business and wealth can be good or bad. The question to ask is, 'Was value created or stolen?' Jesus was not condemning money or business but the fact they were achieving it by stealing. Christ taught us not to obtain wealth through theft and taking from others, which destroys. Instead, He taught us to obtain wealth by creation and production which creates life and abundance, saying, 'The thief cometh not, but for to steal, and to kill, and to destroy: I am come that they might have life, and that they might have it more abundantly.'[6]"

The young thief then said, "I have one last question. Why do people believe they can only succeed at the expense of someone else?"

Bobby's father answered, "The root cause is a belief in scarcity, that there is a fixed amount of wealth. With a scarcity belief, if one person gains more financially it means another has less. A great example of scarcity mentality is population control. Those who believe in population control believe there is a fixed pie of resources. Thus, if there are more people, each person will get a smaller piece of the pie. With a scarcity mentality, the only way to increase the quality of life of each individual is to reduce the number of people. Thus as population is reduced, each person receives a larger piece of the pie.

"Good Christians will not achieve wealth by taking it from others; thus, if they belief the world has a fixed amount of wealth, they will feel guilty the more they receive because that means less for someone else. Once Christians understand that they can create wealth, they will also understand that as they create wealth they are improving the lives of society—not taking from them. A belief that the world is abundant and that wealth can be created is essential to creating prosperity for you and for society. 'The more we develop an abundance mentality, the more we love to share power and profit and recognition, and the more we are genuinely happy for the successes, well-being, achievements, recognition, and good fortune of other people. We believe that their success adds to—rather than detracts from—our lives.'[7]"

In gratitude, the young thief said, "When I was caught stealing, I expected to be punished, but instead you showed me kindness. Thank you. I have learned a lot today."

Bobby's father invited the young boy to walk with them to the farmhouse. When they got there, Bobby's father asked the young thief what items he and his family needed. He graciously gave them to the boy. Voluntarily, month-by-month, the young would-be thief paid for all the food Bobby's father had given him, including the sacks of potatoes.

"ABUNDANCE VS. SCARCITY" AND "CREATION VS. REDISTRIBUTION"

If you believe in scarcity and a fixed number of resources, you will focus on distributing the limited wealth among society fairly. You will not focus on creation because what currently exists is all that there will ever be. Instead of trying to develop a way to divide the current pie, we should focus on creating a new pie big enough for all to share. People who consume more than they create are the only cause of depleting resources and diminishing economics. Fortunately our world is abundant and God has given humans the unique ability to create resources rather than simply use resources. Using our God-given ability to create resources is the key to our economic well being.

Creating a Larger Pie

It would seem logical that the larger share of ownership you have in a company, the more you will make. This is not always the case, as discovered Hyrum Smith, founder of the Franklin Planner. In 1984, early in the creation of the Franklin Quest Company, Hyrum met with the four men who helped start the company. The purpose of the meeting was to decide ownership interest. As the principle founder, Hyrum could have taken a majority interest in the company. Instead he took only 33 percent and gave 67 percent to the other partners. As the company grew, Hyrum gave away additional portions of his stock to employees. On June 3, 1992, the Franklin Quest Company went public and its stock began trading on the New York Stock Exchange. The stock Hyrum had given away was now worth more than $200 million while the stock Hyrum retained was only worth $60 million. One of the investment bankers was amazed that Hyrum had given away $200 million. In response, Hyrum said to this investment banker, "If I hadn't given away that stock . . . then the ownership I retained would not have been anywhere near $60 million . . . What I am worth today, I am worth because I was willing to share the wealth."[8]

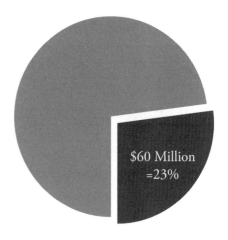

$50 MILLION DOLLAR
COMPANY

$260 MILLION DOLLAR
COMPANY

The investment banker saw that the Franklin Quest stock was worth $260 million in 1992, and Hyrum only had 23 percent of the stock—worth $60 million. The investment banker saw that if Hyrum had retained 50 percent of the company, he would now be worth $130 million instead of $60 million. Hyrum did not believe this was the case. Hyrum believed in abundance and the power of the creation of wealth. Hyrum would rather have a smaller piece of a large pie than a large piece of a small pie. Hypothetically, let's say Hyrum retained the majority interest in the company, 60 percent, and as a result in 1992 the company was smaller and thus only worth $50 million. Hyrum's

60 percent ownership interest would have been worth $30 million or half of what his 23 percent interest in the $260 million company was worth. Would you rather have 60 percent of $50 million ($30 million) or 23 percent of $260 million ($60 million)?

A similar account is found in the early days of McDonald's. The founder, Ray Kroc, was upset about having to give up 22 percent ownership to fund the operations and growth of the company. One of McDonalds' executives said to Mr. Kroc, "You've got to remember, Ray, that 78 percent of something is a lot better than one hundred percent of nothing."[9]

United States Case Study on Wealth Creation

UNITED STATES CASE STUDY ON WEALTH CREATION				
	1960	1980	2000	Increase
Total U.S. Personal Income[10]	$2.65 trillion	$5.26 trillion	$9.37 trillion	3.5 Times
Total U.S. Households[11]	53 million	80 million	105 million	2.0 Times
Average Household Income	$50,062	$65,414	$88,745	77%
* All Dollar Amounts in 2005 Equivalents				

The history of America shows how wealth has been created and increased over time (see chart). All dollar amounts in this case study have been adjusted for inflation to their 2005 equivalent values. In 1960, there were 53 million households in the United States with an average income of $50,062 for a total income of $2.65 trillion. In 2000, there were 105 million households in the United States with average income of $88,745 for a total income of $9.37 trillion. Thus, from 1960 to 2000, the population doubled while total income increased 3.5 times.

If no new income was created and the population had doubled, income would have been cut in half over the 40 years to $25,000. However, this was not the case, because new wealth was created. The population doubled and the average income went up by 77 percent.

CONCLUSION

Through work and industry, Americans increased their abundance from $2.65 trillion to more than $9 trillion. If average income grows at the same rate during the next forty years, the average income of an American household in 2040 will be $157,078 with the total income of America growing to more than $33 trillion. Our focus should be working to create greater abundance rather than redistributing the current wealth.

TRUTH 4

If Each Person Produced to His or Her Potential, the World's Needs Would be Satisfied with a Great Abundance.

Principle II:

Liberty is Given to All Men by Our Creator

"The God who gave us life, gave us liberty at the same time."
—Thomas Jefferson

MYTH 5

BAD THINGS SHOULD NOT HAPPEN TO GOOD PEOPLE

The myth that bad things should not happen to good people is found among congregations today and by Christians in the Old and New Testaments. A friend of our family told me about a faithful Christian in a neighboring state whose home was burned down. When this individual went to church the following Sunday, a member of her congregation asked her what she had done wrong to deserve such a thing.

In the Old Testament the story is told of a righteous man named Job who ". . . was perfect and upright, and one that feared God, and eschewed evil."[1] Despite his righteousness, Job's children were killed, his property destroyed, and his body afflicted with boils. Job's friend Eliphaz tries to explain Job's great suffering as the results of Job's wickedness and sins.[2]

The Savior corrected the disciples who believed a man was blind as a result of sin. The account in the New Testament reads, "As Jesus passed by, he saw a man which was blind from his birth. And his disciples asked him, saying, Master, who did sin, this man, or his parents, that he was born blind? Jesus answered, Neither hath this man sinned, nor his parents."[3]

Just as the disciples believed the man's blindness could have only been caused by sin, we often assume that sin is the only cause of bad things in our lives. There are multiple reasons why things we usually define as bad (such as pain, suffering, trials, afflictions, and hardships) occur in our lives. To help us understand why bad things happen to good people, I have identified four causes of pain. Personal sin is only one of the four causes of pain. It is often one of the other three causes of pain that is the reason why bad things happen to good people.

FOUR CAUSES OF PAIN™
1. Liberty
2. Growth
3. Personal Choices/Sins
4. Choices/Sins of Others

When we experience pain, it is key to ask why it happened. Identifying which of the four causes led to the pain will determine how we respond to it, how we interpret it, and how we feel about it.

1. LIBERTY

Four principles must be in force for there to be liberty:
I.   Laws ordained by God
II. Opposites must exist (good/evil, pleasure/pain, right/wrong)
III. Knowledge of good and evil
IV. The power to choose

Pain as a Result of Laws Ordained by God

One of the laws God created and ordained is the law of gravity. "Gravity makes objects fall. Sometimes they fall on people and hurt them. Sometimes gravity makes people fall off mountains and out of windows. Sometimes gravity makes people slip on ice or sink under water. We could not live without gravity, but that means we have to live with the dangers it causes. Laws of nature treat everyone alike. They do not make exceptions for good people or for useful people. If a man enters a house where someone has a contagious disease, he runs the risk of catching that disease. It makes no difference why he is in the house. He may be a doctor or a burglar; germs cannot tell the difference. . . Laws of nature do not make exceptions for nice people. A bullet has

-49-

no conscience; neither does a malignant tumor or an automobile gone out of control."[4] Christ taught this principle when he said, "[God] makes the sun rise on both good and bad people. And he sends rain for the ones who do right and for the ones who do wrong."[5] Thus, bad things are going to happen to good people and good things are going to happen to bad people.

Pain as a Result of Opposition

For every right, there must be a wrong, and for every good, a bad. As a result of liberty, there will be joy and there will be pain. Since all men are given liberty, pain is inevitable for all. You may now be asking, "Why didn't God create a world where pain and suffering weren't necessary?" or "Wouldn't life be better if there were no adversity, pain, or opposition?"

Parable of the Two Schools

Given these two scenarios below, which of the two schools would you prefer to attend?

School #1

You are required to study and work. Your grade is based on performance, so some will get A's and others will fail. Only those who fulfill the requirements will earn a degree. It is challenging and at times painful.

School #2

You must take tests but all the tests are multiple choice. "C" is always the correct answer. You are required to answer "C" for each question, and everyone who takes the test receives a perfect score. Everyone receives a degree and graduates with a perfect 4.0 GPA. It is easy. It is free from work, pain, and struggle.

When I have posed these two options at various universities, the majority of the students will choose School #2. I will then ask, "How many would like to have a surgery performed by a graduate of School #2?" Obviously, no hands get raised. If such a medical school existed, everyone would graduate with a perfect score and a medical degree. Graduates would be given the title of doctor, but the real purpose of learning the necessary skills of surgery would not have been achieved, and thus the diploma from such an institution would be worthless. Work, pain, struggle, and failure are part of the necessary education process to produce an individual with the skills of a surgeon.

When work, pain, and suffering are taken out of school, the purpose of school is defeated. Likewise, if God changed our current world to one where pain and suffering were eliminated, the purpose of life would be defeated. Life was not designed to be an existence of endless bliss. Life was designed to create greatness in each of us. "The command *Be ye perfect* is not idealistic gas. Nor is it a command to do the impossible. He is going to make us into creatures that can obey that command. . . He will make the feeblest and filthiest of us into . . . a dazzling, radiant, immortal creature, pulsating all through with such energy and joy and wisdom and love as we cannot now imagine, a bright stainless mirror which reflects back to God perfectly (though, of course, on a smaller scale) His own boundless power and delight and goodness. The process will be long and in parts very painful; but that is what we are in for. Nothing less. He meant what He said."[6]

Liberty gives us the power to think, choose, and act for ourselves. It is an eternal principle that has always existed and always will. Liberty creates opportunities for growth and joy and at the same time creates failure, pain, and suffering. "Try to exclude the possibility of suffering which the order of nature and the existence of free-wills involve, and you find that you have excluded life itself."[7] Liberty gives us the power to progress and improve our lives and the lives of those around us. Take away liberty and you take away progression toward greatness.

2. Growth

We are all familiar with growing pains. Growth is a source of pain, but it is good pain. For example, when we lift weights or exercise, we experience pain. We have learned that this is a good pain, because from this pain comes growth and improvement.

We often experience growing pains when we strive to reach the next level of prosperity. Sometimes the best people experience great pain because they are ready to learn and grow. The Savior teaches in the parable of the vine, ". . . every branch that bears fruit He prunes, that it may bear more fruit."[8] Pruning is the process of cutting off branches. Someone unfamiliar with the pruning process may think that the person pruning the vine is trying to punish, destroy, or kill the tree. While pruning does cause pain, its purpose is not to injure, harm, or punish. On the contrary, the pruning process will eventually lead to a higher level of production.

Parable of the Renovated House

"Image yourself as a living house. God comes in to rebuild that house. At first perhaps, you can understand what He is doing. He is getting the drains right and stopping the leaks in the roof and so on: you knew that those jobs needed doing and so you are not surprised. But presently He starts knocking the house about in a way that hurts abominably and does not seem to make sense. What on earth is He up to? The explanation is that He is building quite a different house from the one you thought of—throwing out a new wing here, putting on an extra floor there, running up towers, making courtyards. You thought you were going to be made into a decent little cottage: but He is building a palace."[9] Jesus is the master carpenter and he wants to build us into something great. As taught the apostle Paul, "God began doing a good work in you, and I am sure he will continue it until it is finished . . ."[10]

3. PERSONAL CHOICES/SINS

The power of choice brings with it great responsibility, as well as consequences. The consequences of our choices can lead to pain and suffering or joy. For example, if you choose to touch a hot stove you will experience the pain of getting burned. The choice to smoke cigarettes can result in the pains of lung cancer. How do we avoid the pain of bad choices? One way is by following the commandments of God. God knows which choices result in pain and suffering and which result in joy. Learning and following the commandments of God will lead us to choices that will avoid the pain of personal sin and result in the joys of freedom and prosperity. We can eliminate future pain by learning from past mistakes and not repeating them.

Discipline

Many have asked the question, "Why would a loving God cause me pain because of a bad choice?" Just as loving parents discipline their children to lead them to a desirable result, so the pain of sin is God's way of disciplining us. He ultimately wants us to experience happiness, joy, and eternal life. As taught the apostle Paul, ". . . God disciplines us for our good . . ."[11] "For the Lord disciplines the one he loves. . ."[12] And in the words of C.S. Lewis, "God whispers to us in our pleasure . . . and shouts in our pain."[13] You can stop the pain that results from personal sin at any time by ceasing the sin. You will only experience discipline and the pain of personal sin as long as you choose to.

4. CHOICES/SINS OF OTHERS

Choice must exist for us to have our God-given liberty. With this choice, people are able to help and hurt each other. If God stops people from using their choices in a bad way, he also takes away our liberty and ability to choose to use liberty in a good way. God did not cause or want Hitler to kill millions of innocent Jews. This pain was the result of Hitler choosing to use his God-given liberty for cruel and evil purposes.

My oldest brother works at a pharmacy that has been robbed several times. If one of these robbers were to choose to shoot my brother during the course of a robbery, my brother would experience the pain of a gunshot wound as a result of the robber's choices. The pain would not be my brother's fault, but he would experience pain nonetheless. Throughout our lives we will all experience pain as the result of the choices and sins of others. The apostle Paul expressed this pain in a letter to the Corinthians, "Five times the Jews gave me thirty-nine lashes with a whip. Three times the Romans beat me with a big stick, and once my enemies stoned me. . . During my many travels, I have been in danger from . . . robbers."[14]

Parable of the Wolf and the Shepherd

"The shepherd drives the wolf from the sheep's throat, for which the sheep thanks the shepherd as his liberator, while the wolf denounces him for the same act as the destroyer of liberty."[15] If you do good, the bad will denounce you as the wolf denounces the shepherd, but blessed are those who are persecuted for doing good. The Savior taught, "God blesses those people who are treated badly for doing right. . . God will bless you when people insult you, mistreat you, and tell all kinds of evil lies about you . . ."[16] "Rejoice, and be exceeding glad: for great is your reward in heaven: for so persecuted they the prophets which were before you."[17] It is "better to suffer for a good cause than live safely without one."[18] When people do bad things to us, we should respond with the courage to endure, and then rejoice, for the Lord will bless us with great rewards in heaven.

Four Causes of Pain™	1. Liberty	2. Growth	3. Personal Choices/ Sins	4. Choices/ Sins of Others
Why Pain?	Opposition	Growing Pains	Ressult of Your Negative Action	Result of Others' Negative Action
When Does the Pain Stop?	Never	When Higher Level is Attained	When We Repent	Death
What Is the Proper Response?	Courage	Faith/Good Pain	Guilt/Bad Pain	Rejoice/ Heavenly Reward

To live is to experience pain. To survive and benefit from pain, we must learn why we experience pain and give meaning to the pain. When we experience pain, it is important to identify which of the four reasons caused the pain. This will determine how we respond, interpret, and feel about the pain. "The sorest afflictions never appear intolerable, except when we see them in the wrong light."[19] Misapplying why pain has occurred will cause us to incorrectly respond to the pain. Many convince themselves that they are to blame and deserve the pain, even though it is really the result of liberty, growth, or the sins of others.

Misapplying Pain Caused by Liberty as Pain Caused by Sin

If we experience pain caused by liberty, but attribute the pain to a personal sin, we feel guilt for something we have not caused. A rabbi related the following story: a "middle-aged couple had one daughter, a bright nineteen-year-old, who was in her freshman year at an out-of-state college. One morning at breakfast, they received a phone call from the university infirmary. 'We have bad news for you. Your daughter collapsed while walking to class this morning. It seems a blood vessel burst in her brain. She died before we could do anything for her. We're terribly sorry . . .' I went over to see them that same day. I entered their home feeling very inadequate, not knowing any word that could ease their pain. I anticipated anger, shock, grief but I didn't expect to hear the first words they said to me: 'You know, Rabbi, we didn't fast last Yom Kippur.' Why did they say that? Why did they assume that they were somehow responsible for this tragedy?. . . One of the ways in which people have tried to make sense of the world's suffering in every generation has been by assuming that we deserve what we get, that somehow our misfortunes come as punishment for our sins."[20]

This couple mistakenly blamed themselves for their daughter's death instead of identifying it as a result of liberty and natural laws, resulting in unnecessary guilt. God will never hurt innocent people as a punishment for your sins. Would you punish your child for something your spouse did?

Not All Pain Is Beneficial

In the parable of the vine, pruning led to growth and increased production. If the vine represents man, the cutting during the pruning process is for our benefit. This does not mean that all cutting is for our good, however. The mugger who stabs you with a knife is not pruning. The pain from the stab of the mugger is the result of liberty and sins of another and should be responded to with courage and rejoicing, for great is your reward in heaven.[21] If we interpret the stabbing as a growing pain, we would interpret that we should respond with faith and view this pain as good. This would mean that God wanted you to get stabbed by the mugger so you could learn from the experience. While you can learn from and overcome the pain caused by the mugger, God did not want you to be stabbed. Would you stab one of your children with a knife so they could learn from the experience?

Misapplying Growth Pain and Pain from Personal Sin

There are times when we apply the good pain from growth to pain that is a result of personal sin. Misapplying the cause of pain in this way causes confusion and frustration. This can actually hinder growth. When you begin to drudge up sins you have committed to explain the pain you are experiencing, you will feel guilty and view the pain as a punishment. There are many Christians who are filled with guilt as the result of growth pains. How regrettable. They should be responding with faith and be raised to a higher level of prosperity. Instead, when this pain is misapplied, a person spirals downward with feelings of guilt and unworthiness. This can also damage a person's relationship with God, for they misunderstand His pruning as punishment instead of for their growth and good.

Parable of the Weightlifter

If a weightlifter interpreted the growing pains he experienced as an injury, he would stop lifting and never grow. He would be misunderstanding the good pain of growth and would instead be filled with concern that he was injured. One the other hand, if the weightlifter did an exercise that caused injury but interpreted the pain as a growth pain, he would continue the exercise, resulting in more injury. Like the weightlifter, we too must be careful not to apply the pain from personal sin to growing pains. When we do this, we will continue in a sin that results in a downward spiral when what we need to do is repent.

CONCLUSION—COURAGE

Courage is developing the ability to respond, endure, and, in some cases, overcome the pain, suffering, and hardships life can bring. It is not the ability to eliminate our fears but to act despite our fears. "Don't let the sensation of fear convince you that you're too weak to have courage. Fear is the opportunity for courage, not proof of cowardice."[22]

We are not left to deal with the challenges of life alone. We can call upon God, and He will assist us. The Savior extends to each of us this invitation, "Come unto me, all ye that labour and are heavy laden, and I will give you rest. Take my yoke upon you, and learn of me; for I am meek and lowly in heart: and ye shall find rest unto your souls. For my yoke is easy, and my burden is light."[23] The goal is not to eliminate pain but to properly respond to pain. "Be strong and courageous. Do not be afraid or discouraged . . ."[24]

Paul endured well the pain he suffered. Shortly before his death, Paul wrote to Timothy from his prison cell in Rome, "I have fought a good fight, I have finished my course, I have kept the faith: Henceforth there is laid up for me a crown of righteousness, which the Lord, the righteous judge, shall give me at that day: and not to me only, but unto all them also that love his appearing."[25] We need to have the courage to endure life's pain and face our fears so that the Savior may say to each of us, "Well done, thou good and faithful servant: thou hast been faithful over a few things, I will make thee ruler over many things: enter thou into the joy of thy lord."[26]

TRUTH 5

Pain is Inevitable and Misery is Optional.

PRINCIPLE III:

CONSEQUENCES ARE THE
RESULTS OF OUR CHOICES

*"Every choice carries a consequence. For better or worse, each choice is
the unavoidable consequence of its predecessor. There are not exceptions.
If you can accept that a bad choice carries the seed of its own punishment,
why not accept the fact that a good choice yields desirable fruit?"*
–Gary Ryan Blair

Myth 6

I Choose the Consequences of My Actions

While speaking at a prison to a group of the inmates,[1] I asked for a volunteer from the inmates to describe his dream life. After a long pause and some prodding, one of the inmates began to speak. I was rather surprised by his vivid description of a successful career, a beautiful home, and a loving, happy family. I then asked, "Why are you in prison?" The inmate responded, "For drugs." I then asked if drugs would take him away from or toward the dream life he described. I will never forget his response, "I can have both." I replied by saying, "What would happen if you touched a hot stove with your bare hand?" The inmate replied, "I would get burned." I continued, "What if you don't want to get burned? Can you just choose to touch a hot stove and not get burned?" He, of course, answered no. I then taught that we can choose whether or not to touch a hot stove, but we cannot decide whether or not we get burned. We can choose our actions, but we cannot choose the consequences of our choices. Getting burned is a natural consequence of touching a hot stove just like a prison sentence is the consequence of being involved with illegal drugs.

To this the inmate replied, "I am in prison, have no money, am divorced, and rarely see my kids. If you're so smart, how do I change this?" I answered, "You need to learn and live divine laws." The inmate replied, "What do you mean?" I continued, "Our lives are governed by divine laws, such as gravity. A child, though ignorant of the law, will still fall if he jumps off a ledge and will still get burned if he touches a hot stove. The divine laws that govern wealth, health, relationships, and our spirits are as clear and as binding as those that govern the earth, such as gravity. Regardless of whether or not we know or understand divine laws, they always operate the same. Our success or failure, our happiness or unhappiness, depends on our knowledge and application of these laws in our lives."

The inmate then asked, "So why are some people rich and some poor?" I replied, "Why are some people physically fit and others overweight?" I explained that people's health differs because they have made different choices. Consider someone with a lot of money who is also overweight. This person has learned to live financial laws but does not live the laws of health. Something similar could be said about someone who is in great shape and is poor. They have learned to live the laws of health but not the laws of wealth. The great news is that you can be successful in all areas of your life by living the divine laws related to each area.

The inmate then asked, "You are obviously successful—can I achieve success?" In response, I asked the inmate to climb on the table he was sitting at and I climbed onto the table at the front of the room. I then said, "On the count of three, jump off the table. One, two, three." We both jumped off the table and hit the floor. I continued teaching that the law of gravity affected both of us the same regardless of age, gender, race, or upbringing. This is also true of the laws of success. They are the same now as they were in the past and will be the same in the future. Our knowledge about these laws may fluctuate, but their principles and application will never change. Anyone can be successful, because anyone can learn and follow the laws of success.

God has blessed all men with liberty. This great freedom of choice is what determines who we will become. All men are born equal but become unequal as they make decisions. Every man chooses to obey laws differently. One may choose to play softball while another chooses to build a business. One may choose to turn on the television while another chooses to read books. One may choose to golf on his day off while another chooses to spend time with his family. One man chooses to listen to the radio on his way to work and another man chooses to listen to positive tapes. We are born equal, yet years later live diversely, all because we chose to live divine laws differently. It is really very simple. Following divine laws results in positive outcomes.

A prison guard then asked, "How much money did you make last year?" I replied, "How much money did you make last year?" The guard replied, "$30,000." I then answered his question by saying, "I made ten times more than you did last year. Do you think I am ten times smarter than you or ten times better than you?" The guard thought about the question and replied, "No, you are not ten times smarter or better than me." To make my point clear, I continued, "There is no difference between you and me. I have just learned certain financial principles. There are certain principles for success in a marriage, there are certain principles for spiritual success, and there are certain principles for success in finance. If one desires to, one can dramatically increase his or her income by learning and applying the laws of wealth."

Years later, I was at a chamber of commerce meeting and recognized the inmate I had spoken with at the prison. He approached me and said, "Thank you so much for visiting me in prison; your message changed my life. I always wondered why some men had great lives while mine was miserable. I saw people with successful careers, beautiful homes, and happy families and wondered why my life was just the opposite. Once I learned that there were divine laws to success, my heart was filled with hope and peace. I realized that all I had to do was learn these laws and then have courage, discipline, and the guts to obey them. Once I realized this, I knew that I would one day live in the home of my dreams, have no debt, and be a hero to my wife and children. It has been a long road but I have transformed my life from one of bondage and misery to one of freedom and prosperity."

DIVINE LAW—CHOICE AND CONSEQUENCE

Each divine law creates a choice to obey or disobey. With each choice, comes a divinely appointed consequence. No amount of rationalizing or complaining will alter the consequence. If you pick up one end of a stick (choice), you also pick up the other end of the stick (consequence of that choice).

Every time we make a choice we are either obeying or disobeying a divine law. As we obey divine laws, we move to a more successful state of happiness, peace, power, freedom and prosperity. As we disobey the laws, we move to a state of sadness, weakness, bondage, and misery. Each moment we are progressing toward one of these two states. This gift of choice is like fire: if properly used, it creates warmth and life; if improperly used, it can burn or even kill.

Farm Metaphor

On a farm, you reap what you sow. If you plant corn, you harvest corn. You cannot plant corn and harvest watermelon. Similarly, we reap what we sow in life. Our choices are the seeds and the consequences the harvest. At times, we may attempt to choose the consequences of our choices or misunderstand what the consequence of a choice will be. We might want to eat 10,000 calories a day and not gain weight. We might want to smoke cigarettes, but not get lung cancer. We want to violate divine laws and still have freedom and prosperity. This is as foolish as a farmer planting corn and expecting to harvest watermelon. Some might also expect financial abundance but learn nothing regarding the laws of wealth. This is as silly as a farmer not planting and expecting a great harvest. Further examples can be observed in the following myths.

Myth—Do What You Love and the Money Will Follow

It puzzles me that many so called success and self-help books teach the myth that money will come if you simply do what you love. Any application of this myth to real life proves it is not true. If a person who loves to play video games plays video games all day, will the money follow? Of course not. A person can love genealogy or singing in the church choir, but that does not mean the amount in his or her bank account is going to increase.

One reason many new businesses fail is because someone decides to do what they love to do and then are forced to shut the doors because the money never follows. Liking an area of business and knowing how to operate a profitable business are two different things. A great deal of new businesses fail for two reasons: 1) The business idea is not economically feasible. Robert Noyce, a founder of Intel,® said, "A lot of things are technologically possible but only economically feasible products will become a reality." 2) The person starting the business does not posses the necessary entrepreneurial skills required to succeed.

Simply doing what you love will not produce money. You must develop the necessary entrepreneurial skills to start and manage a business and find a way to make doing what you love economically feasible. For example, a person who loves to cook opens a restaurant. She quickly finds, however, that it takes much more than the technical skill of cooking to turn a profit. This person may make delicious food, however if not coupled with entrepreneurial, managing, and marketing skills the restaurant will most likely not last very long.

Myth—God Will Rescue Me

Following 40 days of fasting, Jesus was tempted three times by Satan. The second temptation is recorded in the New Testament as follows, "Then the devil taketh him up into the holy city, and setteth him on a pinnacle of the temple, And saith unto him, If thou be the Son of God, cast thyself down: for it is written, He shall give his angels charge concerning thee: and in their hands they shall bear thee up, lest at any time thou dash thy foot against a stone. Jesus said unto him, It is written again, Thou shalt not tempt the Lord thy God."[2]

Satan's temptation was an appeal to man's desire to be miraculously delivered from the consequences of an action. We tend to seek divine intervention to rescue us from consequences with little or no effort on our part. This tendency was illustrated by Ancient Greece dramatists' use of the "dues ex machine," meaning "God from a machine." This was a machine in which actors portraying the gods would suddenly be lowered on the scene to save the mortal characters from the consequences of their choices.

Satan's use of this temptation continues today and can easily be seen manifested by the student who fails to study and then prays for an "A" during the examination, or the person who violated the divine laws of health and then prays for deliverance from resulting sickness, or the person who purchases an expensive plasma screen television and then prays for help to pay the rent. We also see this tendency manifested by those who have incurred large amounts of debt and then seek to be delivered from the bondage and obligation of repayment through bankruptcy, or those who seek deliverance from a disease of choice by taking a pill to treat the symptoms instead of changing the behavior that causes the symptoms.

We should respond to such temptations as did the Savior by saying, "Thou shalt not tempt the Lord thy God."[3] We must accept responsibility, which is the willingness and ability to recognize and accept the consequences of our actions.

Myth—Freedom Comes From Doing Whatever I Want

We have all heard someone describe freedom as follows, "No one can tell me what to do. I am in charge of my own life. God's commandments are restrictive and to be free one must not be bound by the laws of God." The laws of God are not restrictive but are a road map to joy. The volition of these laws is not freedom but bondage, pain, and misery. As taught the Savior, ". . . whoever commits sin is a slave of sin."[4] Those who know and live the commands of God enjoy freedom, joy, and prosperity. Thus, obedience to the laws of God is freedom.

The correct use of liberty—the power to choose—will result in more choices. The misuse of our liberty will result in fewer choices. Each time we make a choice we either gain more freedom as a result of our increased choices or digress toward bondage as the result of our diminished choices.

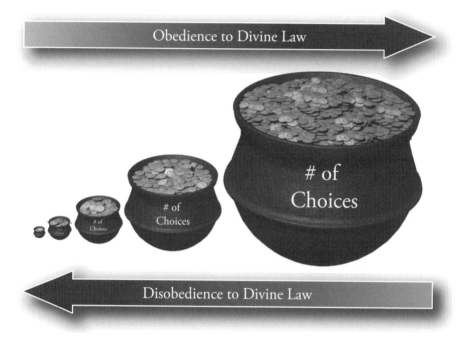

Bank Metaphor

"If someone decides to rob a bank, for instance, he or she may be incarcerated under the law. That person not only lost the ability to rob banks, but is also restricted from other lawful activities in the future. A trip to the park, while lawful, is no longer an option after incarceration. The opposite is also true. If one chooses to open a bank and work hard within the boundaries of the law, they can continue that activity and will have opportunities that they did not have previously. A lawful and successful enterprise would provide funding for additional activities that the person could not afford before their choice to provide banking services."[5]

CONCLUSION

This chapter can be summarized by the following words from the Bible. "Behold, I set before you this day a blessing and a curse; A blessing, if ye obey the commandments of the LORD your God . . . And a curse, if ye will not obey the commandments of the LORD your God."[6]

TRUTH 6

**We Can Choose Our Actions, but
We Cannot Choose the Consequences.**

PRINCIPLE IV:

GOVERNMENT IS CREATED BY THE PEOPLE TO PROTECT OUR GOD-GIVEN RIGHTS

"America didn't give me a dole when I was broke, but she did give me some valuable assets—freedom and the opportunity to work."
–J. Willard Marriott, Founder of Marriott International

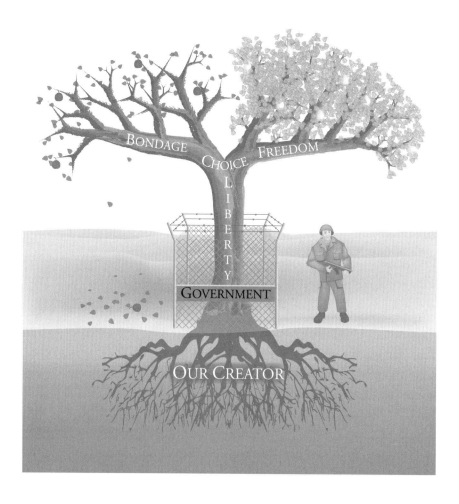

THE CONSTITUTION CALLS FOR THE
SEPARATION OF CHURCH AND STATE

The phrase "separation of church and state" has been used so often by courts and other organizations that many believe it to be a part of the First Amendment of the Constitution. The phrase, however, is nowhere stated in the Constitution or other founding documents. The First Amendment was never intended to remove God from the government. The First Amendment says, "Congress shall make no law respecting an establishment of religion or prohibiting the free exercise thereof . . ."[1]

The First Amendment is a constitutional prohibition of a government-sponsored religion. The founders' purpose was to prevent the formation of a single denomination created and operated by the government as had occurred in Great Britain with the Church of England. The First Amendment simply prohibits the U.S. government from creating and operating a church or interfering with the religious practices of its citizens.

In an attempt to erode and destroy the religious principles on which America was founded, some have wrest and misapplied the First Amendment to mean that any public religious activity is unconstitutional using the fabricated disguise of "separation of church and state." This has now evolved into court-ordered bans which have falsely declared it unconstitutional to pray in school or at public meetings,[2] and to display the Ten Commandments in schools[3] and other government buildings.[4] It has been taken even as far as declaring it unconstitutional for a person to have a cross-shaped planter in a public cemetery,[5] for a teacher to be seen at school with a copy of the Bible,[6] and for nativity scenes to be displayed on public property.[7]

"Although states print hundreds of thousands of custom license plates purchased and ordered by individual citizens, Oregon refused to print, 'PRAY,'[8] Virginia refused to print, 'GOD 4 US,'[9] and Utah refused to print, 'THANK GOD,'[10] claiming that such customized license plates violated the 'separation of church and state.'"[11]

Many are actively seeking legislation which will exclude any mention of God or any display of religious connotation in the public square. Excluding God is undoubtedly counter to the intentions of the First Amendment and the Founding Fathers. God is the foundation upon which the American republic was built. Our currency bears the inscription of the motto, "In God We Trust," and citizens pledge allegiance to a "nation under God." President Dwight Eisenhower said of these words in the pledge of allegiance, "They will help us to keep constantly in our minds and hearts the spiritual and moral principles which alone give dignity to man, and upon which our way of life is founded."[12] "To remove the influence of religion from public policy simply because some are uncomfortable with any degree of moral restraint is like the passenger on a sinking ship who removes his life jacket because it is restrictive and uncomfortable."[13]

GOD'S HAND IN THE FOUNDING OF AMERICA

The Founding Fathers relied upon and called upon God for assistance. They frequently declared that God's hand was working through them in the founding of America. James Madison, commonly called the Father of the Constitution, recognized God's hand in the rising of America. He concluded his inaugural address as president of the United States on March 4, 1809, with this statement, ". . . we have all been encouraged to fall in the guardianship and guidance of the Almighty Being whose power regulates the destiny of nations, whose blessings have been so conspicuously displayed to the rising of this republic, and to whom we are bound to address our devout gratitude for the past, as well as our fervent supplications and best hopes for the future."[14]

In a motion for daily prayers in the Constitutional Convention, Benjamin Franklin declared, "God governs in the affairs of men. And if a sparrow cannot fall to the ground without his notice, is it probable that an empire can rise without his aid? We have been assured, sir, in the sacred writings that 'except the Lord build the house, they labor in vain that build it.' I firmly believe this, and I also believe without his concurring aid we shall succeed in this political building no better than the builders of Babel."[15]

George Washington–Servant Raised Up and Protected by God [16]

George Washington was born in what is now modern day Virginia on February 22, 1732 to Mary Ball and Augustine Washington. George's character was formed and developed early in his youth. His parents instilled in him the values found in the Bible. "At a very early age George was required to memorize the Ten Commandments. His mother found time to see to this . . . [George's father] did his part by explaining the meaning of the Ten Commandments. He made it crystal clear that a member of the Washington family does not lie, does not steal, does not cheat."[17] These early lessons prepared him for the inspired missions he completed later in his life.

In 1754, Washington, age 22, was a colonel in the British army and fought in many battles during the French and Indian War. One such battle was the battle at the Monongahela on July 9, 1755, when the British were ambushed by a party of the French and Indians. "It was a purely Indian-style fight, more one-sided than had ever occurred in the history of woodland warfare. The pandemonium lasted over two hours. A hail of bullets that hardly tested the aim of the French and the Indians had been poured in the British army. It was butchery rather than a battle."[18] The British suffered a decisive defeat with 714 of the 1,300 soldiers being killed or wounded while only 60 of the French and Indians were killed or wounded. During this battle, all of the British officers on horseback were slain or disabled except for Washington. This made him an obvious and important target as he moved about, commanding the soldiers.

Dr. James Craik, a military surgeon, who witnessed the events of the battle, recorded this regarding Washington: "I expected every moment to see him fall. His duty and situation exposed him to every danger. Nothing but the superintending care of Providence could have saved him from the fate of all around him."[19]

Following the battle, Washington wrote to his brother, John, saying, ". . . by the all-powerful dispensations of Providence, I have been protected beyond all human probability, or expectation; for I had four bullets through my coat, and two horses shot under me, yet escaped unhurt, though death was leveling my companions on every side of me!"[20]

An Indian warrior who played a leading part in this bloody battle stated, "Washington was never born to be killed by a bullet! For I had seventeen fair fires at him with my rifle, and after all could not bring him to the ground."[21] Another distinguished young Indian warrior, Redhawk, became acquainted with Dr. Daniel Craig. In a conversion with the doctor, Redhawk inquired what young officer it was who rode with great speed from post to post during the action. The doctor replied, "Colonel Washington." Redhawk immediately stated, "I fired eleven deliberate shots at that man but could not touch him. I gave over any further attempt, believing he was protected by the Great Spirit, and could not be killed."[22]

In 1758, Washington resigned from active military duty and worked as a Virginia planter and politician. In 1770, Colonel Washington and some woodsmen were locating lands in Kanawha, present day Ohio and West Virginia, when they were approached by a group of Indians. One of the Indians, who led the attack at Monongahela on the British 15 years earlier, approached Washington and said through an interpreter, "I am a chief and ruler over many tribes. My influence extends to the waters of the great lakes, and to the far Blue Mountains. I have traveled a long and weary path, that I might see the young warrior of the great battle. It was on the day, when the white man's blood mixed with the streams of our forest, that I first beheld this chief [pointing to Washington]: I called to my young men and said, mark yon tall and daring warrior? . . . Quick, let your aim be certain, and he dies. Our rifles were leveled, rifles which, but for him, knew not how to miss—'twas all in vain, a power mightier far than we, shielded him from harm. He cannot die in battle. I am old, and soon shall be gathered to the great council-fire of my fathers, in the land of shades, but ere I go, there is a something bids me speak in the voice of prophecy. Listen! The Great Spirit protects that man, and guides his destinies—he will become the chief of nations, and a people yet unborn will hail him as the founder of a mighty empire."[23]

The prophecy of the Indian chief would soon be fulfilled as Washington took a leading role in the growing resistance of the American colonies to British rule in the early 1770s. Fighting began on April 19, 1775 with the Battles of Lexington and Concord to begin the Revolutionary War. On June 14, 1775, Congress created the Continental Army and selected Washington as commander-in-chief. The fight for freedom and the creation of a mighty empire had begun.

Washington led the Continental Army in numerous battles. In each battle, Washington escaped unharmed. The Continental Army suffered much sickness, privations and death during the eight years of the Revolutionary War, but Washington's courage, will, and reliance on the power and guidance of the Almighty led the colonies to an eventual victory over the Kingdom of Great Britain. In 1783, the Treaty of Paris officially ended the Revolutionary War and a new nation was born, even the United States of America. To bring about this noble purpose, God raised up, protected, and guided George Washington.

After victory, there were desires by some to make Washington a king. The first Congress voted to pay Washington a salary of $25,000 a year (approximately $500,000 in 2006 dollars). Washington, however, chose to continue his work as an unpaid servant of the people. During his years as commander-in-chief of the Continental Army he took no pay. He would do the same during his 8 years as the first president of the United States. He exemplified the word of the Savior, "But he that is greatest among you shall be your servant."[24]

In 1797, as he ended his presidency, Washington delivered a farewell address that emphasized the proper role and function of government. In this address he stated, "Of all the dispositions and habits, which lead to political prosperity, religion and morality are indispensable supports. In vain would that man claim the tribute of patriotism, who should labor to subvert these great pillars of human happiness. . . It is substantially true, that virtue or morality is a necessary spring of popular government."[25] Washington had completed his divinely inspired work and would shortly be taken home to the God who gave him life.

On December 14, 1799, at age 67, George Washington died, but the nation he helped bring to life lives on. At his death, Congressman Henry Lee said of Washington, "First in war, first in peace, and first in the hearts of his countrymen . . . Correct throughout, vice shuddered in his presence and virtue always felt his fostering hand; the purity of his private character gave effulgence to his public virtues. . . Such was the man for whom our nation mourns."[26]

Washington was a patriot whose soul did joy in the liberty and freedom of his country. A man more concerned with deeds than words, who fought and labored intensely for his people. Through his firm faith in Christ and selfless devotion to country, he lived his motto, "For God and my Country."[27]

DIVINE LAW—THE FOUNDATION OF GOOD GOVERNMENT

Many have wondered what literature influenced the Founding Fathers and assisted them in the formation of their ideas on government. To find out which resources the Founding Fathers drew upon during the founding period, a study was performed that examined the citations in public political literature written between 1760 and 1805.[28] The most frequently cited book in the sample literature was the Bible with 34 percent of the citations. Other major sources of the citations were Montesquieu, a French writer famous for his theory on the separation of powers, with 8.3 percent; William Blackstone, an English jurist and professor who wrote the book *Commentaries on the Laws of England*, with 7.9 percent; and John Locke, an English philosopher who developed the concepts of "government with the consent of the governed" and "rights of life, liberty, and property," with 2.9 percent.[29] While there were numerous historians, philosophers, economists, and lawyers cited by the Founding Fathers, the single most influential reference source for their work on the Constitution and other founding documents was the Holy Bible.

According to James Madison, fourth president of the United States, "We have staked the whole future of American civilization not upon the power of the government—far from it. We have staked the future of all of our political institutions upon the capacity of each and all of us to govern ourselves according to the Ten Commandments of God."[30]

"Displays like the Ten Commandments tell a critically important part of America's history. They make it clear that America is not like other nations. Much of our legal system was deliberately established on principles derived directly from the Bible. In fact, 12 of the original 13 colonies incorporated the entire Ten Commandments into their civil and criminal laws."[31]

John Adams, the first vice president and the second president of the United States, in a letter written to Thomas Jefferson dated December

1813 wrote, "I have examined all as well as . . . my busy life would allow me and the result is that the Bible is the best book in the world. It contains more ... than all the libraries I have seen ..."[32]

John Adams also wrote in his dairy, "Suppose a nation in some distant region should take the Bible for their only law-book; and every member should regulate his conduct by the precepts there exhibited. Every member would be obligated, in conscience, to temperance and frugality and industry, to justice and kindness and charity toward his fellowmen, and to piety, love, and reverence toward Almighty God. In this commonwealth no man would impair his health with gluttony, drunkenness or lust: no man would sacrifice his precious time to cards, or trifling with other mean amusements; no man would steal or lie, or in any way defraud his neighbor, but would live in peace and good will with all men; no man would blaspheme his Maker or profane his worship; but ... a sincere and unaffected devotion would reign in all hearts. What a utopia, what a paradise this region would be."[33]

"We must never forget that nations may, and usually do, sow the seeds of their own destruction while enjoying unprecedented prosperity... At least twenty great civilizations have disappeared. The pattern is shockingly similar. All, before their collapse, showed a decline in spiritual values, in moral stamina, and in the freedom and responsibility of their citizens ... [The Ten Commandments] are the foundation principles upon which all civilized government and our present civilization is built. To disregard them will lead to inevitable personal character loss and ruin. To disregard them as a nation will inevitably lead that nation to destruction."[34]

CONCLUSION

The famous French historian Alexis de Tocqueville traveled to America in the early 1800s to find out what made America great. He said, "I sought for the greatness and genius of America in her commodious harbors and her ample rivers, and it was not there; in her fertile fields and boundless prairies, and it was not there; in her rich mines and her vast world of commerce, and it was not there. Not until I went to the churches of America and heard her pulpits aflame with righteousness did I understand the secret of her genius and power. America is great because she is good, and if America ever ceases to be good, America will cease to be great."[35]

TRUTH 7

America was Built on the Foundation of Divine Law by Wise and Noble Men Inspired by the Almighty.

Myth 8

The U.S. Constitution Established a Pure Democracy

The Founding Fathers' goal was to create a government that could protect God-given rights. To do this, they created a representative democracy rather than a pure democracy. A pure democracy is government by majority vote; therefore, the majority could vote to take away the God-given rights of the minority. Thomas Jefferson stated that, "A democracy is nothing more than mob rule, where 51 percent of the people may take away the rights of the other 49." We are each in some aspect a minority. To protect the rights of all, the Founding Fathers created a new form of government. They created a constitutional, representative democracy, which they called "a Republican Form of Government."[1] The United States is a constitutional democratic republic. In a constitutional democratic republic, there are God-given rights protected by the government, which cannot be violated, even by majority vote.

The Creation of the Constitution

Following victory in the Revolutionary War, the American colonies had the unique opportunity of establishing a new country and government. The Articles of Confederation were the first governing document that loosely tied the newly independent thirteen colonies, but they were incomplete and inadequate to completely govern the new nation. To establish a constitution and a new form of government, the Constitutional Convention was organized and held in Philadelphia from May 25 to September 17, 1787. George Washington presided over the convention and with 54 other great leaders of the new nation and the inspiration of the Almighty, they drafted the Constitution of the United States of America. This document was the first written constitution in the world and the foundation of the newly founded republic.

George Washington called the creation of the Constitution a miracle. He wrote in a letter dated February 7, 1788, "It appears to me, then, little short of a miracle, that the delegates from so many States different from each other, as you know, in their manners, circumstances, and prejudices, should unite in forming a system of national government."[2]

James Madison, often called the father of the Constitution for the key role he played at the convention, said of the 55 leaders assembled, "I feel it a duty to express my profound and solemn conviction, derived from my intimate opportunity of observing and appreciating the views of the Convention, collectively and individually, that there never was an assembly of men, charged with a great and arduous trust, who were more pure in their motives, or more exclusively or anxiously devoted to the object committed to them, than were the members of the [Constitutional] Convention of 1787, to the devising and proposing a constitutional system ... [to] secure the permanent liberty and happiness of their country."[3] He also said of the convention, "It is impossible for the man of pious reflection not to perceive in it a finger of that Almighty hand ..."[4]

Alexander Hamilton said of the constitution, "I sincerely esteem it a system, which without the finger of God, never could have been suggested and agreed upon by such a diversity of interest."[5]

Charles Pinckney, a delegate at the convention, said, "When the great work was done and published, I was ... struck with amazement. Nothing less than the superintending Hand of Providence, that so miraculously carried us through the war ... could have brought it about so complete."[6] Nothing short of a divine miracle resulted in the creation of a Constitution founded on just and holy principles which is now "The Supreme Law of the Land."[7]

FOUR PILLARS OF THE CONSTITUTION™

1. Divinely Granted Rights

2. Limited Power Granted by the People

3. Divine Law

4. Separation of Powers

THE FOUR PILLARS OF THE CONSTITUTION

Pillar 1: Divinely Granted Rights

Our divinely granted rights can be found in the Declaration of Independence and Bill of Rights. "We hold these truths to be self-evident, that all men are created equal, that they are endowed by their Creator with certain unalienable rights, that among these are life, liberty and the pursuit of happiness."[8]

"Starting at the foundation of the pyramid, let us first consider the origin of those freedoms we have come to know as human rights. There are only two possible sources. Rights are either God-given as part of the divine plan, or they are granted by government as part of the political plan. Reason, necessity, tradition, and religious convictions all lead me to accept the divine origin of these rights. If we accept the premise that human rights are granted by government, then we must be willing to accept the corollary that they can be denied by government. I, for one, shall never accept that premise."[9]

If you take God out of government, you also put at jeopardy our God-given rights. Thomas Jefferson asked, "Can the liberties of a nation be thought secure when we have removed their only firm basis, a conviction in the minds of the people that these liberties are of the gift of God? That they are not to be violated but with His wrath?"[10]

Pillar 2: Limited Power Granted by the People

Government is to secure the God-given rights and freedoms of individual citizens. As reads the Alabama Constitution, "… the sole object and only legitimate end of government is to protect the citizen in the enjoyment of life, liberty, and property, and when the government assumes other functions it is usurpation and oppression."[11]

Government is not to rule the people—the people are to rule the government. The Declaration of Independence reads, "to secure these rights, governments are instituted among men, deriving their just powers from the consent of the governed …" The preamble of the U.S. Constitution states, "We, the people of the United States … do ordain and establish this Constitution." The Constitution established a form of government described as "of the people, by the people, and for the people."

We must oppose any action by government that overstep the bound of the limited power to protect the rights of the citizens. George Washington warned, "Government is … like fire, it is a dangerous servant and a fearful master; never for a moment should it be left to irresponsible action."[12] Woodrow Wilson, 28th president of the United States, taught, "The history of liberty is a history of limitations of governmental power, not the increase of it … concentration of power is what always precedes the destruction of human liberty."[13] Always remember, "a government big enough to give you everything you want is big enough to take everything you've got."[14]

Pillar 3: Divine Law

In his first inaugural address, Thomas Jefferson said "a wise and frugal government, which shall restrain men from injuring one another"[15] is necessary to make a happy and prosperous people. Laws are to be created and enforced that protect man's God-given rights. John Locke taught, "The end of law is not to abolish or restrain, but to preserve and enlarge freedom."[16] These laws are not to be founded upon the ideas of man or the vote of the majority but are to be founded upon the laws of God.

Pillar 4: Separation of Powers

The constitution separates the power of government between the national, state, and local governments and divides the national government into three branches: legislative, executive, and judicial. Thomas Jefferson explained it this way: "The way to have good and safe government is not to trust it all to one, but to divide it among the many, distributing to every one exactly the functions he is competent to. Let the national government be entrusted with the defense of the nation, and its foreign and federal relations; the state governments with the civil rights, law, police, and administration of what concerns the state generally; the counties with the local concerns of the counties, and each township direct the interests within itself . . . What has destroyed liberty and the rights of man in every government which has ever existed under the sun? The generalizing and concentrating all cares and powers into one body."[17]

DEPARTURE FROM THE CONSTITUTION

Sadly, America has departed from many of the constitutional principles established by the founders. These departures have violated the U.S. Constitution and the rights of its citizens and have added elements of socialism to our form of government. We must fight to preserve and return to the principles of the U.S. Constitution that have produced the greatest freedom for the greatest number of people in the history of the world. Socialism also has a history—it has been a miserable failure each time attempted.

Constitutional Democratic Republic vs. Socialism

Consider the following illustration using a tree as a metaphor to depict the differences of two forms of government: constitutional democratic republic and socialism (see illustration).

In a constitutional democratic republic, our Creator is represented as the roots of the tree. From the roots of God spring the God-given rights of life, liberty, and the pursuit of happiness. These are represented as the tree trunk of liberty and choice. Government is illustrated as

CONSTITUTIONAL DEMOCRATIC REPUBLIC

CONSEQUENCE =
MISERY

CONSEQUENCE =
PROSPERITY

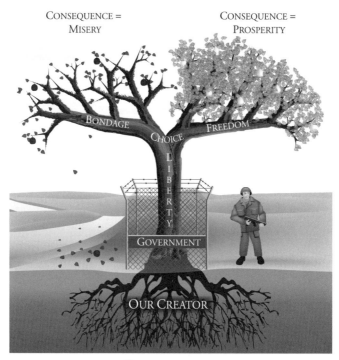

SOCIALISM

CONSEQUENCE=
Misery

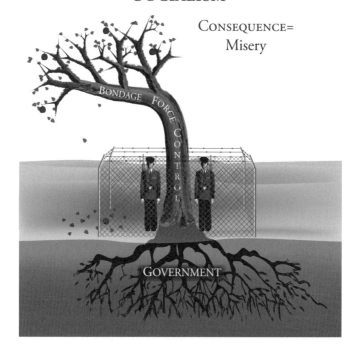

a protective fence with an armed soldier, separate from the tree. The government is created by the people to protect the God-given rights of life, liberty and the pursuit of happiness.

In socialism, the government is represented as the roots of the tree. Socialism and communism are often referred to as godless, because under socialism and communism government replaces God. God-given rights are replaced by the dictates of the government. The government is not created to protect God-given rights but to control and force the citizens to live by it's dictates. The tree trunk of control and force as well as the prison fence with guards preventing escape represent this.

Satan was the first socialist. He desired to replace God, as can be found in Isaiah 14: "How art thou fallen from heaven, O Lucifer . . . For thou hast said in thine heart, I will ascend into heaven, I will exalt my throne above the stars of God . . . I will be like the most High."[18] And C.S. Lewis taught, "How did the Dark Power go wrong? . . . The moment you have a self at all, there is a possibility of putting yourself first—wanting to be the center—wanting to be God in fact. That was the sin of Satan: and that was the sin he taught the human race. . . What Satan put into the heads of our remote ancestors was the idea that they could 'be like god'—could set up on their own as if they had created themselves—be their own masters—invent some sort of happiness for themselves outside God, apart from God. And out of that hopeless attempt has come . . . empires."[19]

Karl Marx, author of the *Communist Manifesto*, declared, "My object in life is to dethrone God." Socialists attempt to set themselves up as gods to rule and reign as masters over their adjuncts. Many are trying to remove God from government through the fabricated disguise of "separation of church and state" so they can then set themselves up as masters. The basic concept of socialism is that the government has full responsibility for the welfare of its citizens and, in order to fulfill that responsibility, must assume control of all their activities. Under socialism, the government controls and distributes the income and wealth of its citizens.

Socialism is not a political plan or party under the American

Constitution. It is a system of government opposite to that of our constitutional democratic republic. Socialism would destroy our American constitutional government and our freedom and rights to life, liberty, and the pursuit of happiness. No American patriot would ever support a socialistic program, because socialism is a system of human slavery and an act of treason against our country and our God-given liberties.

In the 1950s, Khrushchev, the communist leader of the Soviet Union after the death of Joseph Stalin, wanted to learn about American agriculture. President Eisenhower asked the secretary of agriculture, Ezra Benson, to host Khrushchev during his visit to the United States. As Secretary Benson and Khrushchev talked face to face, Khrushchev declared in substance, "You Americans are so gullible. No, you won't accept communism outright, but we'll keep feeding you small doses of socialism until you'll finally wake up and find you already have communism."[20] Today we are being fed socialism not from our enemies overseas but by American socialists in our government, media, schools, and neighborhoods.

EDUCATION

"Education is a better safeguard of liberty than a standing army."
–Edward Everett

Citizens should oppose any infringement of the inspired principles of the Constitution. In order to do this, "we must learn the principles of the Constitution in the tradition of the Founding Fathers. Have we read *The Federalist Papers*? Are we reading the Constitution and pondering it? Are we aware of its principles? Are we abiding by these principles and teaching them to others? Could we defend the Constitution? Can we recognize when a law is constitutionally unsound?"[21]

Benjamin Franklin taught, "A nation of well-informed men who have been taught to know and prize the rights which God has given them cannot be enslaved. It is in the region of ignorance that tyranny begins."[22] Thomas Jefferson warned, "If a nation expects to be ignorant and free, in a state of civilization, it expects what never was and never will be."[23] Education is essential for the preservation of freedom against the aspiring tyrants who would have us ignorantly vote ourselves into bondage.

In the school history textbooks of recent years, some of the greatest phrases in American history have been dropped and principles of socialism have crept in. Are we teaching our children the principles of freedom? This is key to securing liberty for future generations. Abraham Lincoln taught, "The philosophy of the school room in one generation will be the philosophy of government in the next."[24]

Conclusion

When James Russell Lowell, a nineteenth century American writer, was asked, "How long will the American Republic endure?" he replied: "As long as the ideas of the men who founded it continue dominant."[25]

Truth 8

The U.S. Constitution was Founded Upon the Just and Holy Principles of the Almighty.

Government Has a Responsibility
to Provide For the Poor and Needy

Many have acquired the attitude that the government should provide the necessities of life. As responsibility is shifted from the people to the government, freedom is eroded. Many people choose bondage and the illusion of government security over liberty and freedom. A classic example of people selling themselves into bondage for government support is found in the Old Testament. Instead of saving for a future time of need, the Egyptians relied upon the government to support them in the event of a disaster. When the disaster of famine hit, they were unprepared. As a result, they were compelled to exchange their money, livestock, land, and their lives (selling themselves into slavery) for government support.[1]

Today, many Americans are likewise willing to sell their freedom for government-provided health care. People are becoming slaves to the government in exchange for prescription drugs and becoming impoverished and dependant in exchange for government-planned retirement. "There was a time when the American people roared like lions for liberty; now they bleat like sheep for security."[2] Slavery is the result of seeking the illusion of government-supported security. Any society that gives up liberty in hope of security will find they lose both. Freedom and security are only to be found in our own liberty, industry, and production.

Government Welfare is Unconstitutional

James Madison, the father of the Constitution, said that if the government was to "assume the provision of the poor . . . it would subvert the very foundations and transmute the very nature of the limited government established by the people of America."[3]

Thomas Jefferson, third president of the United States, said in his first inaugural address that one of the things required for a happy and prosperous people was "a wise and frugal government … which shall leave them … free to regulate their own pursuits of industry and improvement, and shall not take from the mouth of labor the bread it has earned."[4] He also wrote of the idea to take from the top income earner to give to lower income earners, "To take from one, because it is thought that his own industry and that of his fathers has acquired too much, in order to spare others, who, or whose fathers have not exercised equal industry and skill, is to violate arbitrarily the first principle of association, 'the guarantee to everyone of a free exercise of his industry and the fruits acquired by it.'"[5]

Government welfare is unconstitutional because the money is not the government's to give. Since the government does not produce wealth, it must first take before it can give. For every give-away program the government implements, it has to create an even greater take-away program to pay for it, for "nothing can enter the public treasury for the benefit of one citizen or one class unless other citizens and other classes have been forced to send it in."[6]

"When a portion of wealth is transferred from the person who owns it—without his consent and without compensation, and whether by force or by fraud—to anyone who does not own it, then I say that property is violated; that an act of plunder is committed … How is this legal plunder to be identified? Quite simply. See if the law takes from some persons what belongs to them, and gives it to other persons to whom it does not belong. See if the law benefits one citizen at the expense of another by doing what the citizen himself cannot do without committing a crime."[7]

Unfortunately, the U.S. Constitution designed to protect peoples' rights and property has now been twisted, misinterpreted, and changed to become a system of legal plunder through the many redistribution programs operated by the government. This should shock the conscience of every American. For "it is impossible to introduce into society … a greater evil than this: the conversion of the law into an instrument of plunder."[8]

Davy Crockett—Pioneer and Patriot [9]

Davy Crocket was born August 17, 1786 in Tennessee. His father, John, was a solider in the American Revolutionary War.[10] Davy continued the fight for freedom as a congressman. In 1826, Davy Crocket was elected to the United State House of Representatives. He represented Tennessee as a congressman for six years (1826–1830, 1832–1834). As does each congressman, he began his service with the oath: "I do solemnly swear that I will support the Constitution of the United States."[11]

One winter evening while standing on the steps of the Capitol, Crockett and other members of congress saw, as the result of a large fire, great light coming from Georgetown. Crockett wrote of the experience, "We … drove over as fast as we could. When we got there I went to work … but in spite of all that could be done, many houses were burned and many families made homeless, and, besides, some of them had lost all but the clothes they had on. The next morning a bill was introduced appropriating $20,000 [approximately $400,000 in 2006 dollars] for their relief. We put aside all other business and rushed it through as soon as it could be done."[12]

The following summer, while working for reelection, Crockett stopped to talk with a farmer in one of his districts. The man turned to his plow and was about to start off when Crockett said, "Don't be in such a hurry, my friend, I want to have a little talk with you, and get better acquainted."[13] The man replied, "Yes, I know you; you are Colonel Crockett… I shall not vote for you again."[14]

Crocket asked what was the matter to which the man replied, "You gave a vote last winter which shows that either you have not capacity to understand the Constitution, or that you are wanting in the honesty and firmness to be guided by it. In either case you are not the man to represent me… [If] the Constitution [is] to be worth anything, [it] must be held sacred, and rigidly observed in all its provisions."[15]

Crockett replied, "I admit the truth of all you say, but there must be some mistake about it, for I do not remember that I gave any vote last winter upon any Constitutional question."[16] The man answered, "No, Colonel, there's no mistake . . . last winter you voted for a bill to appropriate $20,000 to some sufferers by a fire in Georgetown. Is that true?"[17]

Crocket answered, "Well, my friend, I may as well own up. You have got me there. But certainly nobody will complain that a great and rich country likes ours should give the insignificant sum of $20,000 to relieve its suffering women and children, particularly with a full and overflowing treasury, and I am sure, if you had been there, you would have done just as I did."[18]

The man responded, "It is not the amount, Colonel, that I complain of; it is the principle. . . The power of collecting and disbursing money at pleasure is the most dangerous power that can be entrusted to man … you see, that while you are contributing to relieve one, you are drawing it from thousands … Colonel, Congress has no right to give charity. Individual members may give as much of their own money as they please, but they have no right to touch a dollar of the public money for that purpose… The people have delegated to Congress, by the Constitution, the power to do certain things. To do these, it is authorized to collect and pay moneys, and for nothing else. Everything beyond this is usurpation, and a violation of the Constitution… So you see, Colonel, you have violated the Constitution in what I consider a vital point. It is a precedent fraught with danger to the country, for when Congress once begins to stretch its power beyond the limits of the Constitution, there is no limit to it, and no security for the people …"[19]

Realizing the man was right, Crockett replied, "Well, my friend, you hit the nail upon the head when you said I did not have sense enough to understand the Constitution. I intended to be guided by it, and thought I had studied it fully . . . If I had ever taken the view of it that you have, I would have put my head into the fire before I would have given that vote, and … if I ever vote for another unconstitutional law I wish I may be shot."[20]

Following this experience, a bill was raised to appropriate money to the widow of a distinguished naval officer. Several beautiful speeches were made in its support. It appeared the bill would pass unanimously when Davy Crockett arose and spoke. "Mr. Speaker—I have as much respect for the memory of the deceased, and as much sympathy for the suffering of the living… I will not go into an argument to prove that Congress has no power to appropriate this money as an act of charity. Every member upon this floor knows it. We have the right, as individuals, to give away as much of our own money as we please to charity; but as members of Congress we have no right to appropriate a dollar of the public money…. We cannot, without the grossest corruption, appropriate this money… We have not the semblance of authority to appropriate it as charity…I cannot vote for this bill, but I will give one week's pay to the object, and, if every member of Congress will do the same, it will amount to more than the bill asks."[21] As a result of Crockett's speech, the bill failed, receiving very few votes. He had honored his oath to "support the Constitution."

Crockett ran for reelection in 1834. Since, in fighting to support the constitution, he had opposed Andrew Jackson, seventh president of the United States, on several key issues, President Jackson exercised his power and influence to prevent Crockett from returning to Congress. Crockett was determined to fight for freedom and if he couldn't do it as a congressman in Tennessee, he would join the patriots in Texas to fight in the Texas Revolution. Crocket said of his campaign for reelection, "I told the people of my district that if they saw fit to reelect me, I would serve them as faithfully as I had done; but if not, they might go to hell and I would go to Texas."[22]

On October 31, 1835, Crockett left Tennessee for Texas to help in their fight for freedom. He arrived at the Alamo on February 8, 1836. The thirteen day battle of the Alamo began February 23, 1836. The Alamo forces only consisted of approximately 200 patriots while by the end of the 12th day of battle, the Mexican forces that were attacking the post were reported to be more than 4,000. Davy Crockett fought courageously and echoed the words of his commander, Lt. Col. William B. Travis, who wrote in his final dispatch, "The enemy has demanded a surrender at discretion, otherwise the garrison are to be put to the sword if the fort is taken. I have answered the demand with a cannon shot, and our flag still waves proudly from the walls. I shall never surrender or retreat . . . I am determined to sustain myself as long as possible and die like a soldier who never forgets what is due to his own honor and that of his country. Victory or Death!"[23]

The Battle of the Alamo played a key role in securing the independence of Texas. The small band of 200 patriots was able to hold off the Mexican army for 13 days, delaying their movement eastward. This gave the Texan revolutionaries more time to gather troops and supplies which lead to a decisive defeat of the Mexican forces at the Battle of San Jacinto on April 21, 1826 and the establishment of the independent Republic of Texas. In life, Davy Crockett fought to preserve the freedoms of the U.S. Constitution and at age 49 he made the ultimate sacrifice by giving his life in the Battle of the Alamo on May 6, 1836. He lived and died a patriot.

The Lord and the government both have an approach to care for the poor and the needy but the approaches are complete opposites (see table).

CARING FOR THE POOR AND NEEDY	
THE LORD'S WAY	THE GOVERNMENT'S WAY
1. Voluntary	1. Force
2. Work/Industry	2. Idleness
3. Personal Responsibility	3. Government Responsibility
4. Self-Reliance	4. Dependence

Voluntary vs. Force

Under the Lord's way, the poor and needy will be taken care of by individual action and charity. It is done voluntarily. The history of America is one of individuals, churches, and other organizations voluntarily taking care of the lame, sick, and destitute. Under the Lord's way, government plays no part in caring for the poor and those in need. When a person is unable to provide for themselves, the family should assist. When the family is unable to meet the needs, fellow citizens ought to stand ready to help and support.

Many countries have attempted to use the power of government to care for the poor and needy by force, but in every case the improvements have been marginal at best. In the long run they have created more poverty. Government welfare rewards negative and undesirable behaviors such as idleness and thus produces more of it. What would happen if every time a child hit his sibling, you paid him a dollar to stop? Would the child hit his sibling more or less?

"Most of the major ills of the world have been caused by well-meaning people who ignored the principle of individual freedom, except as applied to themselves, and who were obsessed with fanatical zeal to improve the lot of mankind in the mass through some pet formula of their own. . . The harm done by ordinary criminals, murderers, gangsters, and thieves is negligible in comparison with the agony inflicted upon human beings by the professional 'do gooders' who attempt to set themselves up as gods on earth and who would ruthlessly force their views on all others—with the abiding assurance that the end justifies the means."[24]

Work/Industry vs. Idleness

Speaking to Adam, the Lord emphasized the need for work saying, "In the sweat of your face you shall eat bread, till you return to the ground."[25] With government welfare, initiative and work are replaced with handouts. If someone gets "something for nothing" that means some else gets "nothing for something." When you accept an unearned handout from the government, you are taking something that does not belong to you. That is the definition of stealing. This is clearly not the Lord's way. The Lord has commanded, "Thou shalt not steal."[26] Some may rationalize the acceptance of government handouts by saying, "It is legal, and I didn't take the money from anyone." What is right and what is legal are two different things. Prostitution is legal in the state of Nevada but still clearly violates the laws of God. By accepting government handouts, you contribute to the problem and willingly participate in a program based on theft by force.

Government welfare creates and promotes a class of people who can get "wealth without work," one of Mahatma Gandhi's seven social sins that will destroy a society.[27] One who gets wealth without work through government welfare is a societal parasite. History proves that once implemented government welfare grows. If it is not stopped, eventually the parasites will kill the host and the economy will collapse.

Personal Responsibility vs. Government Responsibility

The Lord's plan for caring for the poor is based on the principle of individual responsibility. As taught the apostle Paul, "But if any provide not for his own, and specially for those of his own house, he hath denied the faith, and is worse than an infidel."[28] In most instances, government welfare dismisses the principles of work and responsibility and promotes the idea that "the government will take care of you." No able Christian will shift the burden of his own or his family's well-being to someone else.

Self-Reliance vs. Dependence

The following story illustrates the dangers of dependence. "In our friendly neighbor city of St. Augustine, great flocks of seagulls are starving amid plenty. Fishing is still good, but the gulls don't know how to fish. For generations they have depended on the shrimp fleet to toss them scraps from the nets. Now the fleet has moved ... The shrimpers had created a Welfare State for the ... seagulls. The big birds never bothered to learn how to fish for themselves, and they never taught their children to fish. Instead they led their little ones to the shrimp nets. Now the seagulls, the fine free birds that almost symbolize liberty itself, are starving to death because they gave in to the 'something for nothing' lure! They sacrificed their independence for a hand-out. A lot of people are like that, too. They see nothing wrong in picking delectable scraps from the tax nets of the U.S. Government's 'shrimp fleet' ... Let's not be gullible gulls. We ... must preserve our talents of self-sufficiency, our genius for creating things for ourselves, our sense of thrift and our true love of independence."[29] The Lord's way works to restore those in need to a state of self-reliance, while government welfare creates an ever-growing number who are dependant on the government.

In an attempt to eliminate classes, government welfare programs create two classes: slaves and dependants. Government welfare supports idleness through theft and removes the responsibility from the people to care for themselves. These programs violate the U.S. constitution and the Lord's way of caring for those in need. The government's approach to taking care of those in need is a counterfeit alternative to the Lord's way and is wrong and immoral.

GROWTH OF THE WELFARE STATE

Our current federal government clearly violates the U.S. Constitution and the ideas of the founders of a limited government with low, indirect taxes. Thomas Pain taught that when government is just, taxes are few.[30] As government has expanded and grown in areas that are unconstitutional, so have taxes expanded and grown to support them. In 1901, the total spending of the federal government was $525 million. In the year 2000, the federal government spent $1.79 trillion. During those 100 years, federal government's spending has increased by more than 3,000 times, while the population grew by only 6.5 times. Thus, the yearly cost per household increased from $32 in 1901 to $16,949 in 2000—over a 500 time increase in cost per household (see table). Much of this growth has been in welfare spending. Since 1971, more than half of all government spending has been for welfare.[31]

GROWTH OF THE U.S. FEDERAL GOVERNMENT[33]			
Year	Total Spending[34]	# of U.S. Households[35]	Cost Per Household
1901	$525 million	16 million	$32
1910	$694 million	20 million	$34
1920	$6.3 billion	24 million	$260
1930	$3.3 billion	30 million	$111
1940	$9.5 billion	35 million	$269
1950	$42.6 billion	44 million	$977
1960	$92.2 billion	53 million	$1,746
1970	$195.6 billion	63 million	$3,112
1980	$590.9 billion	80 million	$7,351
1990	$1.25 trillion	92 million	$13,622
2000	$1.79 trillion	106 million	$16,949

The government's future unfunded commitments show that this trend will continue. "By commitments, I mean things like unfunded promises for future Social Security and Medicare benefits. Our total accumulated fiscal burden is more than $46 trillion. . . The new Medicare prescription drug benefit represents more than $8 trillion of this accumulated burden. . . To put things into perspective, $46 trillion translated into a burden of $156,000 for every American alive today, or about $375,000 per full-time worker. . . The combined net worth of every American including billionaires like Bill Gates and Warren Buffett, is only about $50 trillion. That means every American would have to hand over more than 90 percent of their net worth to cover the government's current unfunded promises for future spending."[32] If this trend is not reserved, we will see the establishment of a complete socialistic government, the end of liberty and the collapse of the economy that will mirror the effects of the great depression.

CONCLUSION—RESTORING FREEDOM

The greatest way to reduce taxes is to reduce the size and scope of government. If the federal government only provided the services authorized by the constitution, the spending and cost to Americans would be a very small fraction of what it is today. If the current trends of government growth and the increase of government redistribution are not reversed, America will no longer be the land of the free and home of the brave, but the land of the slaves and home of the dependants. Action must be taken to freeze the growth and phase out all redistribution programs until the limited government created by the inspired constitution is restored.

The great men and women of this nation must again unite and work and fight for freedom as did our inspired founders. In a speech delivered to some who thought it better to have peace and bondage then fight for freedom, Patrick Henry said, "If we wish to be free . . . we must fight! . . . Is life so dear, or peace so sweet, as to be purchased at the price of chains and slavery? Forbid it, Almighty God! I know not what course others may take; but as for me, give me liberty or give me death!"[36] And in the words of George Washington, "We must now determine to be enslaved or free. If we make freedom our choice, we must obtain it by the blessing of Heaven on our united and vigorous efforts."[37]

TRUTH 9

Government Welfare Violates the U.S. Constitution and the Lord's Way of Caring for Those in Need.

THE RICH GET RICHER AND
THE POOR GET POORER

Many falsely assume that once a person is "rich" he or she is always "rich," and that once someone is "poor" he or she is always "poor." Opposition to free enterprise is often expressed with the saying, "the rich get richer and the poor get poorer." Some people strongly oppose free enterprise believing that it results in the unfair distribution of wealth. This chapter analyzes several studies, which show these statements to be monumentally wrong.

THE RICH WERE ONCE THE POOR

The majority of those who are wealthy in American have become so after starting at the poverty level. A study of the 4,047 American millionaires in 1892 found that 84 percent became millionaires without the benefit of inherited wealth.[1]

"In 1996, approximately 3.5 million households in America (out of a total of 100 million households) had a net worth of $1 million or more [and] . . . fewer than 20 percent inherited 10 percent or more of their wealth."[2]

These statistics mean that more than 80 percent of American millionaires began poor. Those now considered rich were at one point in their life the poor. In the first 8 years of adult life, I never earned an income above $20,000 per year. The ninth year, I earned more than $100,000 and every year since have earned an income in the top 5 percent of income earners. When I began, I had no money or capital; however, I went from the bottom level of income earners to the top level of income earners within a matter of years. Studies of American millionaires have found that income growth occurred in a similar pattern for the great majority of millionaires.

U.S. Treasury Department Study

A study was done by the U.S. Treasury Department to determine if, over time, Americans move from one income class to another. The study analyzed a random sample of 14,351 tax returns from 1979 to 1988. This sample was broken into five groups based on income in 1979 with the lowest 20 percent of income earners in the 1st group and the top 20 percent of income earners in the 5th group. In 1988, the 14,351 tax returnee's income was again analyzed. During the 10-year period, 86 percent of the lowest income earners had increased their income and moved to a higher earning group. In addition, more of the lowest income earners (1st group) became the highest income earners (5th group) than remained in the lowest group (see table). During this 10-year study, the poor did not get poorer; they got richer and became the rich. For most people poverty is temporary. Even those who choose to stay poor still get richer as the economy grows.

AMERICA ON THE MOVE[3]					
	Percent in Each Group in 1988				
1979 Group	1st	2nd	3rd	4th	5th
1st (lowest 20%)	14.2%	20.7%	25.0%	25.3%	14.7%
2nd	10.9%	29.0%	29.6%	19.5%	11.1%
3rd (Middle 20%)	5.7%	14.0%	33.0%	32.3%	15.0%
4th	3.1%	9.3%	14.8%	37.5%	35.4%
5th (Highest 20%)	1.1%	4.4%	9.4%	20.3%	64.7%

The Urban Institute did a similar study from 1977 to 1986. They found that during the ten-year period, the income of the bottom fifth of income earners increased by 77 percent ($12,145) while the income of the top 20 percent of income earners increased by 5 percent ($4,609) (see table). The poor are not getting poorer. From this study, you could say the rich get a little richer and the poor get a lot richer.[4]

Average Family Income[5] (in constant 1991 dollars)				
	Average Family Income		Change in Average	
Group	1977	1986	Amount	Percent
1st (Lowest 20%)	$15,853	$27,998	$12,145	77%
2nd	$31,340	$43,041	$11,701	37%
3rd (Middle 20%)	$43,297	$51,796	$8,499	20%
4th	$57,486	$63,314	$5,828	10%
5th (Highest 20%)	$92,531	$97,140	$4,609	5%

From Poverty to Abundance

One of my mentors, Curtis, lived a rough impoverished childhood. His father worked for the railroad and was killed in a train accident when Curtis was five years old. Curtis failed the third grade several times. He has scars on his back and head from being stabbed and hit by bricks in his youth. He had a very difficult childhood. While in high school, Curtis was invited to a school dance. Curtis walked across town to the girl's house to meet her before going to the dance. Before they left the house, the grandmother came in and said, "I didn't know you were going to the dance with Curtis." The young girl said, "Yes, that's who I've asked." The grandma replied, "Well, you can't go with him. He's nothing but poor, white trash." The grandma refused to let her granddaughter go to the dance with Curtis so he walked home and missed the dance.

Curtis was raised in a poor environment, but he chose not to stay there. Curtis received multiple doctorate degrees and became a Methodist minister. He served as a minister for 14 years and then taught religion at a university. While at the university, he started a business and became a multimillionaire. After his financial success, he was invited to a large political function where many extremely wealthy people were present. One of the politicians came up to Curtis and said, "The problem with you rich guys is you don't know how the poor people live. If you come with me for the next two or three days, I'll show you how the poor people live and that will change your attitude and your thoughts." Curtis responded to the man, "Sir, I don't need to go with you to see how poor people live. I've been there, I lived there, I just didn't choose to stay there."

Free Enterprise vs. Socialism

Free enterprise is a system based on work and production. There is a direct correlation between hours worked and income earned. As taught the apostle Paul, "But this I say, He which soweth sparingly shall reap also sparingly; and he which soweth bountifully shall reap also bountifully."[6]

Share of Hours Worked
(Based on Unequal Census Income Quintiles)

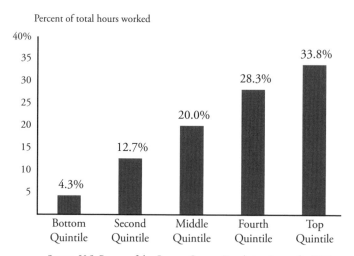

Source: U.S. Bureau of the Census, Current Population Survey for 2002

"In many respects, economic inequalities between the quintiles are a direct reflection of disparities in work performed (see chart). The chart shows the total annual hours of paid labor in each quintile. In 2002, individuals in the bottom quintile performed 4.3 percent of all the work in the U.S. economy, while those in the top quintile performed

33.8 percent. Thus, the top quintile performed almost eight times as much labor as did the bottom quintile."[7] It is very simple; those who work more make more.

Production

The United States has the freest economy in the world. With less than 5 percent of the world's population,[8] it produces more than 28 percent of the world's goods and services.[9] China has the most socialist economy and with 20 percent of the world's population[10] produces 5 percent of the world's good and services.[11] Based on these numbers, the United States is 25 times more productive than China. China's production numbers would be much, much lower if the government did not allow some elements of free enterprise into the economy in the 1970s. As a result of free enterprise, China has seen a 10-time increase in production since 1978.[12] The facts clearly show that free enterprise is much more productive than socialism. The free enterprise system is superior by far to any economic system the world has ever known. As countries implement the principles of free enterprise, they will see higher levels of production and wealth.

Distribution

Some falsely claim that a socialist economy provides a more equal distribution of wealth than does free enterprise. The opposite is actually true. Under socialism, all property and capital is owned and controlled by the government. As a result, the government leaders take a large share of the wealth before it is distributed to the citizens. Over time, this results in the government leaders holding most of the country's wealth. A study of socialist countries proves this fact. "For example, the largest item of personal wealth in socialist nations is the automobile. In 1971, in the socialist countries of U.S.S.R and Poland, the top 1 percent of population owned respectively 60 percent and 59 percent of the nation's automobiles. While in the U.S., the top 1 percent owned 3 percent of the nation's automobiles."[13] Free enterprise creates "a better distribution of all that has been produced so that more people enjoy more of our abundance than under any other system."[14]

Socialism results in a society where all citizens are equal in their bondage and poverty. Winston Churchill taught, "The inherent virtue of socialism is the equal sharing of miseries." The inherent virtue of free enterprise is the equal opportunity for all to achieve wealth and prosperity, which results in an ever-increasing standard of living for all.

Social Security Case Study

A comparison between socialism and free enterprise can be seen by analyzing the retirement program of Social Security, which is founded on the principles of socialism and retirement planning in a free enterprise economy. According the Social Security Administration web site, Social Security is "the most successful domestic program in our nation's history." Let's see how the greatest federal program in U.S. history compares to retirement under a free enterprise economy.

For illustrative purposes, we will look at a low income and middle-class income earner. In both cases, the person began working at age 22, worked for 45 years, and retired at age 67 (the required age to receive full benefits from Social Security in 2006). The low-income person earned an average of $18,000 per year and the middle-class person earned an average of $48,000 per year during the 45 years.

Social Security (Socialism) Retirement Results

During the 45 years, the low-income person paid $100,440 in Social Security tax and the middle- class person paid $267,840 (Social Security tax rate in 2006 was 12.4 percent of income). At retirement, the low-income person receives a monthly retirement benefit check of $892 a month or $10,704 annually, while the middle class person receives $1,714 a month or $20,568 per year.[15]

Free Enterprise Retirement Results

Instead of 12.4 percent of their earnings going to Social Security tax, $100,440 of the low-income person's and $267,840 of the middle class person's earnings are put into a personal retirement account over the 45 years.[16] At retirement, the low-income person has $682,438 in his retirement account and the middle class person has $1.8 million. If they were each just to live on the interest (7 percent) generated from their retirement accounts, the low income person would receive a monthly payment of $3,981 and the middle class would receive a monthly payment of $10,616 for annual incomes of $47,771 and $127,388 respectively without ever touching the money in their retirement accounts. Each could increase his or her retirement lifestyle by using the money in the retirement account or could choose at death to pass the money to heirs or favorite charities. The facts show that free enterprise retirement planning would dramatically improve the retirement standard of living of all segments of U.S. society.

FREE ENTERPRISE vs. SOCIAL SECURITY RETIREMENT PROGRAMS						
	Social Security Retirement Benefits			Free Enterprise Retirement Benefits		
	Savings	Monthly Income	Annual Income	Savings	Monthly Income	Annual Income
Low Income	$0	$892	$10,704	$682,438	$3,981	$47,771
Middle Class	$0	$1,714	$20,568	$1.8 million	$10,616	$127,388

America lost a great portion of its liberty when the government took control of retirement planning through the Social Security system. Some have embraced the bondage this program creates for the illusion of a secure retirement. "Social Security is unconstitutional. The Social Security system in the U.S. is compulsory, unfair, and immoral. The Social Security system, as it is conceived and operated today, is not social, does not provide security, and does not qualify as a real system. It should be made voluntary in order to become social; it should be backed by reserves in order to become secure; and benefits should be computed on an actuarial basis to make it a system that is fair."[17] Social Security is one of the greatest scams ever perpetrated against the American people. Social Security is not a retirement plan. It is simply a disguise used by the federal government to tax its citizens.

TAXES IN A FREE SOCIETY VS. TAXES UNDER SOCIALISM

Unfortunately, since the 1930s laws have been passed to redistribute the income of American citizens through the federal tax system—which is by definition socialism. There are many in government and throughout society who continue to advocate and expand this practice. *The Communist Manifesto* written by Karl Marx and Friedrich Engels lists 10 objectives of the communist party. The second objective is, "A heavy progressive and graduated income tax,"[18] for the purpose of income redistribution on a grand scale. This clearly describes the current progressive and graduated federal tax system in the United States where the lowest income earners have a negative tax rate and the percent increases as income increases with a tax rate of 38.6% percent for the top income earners.[19]

Anyone who tells you the rich don't pay taxes because they use loopholes in the tax system hasn't looked at the facts. In 2002, the top 10 percent of income earners paid more than 67 percent of all federal income tax while the bottom 20 percent received more in welfare than they contribute in federal income taxes (see table).

SHARE OF FEDERAL TAX LIABILITIES, 2002	
Income Category	% of Federal Income Taxes Paid
Lowest Quintile	-2.6%
Second Quintile	-0.2%
Middle Quintile	5.3%
Fourth Quintile	14.8%
Highest Quintile	82.8%
Top 10%	67.4%

"In a fully free society, taxation—or, to be exact, payment for governmental services—would be voluntary. Since the proper services of a government—the police, the armed forces, the law courts—are demonstrably needed by individual citizens and affect their interests directly, the citizens would (and should) be willing to pay for such services, as they pay for insurance . . . In a free society . . . there would be no legal possibility for any redistribution of wealth."[20]

Lunch Metaphor

If a lunch bill was divided the way federal taxes are divided between Americans, the bill would be broken down this way.[21] Ten people go to lunch and the meal costs $10 a person for a total of $100. The two people with the lowest income would each get paid $1.30 for eating lunch. The next two people with the lowest income would each get paid 10 cents for eating lunch. The two with the middle incomes would pay $2.65 each for lunch. The two people with the third- and fourth-highest incomes would each pay $7.40. The person with the second-highest income would pay $15.30 for his lunch and the person with the highest income would pay $67.40. The highest income earner would pay $67.40 for the same lunch the lowest income earners got paid $1.30 to eat.

Citizens should each pay for their use of government services. For one to get paid $1.30 for a government service while another pays $67.40 for the same service is as silly as a restaurant paying one person $1.30 to eat lunch and charging another $67.40 for the same lunch. The portions of taxation that are not for services but for redistribution from one person for the benefit of another is comparable to a restaurant owner stealing money from his neighbor to pay for his customers to eat free. In a truly free society, citizens would pay for government services like they pay for lunch in the free enterprise marketplace.

DIVINE LAW AND FREE ENTERPRISE

Free enterprise does not mean the economic freedom to do anything you wish, any more than a free country allows you to steal or kill. Laws and morals are required for a free society and divine laws are the foundation of a successful free economic system. The same divine laws that govern the free society should also govern economic practices. Thus, free enterprise is the freedom to do anything that does not violate divine law and the rights of others. To say this restricts trade or the economy would be the same as saying the laws not to steal or kill restrict freedom. Laws protecting God-given rights are required for there to be economic freedom. If personal interests and profits were the sole driver of our free enterprise system, there would soon be no freedom, for the violation of another's rights would surely result, as one stood to gain financially by killing, stealing, or taking advantage of others.

A Christian will not participate in any business which violates divine laws. For example, the Omni Hotels® refuse to sell pornography—a product that would result in millions of dollars in profit each year.[22] Many others hotels choose to sell pornography. They violate divine law in exchange for profit. Money acquired through the violation of divine laws is never worth its cost. As taught the Savior, "For what is a man profited, if he shall gain the whole world, and lose his own soul? Or what shall a man give in exchange for his soul?"[23] Money obtained by theft, bribery, false advertising, excessive charges, exploiting employees,[24] or from the sale of gambling, pornography, harmful drugs, or other sinful practices is what the Bible calls filthy lucre.[25]

CONCLUSION

Free enterprise "offers the greatest opportunity for man to become what God intended."[26] Thomas Jefferson taught, "The true foundation of republican government is the equal right of every citizen, in his person and property, and in their management. . . Our interest [is] to throw open the doors of commerce, and to knock off all its shackles, giving perfect freedom to all persons."[27]

Abraham Lincoln taught, "It is best for all to leave each man free to acquire property as fast as he can. Some will get wealthy. I don't believe in a law to prevent a man from getting rich; it would do more harm than good... When one starts poor, as most do in the race of life, free society is such that he knows he can better his condition... I am not ashamed to confess that twenty-five years ago I was a hired laborer... I want every man to have the chance ... in which he can better his condition—when he may look forward and hope to be a hired laborer this year and the next, work for himself afterward, and finally to hire men to work for him. That is the true system... Property is the fruit of labor; property is desirable; is a positive good in the world. That some should be rich, shows that others may become rich, and hence is just encouragement to industry and enterprise. Let not him who is houseless pull down the house of another; but let him labor diligently and build one for himself."[28]

Truth 10

Free Enterprise Is the Only Economic System That Recognizes Our God-Given Rights of Life, Liberty, and the Pursuit of Happiness.

Choice 1:
Blame or Responsibility

"The price of greatness is responsibility."
–Winston Churchill

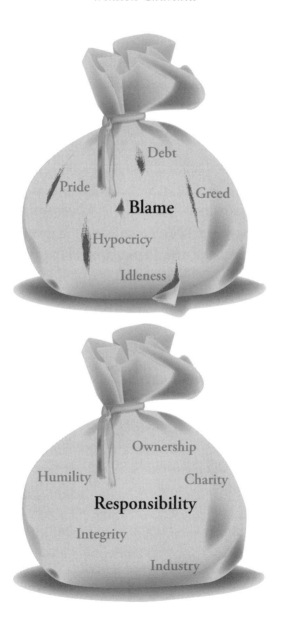

MYTH 11

THE GRASS IS ALWAYS GREENER ON THE OTHER SIDE

Prosperity is elusive to many because it is always on the other side of the fence. People look elsewhere for opportunity, happiness, and financial freedom. The circumstances of others always seem to be more desirable than their own. For many, happiness, opportunity, and fortune are always on the other side of the fence. We have all heard people say, "I'll be happy when …" or "If I just had the right opportunity, I could become wealthy" or "If I wasn't abused as a child, then I could have loving relationships."

The quest for happiness and wealth does not begin by crossing the fence to a new environment, circumstance, opportunity, or relationship. Those who begin the quest with this attitude do not find happiness and wealth. They find another fence. The most significant changes in life will be made not by changing our environment but by changing our choices. Your life story is not written by what happens to you but by what you choose to make happen. The realization that you are responsible for your fate will produce a power and drive to make choices that result in the life you desire. "When the grass looks greener on the other side of the fence, it may be that they take better care of it there."[1]

BLAME VS. RESPONSIBILITY

Blame has been used by mankind since the very beginning to avoid taking responsibility. In the Garden of Eden when Adam and Eve ate of the forbidden fruit, the Lord asked Adam, "Have you eaten from the tree of which I commanded you that you should not eat?"[2] To which Adam blamed Eve saying, "The woman whom You gave to be with me, she gave me of the tree, and I ate."[3] The Lord then asked Eve, "What is this you have done?"[4] To which Eve blamed Satan answering, "The serpent deceived me, and I ate."[5]

We must learn to be responsible for our actions and not blame others or circumstances. During the last supper, while Jesus was eating with the 12 apostles he declared, "Verily I say unto you, that one of you shall betray me."[6] Each of the apostles replied, "Lord, is it I?"[7] They did not reply, "Is it Judas? They were concerned about their own actions and not the actions of the other apostles. "People are always blaming their circumstances for what they are. I don't believe in circumstances. The people who get on in this world are the people who get up and look for the circumstances they want and, if they can't find them, make them."[8]

Taking Responsibility

During his career, Steve Young threw 203 interceptions, and he threw two interceptions in a row 6 times. Steve Young commented that after each interception, "The coaches, my teammates, and the fans want an explanation. I could give excuses like 'the receiver ran the wrong route,' 'the lineman missed a block,' 'the ball slipped,' 'I lost my footing.' I found that using excuses was never very effective. I learned to take responsibility for the mistake. When I would throw an interception, I would say, 'I messed up' with no excuses and I would then tell my teammates that we are going to go to the sideline and when we get the ball back we are going to try again. We are going to go back on the field and score a touchdown. My teammates and coaches responded much better when I took responsibility for the mistake than when I looked for someone or something to blame."[9]

Victor Mentality Instead of Victim Mentality

"Since the 1970s several sociologists and social critics have noted the increase in individuals claiming to be victims and then using that status to relieve themselves of responsibility . . . [and] the tendency to use victimization as a justification, excuse, and explanation for wrongful behavior and personal irresponsibility."[10] "Instead of making an effort, some people make excuses for not doing what they could be doing. We hear the argument, 'I was denied the advantages others had in their youth.' Others say, 'I am physically handicapped.' But history is full of examples of people with physical handicaps who went on to greatness. The Greek poet Homer, the English poet John Milton, and the American historian William Prescott, had good excuses—they were blind. Athenian Demosthenes, greatest of all great orators, had a wonderful excuse—his lungs were weak, his voice was hoarse and unmusical, and he stuttered. The great German composer Ludwig van Beethoven continued to compose even after he became totally deaf. They all had good excuses for not doing anything—but they never used those excuses."[11]

THE POWER TO CHOOSE OUR RESPONSE

There are some who believe man is the product of his environment. Sigmund Freud once asserted, "Let one attempt to expose a number of the most diverse people uniformly to hunger. With the increase of the imperative urge of hunger all individual differences will blur, and in their stead will appear the uniform expression of the one unstilled urge."[12] Viktor Frankl disputed this notion. Writing of his experience in Nazi prison camps Mr. Frankl declared, "The 'individual differences' did not 'blur' but, on the contrary, people became more different; people unmasked themselves, both the swine and the saints."[13] "In the midst of the most degrading circumstances imaginable, Frankl used the human endowment of self-awareness to discover a fundamental principle about the nature of man: Between stimulus and response, man has the freedom to choose."[14] Those in the prison camp were in a similar negative environment but the people were very different depending on how they chose to respond and act.

At the conclusion of World War II, the survivors in the concentration camps were freed. Many prisoners were weak and filled with anger. In one of the camps, the American soldiers observed a man who appeared to be strong, happy, and peaceful. "His posture was erect, his eyes bright, his energy indefatigable." The soldiers assumed he had recently been imprisoned or had not suffered as the other prisoners had. As this prisoner was questioned, it was learned that "for six years he had lived on the same starvation diet, slept in the same airless and disease-ridden barracks as everyone else, but without the least physical or mental deterioration." Explaining what made the difference, he related the following: "We lived in the Jewish section of Warsaw [capital of Poland], my wife, two daughters, and our three little boys. When the Germans reached our street they lined everyone against a wall and opened up with machine guns. I begged to be allowed to die with my family, but because I spoke German they put me in a work group. I had to decide right then whether to let myself hate the soldiers who had done this. It was an easy decision, really. I was a lawyer. In my practice I had seen too often what hate could do to people's minds and bodies. Hate had just killed the six people who mattered most to me in the world. I decided then that I would spend the rest of my life—whether it was a few days or many years—loving every person I came in contact with."[15]

We have within us the power to choose how we respond to a hurtful situation. We cannot control the actions of others, but we control how we will respond. As we understand our power to choose, we see that we are in control. Our life is not a result of our environment or upbringing but is a result of our choices. We have the ability to determine the kind of life we want to live and the type of person we wish to be.

Thermostat vs. Thermometer

This idea of choice can be illustrated through an analogy between a thermometer and a thermostat. A thermometer is stationary and only reflects what is happening around it. It simply responds to its environment. If it is hot outside, it reports it is hot. If it is cold outside, it reports it is cold. A thermostat, on the other hand, measures what the temperature is and then responds by changing the temperature to the conditions it desires. If it wants the temperature to be cooler, it turns on the air conditioner and cools the room down. If it wants the temperature to be warmer, it turns on the heater. Some people are like a thermometer. If their environment is negative, they are negative. If bad things happen, they are sad. If good things happen, they are happy. They are simply a product of their environment. Successful people, on the other hand, are more like a thermostat. Even if their environment is negative, they choose to be positive.

Happiness Comes from Within

My grandmother passed away several years ago, and I was asked to speak at her funeral. In my comments, I shared the following: "What qualities did Grandma Taylor radiate throughout her life? She radiated many—strengthening thousands of people—but there are a few qualities that stand paramount in my mind. One was that of happiness and encouragement. I cannot remember a single encounter with Grandma when she was not happy and positive. Even as her health declined, and though her circumstances were far from ideal, she always maintained a happy, positive attitude. It would have been easy and justifiable as she struggled with many physical alignments, such as broken bones and lost memory, to have become sad and discouraged, but this was never the case. She continued to strengthen and build those around her. I recall that after visiting she would often give departing words of encouragement such as, 'Be good.' From this I have learned the powerful lesson that happiness doesn't depend on outward conditions but on those inside."

The Perfect Example

Jesus is our perfect example. When His captors slapped and spit on him during and after His trial, He did not seek revenge. When paid witnesses testified falsely against Him, He was calm and unflustered. When the soldiers whipped him and placed a crown of thorns on His head, He expressed no hatred. As they mocked Him as He hung in agony on the cross He prayed, "Father, forgive them; for they know not what they do."[16] His enemies inflicted upon Him all the pain and suffering possible, but it was impossible to break the character of Jesus. His enemies could control His environment and torture His body, but they could not control how their acts would affect him. Through it all, he remained full of strength, love, peace, and power. His power, strength, and control are illustrated by His last words on the cross. They were not spoken softly by a broken and weak man, but they were shouted by a man full of strength and power. The New Testament reads, "Jesus called out with a loud voice, 'Father, into your hands I commit my spirit.' When He had said this, He breathed his last."[17] They did not kill Him. When His mission was complete and the will of the Father accomplished, He returned home.

RETURN GOOD FOR EVIL

"Hatred is never ended by hatred but by love." –Buddha

We have a natural tendency to treat others as they treat us. Returning good for good and evil for evil is known as the law of reciprocity. This law results in either the improvement or decline of a relationship. For example, if someone is unkind to you, you respond naturally by being unkind to them. Your unkindness leads to their continued unkindness to you, and suddenly you have produced a cyclical relationship with each person returning more and more unkindness. The end result is a very unproductive and destructive relationship.

The law of reciprocity can also work in a positive direction. For example, if you show someone kindness and love, they respond naturally with kindness. This causes you to respond with even more kindness and love. This cyclical effect returns more and more kindness and love, producing a more meaningful and loving relationship.

The Savior taught, "Ye have heard that it hath been said, Thou shalt love thy neighbor, and hate thine enemy. But I say unto you, Love your enemies, bless them that curse you, do good to them that hate you, and pray for them which despitefully use you, and persecute you."[18] The Lord's command to return love for hate, concern and prayer for persecution, and blessing for cursing enables us to reverse the negative cycle of reciprocity.

The Accidental Gift

My wife, Paula, is one of the most loving, friendly, outgoing people I know. A few years ago she was in a car accident. She was stopped at a traffic light when a person three cars back failed to stop causing a four-car accident. My wife did not have her insurance information with her. When I arrived with the insurance information, the police were taking statements and information. The drivers of the other damaged cars were upset and angry, but Paula was happy and making friends. Paula went up to the driver responsible for the accident and gave her a hug and said, "You need a present." My wife then gave her two tickets to a local college football game taking place on the upcoming Saturday. The girl said in shock, "I damaged your car and caused you and your baby a great deal of stress, and you're giving me a present?" Driving can only cause us frustration and anger if we choose to respond that way.

The Golden Rule

The Savior sums up effective customer service with the golden rule "Treat others as you want them to treat you."[19] In 2003, one of our clients, Dr. Wilk, sent me an e-mail accusing my company of not refunding $3,000 for merchandise he had returned. He demanded his money with interest and threatened to report us to the Better Business Bureau as a scam. He had also sent this e-mail to the director of his professional association whom we had a relationship with. I looked into the matter and found that his money had been returned a month ago shortly after we received the merchandise. I replied to his e-mail, which I copied to the director of his professional association, explaining when

REVERSING THE RECIPROCITY CYCLE

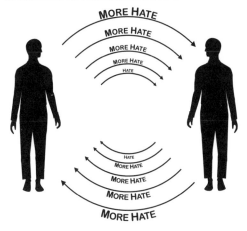

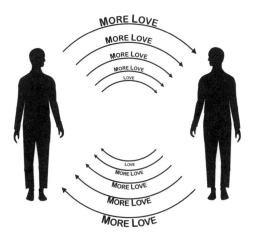

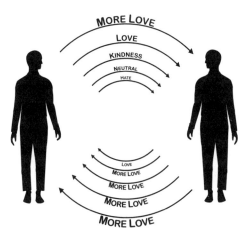

ENEMY

YOU

the money was returned and how he could verify it. I then wrote: "I apologize for the miscommunication. I have put a gift in the mail to you to apologize for the mistake. Let me know if you have any other concerns and I will make sure they get taken care of." Dr. Wilk sent me an e-mail thanking me for the gift, and I received an e-mail from the director of the association, which read:

> "Dear Cameron,
> Thank you for your continued patience and kindness. I did learn just recently that Dr. Wilk lost a son in just the past few months to a long and horrible death from a brain tumor. His son was only in his early 40s and folks here have said Dr. Wilk has slowed a little. So again, thanks for taking the extra time.
> Take care, M—"

Be a Transition Person

Often in life we see people participating in behavioral cycles. Those who are abused as children often become abusers as adults. We see generation after generation of people on welfare. I believe that everyone can be a transition person. In the Old Testament, Abraham came from a family of idol-worshippers, yet he became the father of generations who are the righteous followers of the Lord God. Moses was born in poverty and slavery yet rose to be a leader of Egypt and Israel. Joseph was sold by his brothers into slavery, yet he became a ruler in Egypt, second only to Pharaoh. These examples prove that people can be better than their upbringing.

FORGIVENESS

*"Obsessing on grudges keeps them alive; forgiveness forces them to die.
Moving on gets you back to business."*
–Jon Huntsman, Sr., Billionaire and Philanthropist

One of my mentors shared the following story about a group of teenagers who went for a picnic in the desert outside of Phoenix. While they were playing, a rattlesnake bit one of the girls on the ankle. The girl and her friends pursued the snake and after about 20 minutes were able to find the snake and kill it. Once the snake was destroyed they headed to the emergency room. A couple days later her foot and leg had swollen almost beyond recognition. The tissues in her limb had been destroyed by the poison, and a few days later it was found her leg would have to be amputated below the knee. It was a senseless sacrifice, the price of revenge. How much better it would have been if after the young women had been bitten, there had been an extraction of the venom.[20]

It is difficult for us to forgive those who have injured us. Dwelling on the evil done to us becomes an erosive and destructive poison. Holding a grudge has the power to pull us to the depths of hell while forgiveness exalts us to the heights of heaven. The Lord directs us to forgive those who injure us but that does not mean that feelings of resentment, anger, and injustice are ignored or eliminated. We must learn to respond to the feelings of resentment, anger, and injustice with forgiveness, and guard against the natural tendency to respond with the sins of bitterness, hate, and revenge.

In reference to the sermon "Upon Resentment" given in 1726 by the English Bishop Joseph Butler, Jeffrie Murphy writes, "In that sermon, Butler started to make a case for the legitimacy of resentment and other vindictive passions—arguing that a just and loving God would not have universally implanted these passions within his creatures unless the passions served some valuable purpose. The danger of resentment, Butler argued, lies not in having it, but rather in being dominated and consumed by it to such a degree that one can never overcome it and acts irresponsibly on the basis of it. As the initial response to being wrong, however, the passion stands in defense of important values—values that might be compromised by immediate and uncritical forgiveness of wrongs."[21]

Although we forgive our neighbors of their wrongs against us, we still work to prevent the injury from being repeated. people who are abused should forgive their abuser but also work to hold the abuser accountable for his or her actions and prevent further abuse. A person who was the victim of a dishonest businessperson should not seek revenge or hate the offender but could take action to remedy the wrong. We must fight against sin but not allow bitterness, hatred, and revenge to control our thoughts and actions. As the apostle Paul taught, "Be ye angry, and sin not."[22]

From Bitterness to Love

The abuse of children, whether sexual, physical, or emotional, is one of the most serious problems society faces. The emotional, spiritual, mental, and physical damage of abuse is very real. I know this first-hand because when I was a little boy, I was sexually abused over many years by a close relative. I pray that no child will ever have to experience the hell I have gone through as a boy and as an adult as I have overcome and conquered the harmful effects of abuse. Initially, my reaction to the abuse were feelings of anger, hatred, bitterness, and vindictiveness. I prayed for help in dealing with these emotions and felt directed to forgive and let go. As I forgave my offender, the Spirit filled by heart and soul. The feelings I had of hate and revenge were replaced by feelings of love and concern. It is hard to describe the emotions that resulted from forgiving. Initially, I felt there was no way I could love someone who was guilty of such horrendous crimes against me, but through the power of Christ and forgiveness it was made possible. That is one of the miracles of forgiveness—it not only removes hate, bitterness, and vindictiveness, but it also replaces it with love, peace, and concern.

In January 2001, I was talking to my mom on the phone, and we began talking about the abuse of my childhood. My mom asked, "Have you forgiven him?" I said, "Yes, I have. I forgave him years ago." Tears came to my eyes and pain filled my heart as my mom described the pain and struggles she experienced as a result of her son being abused by someone she trusted—someone she loved. My mom then said, "I can't forgive him." Although she is one of the kindest, most caring Christians in the world, she could not forgive him for hurting her son.

In the fall of 2005, I got a call from my mom to tell me she had forgiven the relative responsible for the abuse. She related the experience to me over the phone, and I asked that she write it down and send it to me. Below is my wonderful mother's experience with forgiveness:

I had known for a long time that I needed to forgive Henry [name has been changed] for sexually abusing my son. I kept postponing it because I felt that if I forgave him, then I would be condoning it somehow. One morning I felt prompted that I needed to go through the process of forgiving him and letting go of all the hurt and anger.

I felt prompted to go the cemetery where he was buried and prayed for the help of the Lord to take away this burden that I had carried with me for so many years. I began to share my feelings and told the Lord that I was really ready to let it all go. I knew that holding onto it was keeping me from progressing spiritually.

I went to the cemetery where Henry was buried. After spending some time at Henry's grave site, I felt prompted to go and run around the track at the high school. I thought that was strange because I am definitely not a runner. I usually walk for exercise but cannot run very far. As I was thinking about this, the story of the leper Naaman who went to Elisha to be healed came to my mind. Elisha told Naaman, "Go and wash in the Jordan seven times, and your flesh shall be restored to you, and you shall be clean."[23] But Naaman rejected the counsel for he expected a mighty miracle. "Naaman became furious"[24] "and went away in a rage."[25] Naaman's servant then spoke to him saying, "If the prophet had told you to do something great, would you not have done it? How much more then, when he says to you, 'Wash, and be clean'?"[26] Naaman then went and washed seven times in the Jordon and was healed.

I figured I better follow the prompting, so I went to the track and thought maybe I could run around one time. As I began to run and my heart began to beat faster, I felt a burden being lifted off of me. My heart felt good, and I knew that the Lord was blessing me with the ability to forgive. I then felt a great remorse for being unforgiving for so long. I asked the Lord for forgiveness for not acting upon this sooner. I felt a peace come over me that was so wonderful and I actually felt changed physically and spiritually. I walked around the track another lap and said a prayer of gratitude to Heavenly Father for his great love for me and expressed appreciation for the power of the atonement of Jesus Christ, which heals what we cannot heal on our own. Just as Naaman's leprosy was healed by washing in the Jordon, my hurt and anger were healed by forgiving.

Blame and grudges keep wounds open and allow the wrongs of others to control our lives. Forgiveness is not easy, but it is the balm that heals our wounds and frees us to choose our destiny.

CONCLUSION

A monk wrote more than 900 years ago, "When I was a young man, I wanted to change the world. I found it was difficult to change the world, so I tried to change my nation. When I found I couldn't change the nation, I began to focus on my town. I couldn't change the town and as an older man, I tried to change my family. Now, as an old man, I realize the only thing I can change is myself, and suddenly I realize that if long ago I had changed myself, I could have made an impact on my family. My family and I could have made an impact on our town. Their impact could have changed the nation, and I could indeed have changed the world."[27]

TRUTH 11

Happiness Is a Choice. Happiness Does Not Depend on Outward Conditions But on Inward Decisions.

MYTH 12

EVERYONE IS ENTITLED TO A HIGH STANDARD OF LIVING

A major political party's platform misuses the word "right" to claim that every American has a right to a job, food, clothes, recreation, medical care, a house, retirement, and education. "The right to life means that a man has the right to support his life by his own work; it does not mean that others must provide him with the necessities of life. The right to property means that a man has the right to take the economic action necessary to earn property ... it does not mean that others must provide him with property. . . There is no such thing as 'a right to a job' ... there is only ... a man's right to take a job if another man chooses to hire him. There is no 'right to a home' only ... the right to build a home or to buy it."[1] Our rights bring with them obligations and responsibilities, not handouts and entitlements.

ENTITLEMENT VS. EARNING

"Charity is injurious unless it helps the recipient to become independent of it."
–John D. Rockefeller, Jr.

There's a story about a wealthy family in which the father had built a large and very successful business from the ground up. As the father approached retirement, he called his son into his office and told his son that he wanted him to eventually take over his company. The son was excited and asked, "When are you going to give it to me?" The father replied, "I am not going to give you anything, you must earn it." The son replied, "How am I supposed to do that?"

The father answered, "First, you must earn $10,000 to purchase a small portion of ownership in the company." As the son left to begin his quest, his mother grabbed him and shoved $10,000 into his hand and told him to give the money to his father. Thrilled by his good fortune, the son ran to his father. His dad was sitting by the fireplace reading a book. The son approached his father and said, "Dad, Dad, here's $10,000 for the business." Without looking up, the father took the money and tossed it into the fire. The son stood, frozen with amazement and watched. As the money burned, the father said, "Come back when you have earned the money."

As he left the room, his mother once again gave him $10,000 and told him to be more convincing in selling his father on the idea that he had actually worked for the money. So the boy scuffed himself up a little, jogged around the block a few times, and then went to find his father again. His father was still sitting in front of the fireplace reading a book. The boy approached his father and said, "It sure is tough earning money. Here's the $10,000. I really do want to own the business." Once again the father took the $10,000 and tossed it in the fireplace. As the money burned, the son asked, "How did you know I didn't earn the money?" The father replied, "It is easy to lose or spend money that is not your own."

At this point, the son realized he wasn't going to get the business unless he actually earned the $10,000. He wanted the business, so when his mother offered him the money again, he declined her offer. He went out and picked up some odd jobs. His jobs required him to get up early and stay up late, but he worked and worked until he earned $10,000. Proudly, he walked into his father's office and presented him with the money. Like before, his father was sitting by the fire reading a book. And like before, the father took the money and threw it in the fire place. As the money hit the flames, the son dove to the floor, and stuck his hands into the fire and pulled out the money. The father looked his son in the eyes and said, "I see you really did earn the money this time."

Harmful Help

Many parents make the mistake of providing damaging financial assistance to their children. With good intentions, they want to help their children get started in life and offer assistance when a financial need arises. Unfortunately, the result is often opposite to the one desired. Instead of helping children become self-sufficient, they become dependant. Rather than sparking initiative and discipline, the children become idle and indulgent. Instead of being achievement oriented, they become entitlement oriented. Instead of becoming grateful, they become demanding. "Children who always get what they want will want as long as they live."[2] Research has shown that "in general, the more dollars adult children receive [from their parents] the fewer they accumulate, while those who are given fewer dollars accumulate more."[3]

If you keep your children from experiencing struggle and responsibility, you will also prevent them from growing. Work ethic, discipline, and initiative cannot be purchased with money but are developed through work, experience, and education. Living off others is a form of bondage—for if you take from a person his responsibility to care for himself, you also take from him the opportunity to be free. If you help too much, you will make an individual helpless. Do not give your kids money, give them education and opportunity. It costs a lot less and will develop the productive, self-sufficient children you desire.

The Story of the Caterpillar

While starting my first business, I often relied on one of my business partners and mentors who was a multimillionaire for advice. My business was growing but struggled to turn a profit. I continued to work hard, but things were getting tighter and tighter financially. I went to my rich partner and asked for a small monthly salary or a loan to help me get by until the business was profitable. He declined to give me any assistance. I was frustrated and said, "You are making millions a year, and I am struggling to stay alive. Please help me." He looked at me and I could tell he was close to giving in and wanted to help me. However, he replied, "If I take away your struggle, I will also take away your victory." He then shared the following story:

"There was a young boy who came across a caterpillar hanging in a cocoon. He visited the cocoon several times a day watching it grow and change and waiting for a butterfly to emerge. After a few days, the young boy began to see the cocoon move and watched as a butterfly struggled to emerge. The boy wanted to help the caterpillar so he ran home and got a pair of scissors. He returned and carefully cut open the cocoon and out fell a partially developed butterfly. This caterpillar would never fly as a butterfly. The young boy innocently killed the butterfly he was trying to help." At the time, I didn't find this advice helpful, but today I am grateful to a wise partner and mentor who resisted the temptation to cut open my cocoon.

TAKING THE INITIATIVE

To achieve financial success, God requires us to take initiative. Wealth does not fall from the heavens but is created through work and the gaining and application of knowledge. Some believe they deserve a high standard of living because they are righteous and live the commandments of God. They see no need for additional effort on their part. This is as foolish as the farmer who neglects to plant his crops and says, "God will make my crops grow because I am a good person." God does make seeds grow, but in order to receive a harvest planting, watering, tending, and harvesting are all required. Prosperity is not the result of simply being good. To say something like, "If I pay my tithe, God will take care of everything else" or "If God wanted me to have money, he would give it to me," is as foolish as saying, "If God wanted my hair combed, he would comb it for me." The truth is that God will not do for man what he can do for himself.

The Wright Brothers—Creating the Wings God Wanted for Man

William J. Tate, a man who helped the Wright brothers in assembling the Wright's first glider in North Carolina, wrote of the early flights, "The mental attitude of the natives toward the Wrights was that they were a simple pair of harmless cranks that were wasting their time at a fool attempt to do something that was impossible. The chief argument against their success could be heard at the stores and post office, and ran something like this: 'God didn't intend man to fly. If He did, He would have given him a set of wings on his shoulders.'"[4]

Wilber was born in 1867 and Orville was born in 1871 to Susan and Milton Wright in the Midwest. They were taught the gospel by their father who was a bishop in the Church of the United Brethren in Christ. In their youth, Wilber and Orville read the Bible as well as many other books from their father's library. Throughout his life, Milton "never tired of relating the positive effect the Bible had had on his children."[5] The Wright brothers exemplified their Christian values through their daily living. They refused to fly or work on Sunday[6] and abstained from alcohol, tobacco, and gambling.[7]

Orville and Wilber's interest in flying began in 1878 when their father gave them a toy helicopter.[8] This interest turned into an active pursuit at the end of the 19th century. Wilber began reading "everything he could lay his hands on, everything in sight. His father had some simple books on flight in nature in his library, and the Dayton Public Library had a handful of things on flight. When he had exhausted the local resources, Wilbur wrote to the Smithsonian Institution asking for more information on flight."[9]

In 1899, they began their flight experiments. At this time, the Wright brothers were running a bicycle repair and sales shop. It was revenues from this company that supported their living expenses and funded the development of the airplane. During the next four years, the Wright brothers performed thousands of tests, experiments, and flights. In

1901, they created the world's first wind tunnel and tested more than 200 different wing shapes,[10] and just in the months of September and October of 1902 they made 700–1,000 glides.[11] On December 17, 1903, Orville, age 32, and Wilber, age 36, achieved their dream of a controlled, powered flight. The flight covered a distance of 120 feet in 12 seconds—about half the length of a 747 jumbo jet. This flight was the beginning of modern aviation.

In 1904, the Wright brothers decided to take a financial risk and withdraw from the bicycle business to focus on developing a practical airplane that they could sell. Wilbur explained to an acquaintance, "… we believed that if we would take the risk of devoting our entire time and financial resources we could conquer the difficulties in the path to success … as our financial future was at stake [we] were compelled to regard it as a strict business proposition."[12] They would have to make the airplane a profitable business to survive, but they never compromised their values. The Wright brothers expected their employees to observe their family rules and among those who worked for them "there was no drinking, gambling, or flying on Sundays."[13]

In February 1908, the company obtained a contract from the U.S. Army to build a two-seat aircraft that could fly for an hour at an average speed of 40 miles per hour and land undamaged. In July 1909, they completed a flight that met the U.S. Army's requirements and received $30,000 ($645,000 in 2006 dollars) for their aircraft. In 1910, they added air shows and commercial air cargo shipping to their business, earning nearly $100,000 ($2 million in 2006 dollars) in profit that year.[14]

Flying was a risky venture. Otto Lilienthal, an early aviator pioneer whose work assisted and inspired the Wright brothers, died after a gust of wind threw his glider out of balance, causing him to fall fifty feet, breaking his spine. His last words were quoted as "sacrifices must be made" and these words were carved on his tombstone.[15] The brothers wrote of Lilienthal and other early aviator pioneers that their work "infected us with their own unquenchable enthusiasm, and transformed idle curiosity into the active zeal of workers."[16]

Orville and Wilber experienced their share of crashes. One occurred on September 17, 1908, when a propeller malfunctioned, and the aircraft crashed, killing the passenger. Orville suffered multiple serious injuries, including a broken leg and broken ribs. Because of the dangers in flying, and at the request of their father, Wilber and Orville never flew together. However, on May 25, 1910, after they had made many improvements that increased the safety of the airplane, and for the sake of history, the father agreed to let Wilber and Orville fly together. This was the only time the brothers flew together. After this flight, Orville took his 81-year-old father on the only flight of his life, which lasted 6 minutes and 55 second. "At one point during the flight, Milton leaned close to his son's ear and shouted … 'Higher, Orville, higher!'"[17]

Wilber died from typhoid fever in 1912 at age 45. "Twenty-five thousand people viewed his casket and for three full minutes the citizens of Dayton stopped everything they were doing as they mourned an American hero. Orville had lost his brother, his best friend, his other half who knew the secrets of flying. He was devastated, but he carried on."[18] Orville continued to run The Wright Company for three more years until he was 44 years old. On October 15, 1915, Orville sold his interest in the company. "*The New York Times* reported that Orville received roughly $1.5 million [$30 million in 2006 dollars], plus an additional $25,000 [$500,000 in 2006 dollars] for his services as chief consulting engineer during the first year of the new company's operation."[19]

God did not give men wings upon their shoulders, but He did give them minds and hands to create. It took faith, study, courage, work, and persistence of these two men to achieve the miracle of flight. Two men with a dream to fly created wings for us all—the wings God intended for man.

CONCLUSION

"You cannot establish security on borrowed money. You cannot build character and courage by taking away men's initiative and independence. You cannot help men permanently by doing for them what they could and should do for themselves."[20] Courage, discipline, and achievement are gifts you can give to no man—they only can be obtained through individual struggle, initiative, and effort.

"The world bestows its big prizes, both in money and honors, for but one thing. And that is initiative. What is initiative? I'll tell you: It is doing the right thing without being told. But next to doing the thing without being told is to do it when you are told once . . . but their pay is not always in proportion. Next, there are those who never do a thing until they are told twice: such get no honors and small pay. Next, there are those who do the right thing only when necessity kicks them from behind, and these get indifference instead of honors, and a pittance for pay . . . Then, still lower down in the scale than this, we have the fellow who will not do the right thing even when someone goes along to show him how and stays to see that he does it: he is always out of a job ... To which class do you belong?"[21]

We must each develop the capacity for independent action. The Wright brothers should inspire each of us to ask, "What cause or endeavor can I take the initiative to move forward?"

TRUTH 12

The Blessings of Prosperity Are Poured upon Those Capable of Independent Action— Those Who Take the Initiative.

CHOICE 2: PRIDE OR HUMILITY

"Humility is the most difficult of all virtues to achieve;
nothing dies harder than the desire to think well of oneself."
—Thomas Stearns Eliot

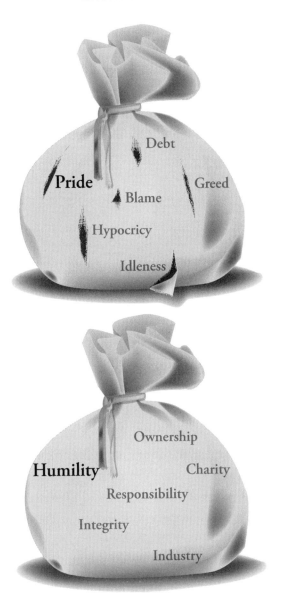

I KNOW ALL I NEED TO ABOUT MONEY

A survey revealed, "70 percent of Americans say they're good or excellent at managing their finances."[1] Since many people think they are good at managing their finances, they have the false belief that they know all they need to about money and fail to learn the principles of financial success and prosperity. In turn, they struggle financially or do not achieve their full financial potential. While most people claim they are good at managing their finances, real life results indicate otherwise, as "96 percent of all Americans will retire financially dependent on the government, family, or charity."[2] The weakest part of each person is where he or she thinks himself or herself the wisest. In the words of the great basketball coach John Wooden, "It's what we learn after we think we know it all that really counts." Those who are teachable and continually seeking to improve and grow rarely contract the disease of pride.

BE TEACHABLE

"Listen to advice and accept instruction, and in the end you will be wise."
—Proverbs 19:20, New International Version

Achieving financial abundance and self-reliance requires more than a desire to obtain financial freedom. Just as it takes thousands of hours of study and practice to develop the skills of a successful engineer, so it also takes hours of study and practice to master the principles of prosperity. Becoming financially free requires developing attributes, skills, and abilities. Those who achieve financial abundance have invested in their financial education. Many talk about the great returns they have received from real estate or the stock market, but the greatest return you will ever get on an investment is the money you invest in education. Benjamin Franklin taught, "An investment in knowledge always pays the best interest."[3]

Education and transportation are tools that get us to our destination. Over the years, transportation has moved from the horse and buggy to trains, cars, and airplanes. Each new mode of transportation has enabled us to reach our destination in a shorter period of time. In the 1800s it took months to cross the plains to the west. Today, with improved tools, we can make the same journey in a matter of hours. Education is also a tool that can speed up your journey to financial independence and prosperity. Studies of those with a high net worth have revealed that they spend significant time each month on financial education.[4] Studies also show there is direct correlation between the amount of time spent on financial education and net worth. The more you learn, the more you earn.

There are three resources I look to for financial education:
1. Reading books
2. Attending seminars
3. Listening to audio programs

Reading Books

"Reading is to the mind what exercise is to the body: as by the one, health is preserved, strengthened, and invigorated; by the other, virtue (which is the health of the mind) is kept alive, cherished, and confirmed."[5] "When we read inspired, thought-provoking books, we grow richer in all phases of our lives. In short, reading has the power to transform us from what we are right now to what we could be in the future."[6]

Reading is a shortcut to success. The Greek philosopher Socrates taught, "Employ your time in improving yourself by other men's writings, so that you shall gain easily what others have labored hard for."[7] A book provides a powerful way to learn in a few hours what others have learned in a lifetime.

Block out time each day to read positive, inspiring books. In 2006, the average American watched 4 hours and 45 minutes of television a day and read 18 minutes a day from books.[8] As you spend more time reading books on positive, inspiring, and financial topics, you will see an increase in your net worth. The libraries of the world are full of knowledge free for the taking but "the man who does not read good books has no advantage over the man who can't read."[9]

Attending Seminars

In addition to reading, you can attend seminars and workshops designed to help you achieve your dreams. Robert Kiyosaki, author of *Rich Dad, Poor Dad*, wrote, "I go to seminars. I like it when they are at least two days long because I like to immerse myself in a subject. In 1973, I was watching TV and this guy came on advertising a three-day seminar on how to buy real estate for nothing down . . . and that course has made me at least $2 million, if not more. But most importantly, it bought me life. I don't have to work for the rest of my life because of that one course. I go to at least two such courses every year."[10]

Listening to Audio Programs

In 2004, the national average commute to work was 24 minutes. How do you spend time in your car? Why not utilize driving time learning the principles that will bring success in every facet of your life? There are audio programs and audio books to teach you on every success topic imaginable. If you want to increase your net worth, decide to make your time in the car a time for education instead of a time for entertainment.

To get started, check out the audio book selection at your local library and utilize this form of education while commuting, during flights, or even on your iPod while exercising. Many people ask how many songs their iPod holds. I ask how many audio books it can hold.

"The illiterate of the 21st century will not be those who cannot read and write, but those who cannot learn, unlearn, and relearn."[11]

CONSTANTLY SEEK IMPROVEMENT

"True nobility is in being superior to your own previous self."
–Hindu Proverb

Satan tries to persuade us to be content with just getting by. The Lord rebukes those who are satisfied with their condition in life, who are content with the way things are, and who don't seek change and improvement. We are always in need of improvement. If you say "I ... have need of nothing"[12] and "do not realize that you are wretched, pitiful, poor, blind and naked,"[13] the Lord will see you as being lukewarm (apathetic) and will cast you out as He said in the book of Revelations, " . . . because you are lukewarm, and neither hot nor cold, I will spit you out of my mouth."[14] The Lord expects us to continually seek improvement.

The Parable of the Fig Tree

The Savior teaches this principle further in the miracle and parable of the fig tree found in Chapter 11 of Mark. Jesus, walking with His disciples, came to a fig tree that had no figs on it. When Jesus saw that there were no figs upon the fig tree, He cursed the fig tree, and the next day it was withered and dead. This miracle is different from all the other recorded miracles of Jesus that were performed for relief, blessing, and beneficent purposes. This appears to be an act of judgment and destructive execution. A key to understanding this miracle and parable is found in verse 13, which reads, "It was not the season for figs."[15] The fig tree didn't have figs on it because figs were not in season. None of the trees had figs on them—why did Jesus destroy this tree? On his tape entitled *A Higher Standard of Excellence*, Mark Gorman states that at 2 a.m. God told him the meaning of these passages. When the inspiration came, he sat straight up in bed and God spoke to him saying, "If all you are doing is what comes naturally to you, I am not impressed. If you are only producing when everyone else is producing, so what. If you are just keeping up with the crowd, big deal." To impress the Lord, we must strive for excellence and do more than just what comes naturally.

We must not just produce fruit when it is in season—we must produce fruit everyday. We must rise above mediocrity. We must rise above just getting by. We must excel.

Growing or Decaying

Life is like trying to go up a downward escalator, where if you're not stepping up (putting forth effort), you're going down. Life is not like a stairway where you can reach a certain step and then stop and maintain your position. Just as a tree is either growing or decaying, so we are either progressing or digressing. In life, you cannot be at a standstill.

Don Soderquist, retired senior vice chairman of the board for Wal-Mart, shares this story: "I was at a banquet one evening and had the opportunity to visit with Harry Cunningham, the former CEO of K-Mart stores. In fact, he was the legendary character who dramatically changed retail in America by developing the concept of the K-Mart stores for the former Kresge company—a model we carefully studied and considered when developing Wal-Mart stores. I thanked him for what he had done in pioneering the successful discounting format as we know it today. He was gracious in accepting my praise, but was quick to add how much he appreciated what Wal-Mart had done in developing the concept even further. He went on to say, 'We made a serious mistake along the way by not changing and updating our stores over the years. We had a successful formula that was working and saw no reason to change. You folks at Wal-Mart continued to improve until you were much better than we were, and by that time, you passed us by.' The lesson for me in that conversation was that while success can lead to success, it could also lead to failure if you refuse to focus on improving."[16]

Line Upon Line

The Lord gives us a little knowledge, and if we give heed to this knowledge, he will give us more. The prophet Isaiah taught, "But the word of the LORD was unto them precept upon precept, precept upon precept; line upon line, line upon line; here a little, and there a little."[17]

God will allow us to know more than we do presently. This gift enables a person to continually seek improvement without becoming overwhelmed. God reveals a few of our weaknesses so we can have hope in overcoming them. If he revealed all our inadequacies at once we would be devastated. As we overcome some of our faults, we receive more knowledge and we see additional areas that can be improved. As we begin doing what we know to be right, we will learn more. We continue this process of gaining knowledge and aligning our behavior with that knowledge until we have learned to live in accordance with all the principles of success.

A great hindrement to our progression is not living in accordance with the things we know to be right—for those who do not give heed to the knowledge given them will receive no more and will also have taken from them that which they had been given. The Savior teaches this principle saying, "For whosoever receiveth, to him shall be given, and he shall have more abundance; but whosoever continueth not to receive, from him shall be taken away even that he hath."[18] In the parable of the fig tree, Jesus took from the tree which was not producing figs that which it did have (leaves) causing them to wither. The Lord said in the book of Jeremiah that those with "no figs on the tree . . . [will have] what I have given them taken from them."[19]

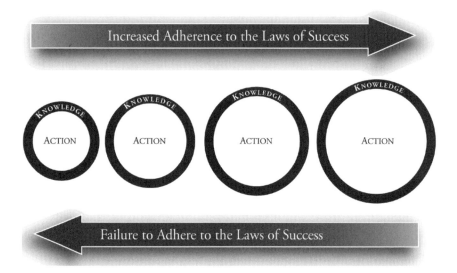

Growth and the 80/20 Rule

It is by pushing ourselves to our current maximum that we open the door of growth to a new maximum. For example, much of the growth from weight lifting comes from the final reps before you can lift no more. If you could bench press 200 pounds a maximum of 10 reps, 80 percent of muscle growth and increased strength will result from the final 2 reps and 20 percent of the growth results from the first 8 reps. The last two reps are the hardest, but if neglected will cost you 80 percent of your growth. It does not require twice the effort to achieve twice the improvement, because the final efforts of maximum exertion result in exponential returns.

In business, if you were to simply work an additional 40 minutes a day, which could be achieved by taking your lunch to work and eating quickly in your office instead of going out to lunch, you would complete an additional month of fulltime work each year. While 40 minutes a day represents only an 8 percent increase in hours worked (based on an 8 hour work day), it could translate into twice the pay.

DOING OUR PERSONAL BEST

"Whatever your hand finds to do, do it with all your might."
–Ecclesiastes 9:10, New International Version

The Lord has set the ultimate goal when he said, "Be ye therefore perfect, even as your Father which is in heaven is perfect."[20] As perfection is unattainable while on Earth, Christ is more worried about our desire to obtain perfection and our doing our personal best even if this is far from perfection. Sometimes our personal best is not high quality, but if it is our best it is acceptable to the Lord.

The Parable of the Talents

The Lord illustrates this point in the parable of the talents. In this parable, a lord gave to one of his servants five talents ($1.5 million in 2006 dollars), to another two talents ($600,000 in 2006 dollars), and to another one talent ($300,000 in 2006 dollars).[21] The servants who received two and five talents both returned to the Lord more talents than he had given them, to which the Lord replied, "Well done, [thou] good and faithful servant: thou hast been faithful over a few things, I will make thee ruler over many things: enter thou into the joy of thy lord."[22] The servant who received one talent was afraid and hid his talent in the ground and returned to the lord only the one talent he had received, for which the lord rebuked him saying, "You wicked, lazy servant! . . . you should have put my money on deposit with the bankers, so that when I returned I would have received it back with interest . . . throw that worthless servant outside, into the darkness, where there will be weeping and gnashing of teeth."[23] In the parable, there was no comparison between the servants—each received an individual accounting. The servant who received one talent was not punished for having less than the other servants, but he was punished for not doing his personal best. It doesn't matter if your neighbor has greater or fewer talents than you. What matters is what you do with your talents. Life is not a competition with others. Life is a competition with yourself—to each day do your personal best.

Curve Analogy

Some view life as a class graded on a curve—where your grade depends on how well others in the class perform. A teacher utilizing a curved grading system may give only the top 10 percent of the class A's. It doesn't matter how much time they put in or how hard they tried. It only matters that they did better than 90 percent of the class. Only those who are top performers compared to others will receive A's. Curves breed a sense of competition and comparison. In the gospel, there is no place for competition and comparison. God's plan is completely individualized; there will be some in the bottom 10 percent in performance compared to others who will receive eternal life. There will be those in the top 10 percent in performance when compared to others who will not receive eternal life, fulfilling the scripture, "But many that are first shall be last; and the last shall be first."[24]

The Broken Kneecap

While in college, I hyperextended my knee and fractured my kneecap playing basketball. I was unable to walk and was on crutches. Every Tuesday morning I had a meeting on campus. It usually took me 12 minutes to walk from my apartment to the building where the meeting was, but on the crutches it took me 35 minutes. As I made my way to the building, everyone was passing me. I was the slowest person on campus, yet I continued toward the building and eventually made it. Even though it took me almost three times as long, I still made it. I went as fast as I could according to my circumstances and abilities. We cannot judge others in how far they have progressed in the gospel or judge their level of obedience, because we do not know their circumstances and abilities. It would have been foolish for someone to say, "Cameron is a real loser. It took him 35 minutes to do something I can do in 12 minutes" or "I am better than Cameron because I can get to the building 3 times as fast as he can." When you take into consideration my circumstances and abilities (broken kneecap and on crutches), I was doing a good job. The same concept applies to the gospel. We can't judge others because we don't know their circumstances. We should not ask the question, "How am I doing compared to so and so?" We should ask, "Am I doing my personal best?"

CONCLUSION

The great football coach Vince Lombardi taught, "Constantly seek ways to do better whatever needs to be done. If a person with this quality will continue positive application of this negative factor, that person will have a leadership role. The quality: dissatisfaction. To make the unsatisfactory satisfactory or better is the mark of leadership. Never be satisfied with less than top performance, and progress will be the reward." Each time we achieve a goal we should ask, "How can it be done better? How can it be improved? "Never [be] satisfied with the status quo or with past attainments. Reaching a goal is merely a signal to set a higher one, goal-setting is done in small increments so that people never become discouraged: at the same time, they are never permanently satisfied."[25]

Captain James Cook, an 18th century English explorer, showed the spirit of excellence by saying of his many voyages of discovery, "I had an ambition, not only to go farther than any man had ever been before, but I wanted to go as far as it was possible for any man to go."

TRUTH 13

Life Should Be a Never-Ending Quest for Improvement.

MYTH 14

RICH PEOPLE ARE PROUD

It is not riches that make a person proud, but his or her motives. Pride is not a result of net worth or income but of attitudes, beliefs, and motives. For example, prayer can be an act of pride or an act of humility. The Savior taught, "Two men went up to the temple to pray, one a Pharisee and the other a tax collector. The Pharisee stood and prayed thus with himself, 'God, I thank You that I am not like other men—extortioners, unjust, adulterers, or even as this tax collector. I fast twice a week; I give tithes of all that I possess.' And the tax collector, standing afar off, would not so much as raise his eyes to heaven, but beat his breast, saying, 'God, be merciful to me a sinner!' I tell you, this man went down to his house justified rather than the other; for everyone who exalts himself will be humbled, and he who humbles himself will be exalted."[1] The Pharisee's prayer was motivated by pride to lift himself above others and "to be seen by men."[2] It is not the act, but the motive for the act, which reveals pride or humility.

PRIDE VS. HUMILITY

One way in which Satan tricks us is when he tries to get us to do the right things for the wrong reasons. To lead us astray, Satan does not have to get us to stop praying or working, he only has to get us to pray or work for the wrong reason. To protect against the universal sin of pride and to cultivate the heavenly attribute of humility, we must understand the underlying motives of each. This knowledge will help us defend against Satan's temptations to gradually lead us astray with the subtle misdirection of our intentions.

MOTIVES	
HUMILITY	**PRIDE**
1. Learn/Grow	1. Impress Others
2. Do Your Personal Best	2. Be Better Than Others
3. Self-Reliance	3. Social Status
4. Mission	4. Money
5. Love	5. Power
6. Joy of Gratitude	6. Pain of Lack

1. Learn/Grow vs. Impress Others

A humble person is genuinely interested in what others have to say. They know they do not have all the answers and continually seek to learn from the insights and experiences of others—they "approach others with open minds and are willing to be taught."[3] The humble usually listen more than they talk. Of their accomplishments, the humble will most likely say nothing or something along the lines of "God has done it" or "We have done it." The humble follow the Lord's council, "Don't brag about your wisdom or strength or wealth. If you feel you must brag, then have enough sense to brag about . . . the LORD."[4] The humble acknowledge the work, help, and support of others and give thanks to them and God. They follow the counsel of Paul to ". . . give more honor to others than to yourselves."[5]

A proud person will often speak in a boastful or bragging manner of their accomplishment and possessions in an attempt to impress others. They are more interested in talking about themselves than learning from others. The proud person says, "I have done it. Look at me. Aren't

I impressive!" The proud will even take credit for the accomplishments of others in their quest to receive attention and praise from others.

2. Do Your Personal Best vs. Be Better Than Others

The humble realize that life is not a competition. They view others as children of God—their brothers, sisters, and equals. They are not worried about how they are doing in relation to others but whether or not they are doing their personal best. The humble are cooperative and always seek to lift others. They celebrate the success of others. Humble people consider themselves smart, beautiful, or athletic, but they will not think themselves prettier, smarter, or a better athlete than others. "To paraphrase C.S. Lewis, humility is not handsome people trying to believe they are ugly and clever people trying to believe they are fools."[6] Comparison with others will not even enter the mind of the humble.

The proud see life as a competition—viewing others as their opponents and enemies. They belittle the successes of others with the belief that the success of others detracts from their success. They continually measure their value, accomplishments, work, wealth, and talents in relation to those of others. The proud are more concerned that their income is more than others' than that it meets their needs. "Pride gets no pleasure out of having something, only out of having more of it than the next man. We say that people are proud of being rich, or clever, or good-looking, but they are not. They are proud of being richer, or cleverer, or better-looking than others. If everyone else became equally rich, or clever, or good-looking there would be nothing to be proud about. It is the comparison that makes you proud: the pleasure of being above the rest. Once the element of competition has gone, pride has gone."[7] The proud seek to create hierarchies and class system where they are above others.

3. Self-Reliance vs. Social Status

For the humble, their worth and respect comes from within. Self-reliance is their source of worth and respect. The humble seek the bounties of life they enjoy without a thought of what others think or say about it. They value freedom and independence and do not submit to the bondage of men's judgment.

For the proud, their worth and respect comes from without. Social status is their source of self-worth and respect. The proud abandon the bounties of life they enjoy for those the world says are the best or most important. Once you love "the praise of men more than the praise of God,"[8] you surrender your independence and freedom to become a slave to men's judgment.

When purchases are motivated not by need and function but to build social status, pride will enter our hearts and lives. For example, the proud will purchase clothes, not for warmth and functionality, but because they are the best clothes and are a symbol of their social status. The prophet Haggai warned of this 2,500 years ago saying, "You put on clothes, but are not warm."[9] This can apply to most purchases. In the book *The Millionaire Next Door*, a doctor shares the following, "I have only had two cars. The first, a Mercedes, I purchased . . . [and] kept it twenty years. Then I bought my second car . . . a three-year old Mercedes. I went to a dealer . . . He wanted to sell me a new one. But it was $20,000 more than the used one on the lot. Then I just asked myself a simple question: Is the 'pride of new car ownership'— and that's all it is, pride—worth $20,000? The cars are the same. The answer is no. The 'pride of new car ownership' is not worth $20,000."[10] Indulgences and ego trips are detours from the path to true success.

4. Mission vs. Money

Near the end of his life, Sam Walton, the founder of Wal-Mart, said, "I have concentrated all along on building the finest retailing company that we possibly could. Period. Creating a huge personal fortune was never a goal of mine."[11] The humble are driven by a mission to help others. Their financial success will be a byproduct of their mission to help others. They lay up for themselves treasures in heaven.[12] The proud are selfish and are driven by money. Financial success is not a byproduct of their mission, but is their mission. They focus on the accumulation of earthly possessions.

5. Love vs. Power

The humble are motivated by love. They lead by persuasion, gentleness, and long-suffering. It is a misconception to think that the humble are doormats to the proud—the influence of the humble is far superior to the power of the proud.

The proud are driven by power. They rule by control and force. "Nothing makes a man feel superior to others as being able to move them about like toy soldiers."[13] "The proud man, even when he has got more than he can possibly want, will try to get still more just to assert his power. Nearly all those evils in the world which people put down to greed or selfishness are really far more the result of pride."[14] "If you want to test a man's character, give him power."[15]

6. Joy of Gratitude vs. Pain of Lack

The humble realize that all they have and are is a gift from God and are thus filled with the joy of gratitude. The humble focus on what they have, while the proud focus on what they lack. Many only think of pride in terms of what we have, but there is another type of pride in that which we lack called envy. "Envy is pained at what another person has and desires to spoil it. Envy is an urge to spoil or devalue what is good in another. Envy is born out of the pain of emptiness, of lack; the urge is to regain some internal balance by denigrating the goodness of the other. My cup is empty; I can't tolerate the fullness of yours, so I spoil it. Destructive envy represents an urgent need to spoil so as not to have to experience the pain of lack."[16]

A classic example of envy is found in the book of Genesis: "Now Israel loved Joseph more than all his children, because he was the son of his old age: and he made him a coat of many colours. And when his brethren saw that their father loved him more than all his brethren, they hated him."[17] To eliminate the pain of lack, his brothers "moved with envy, sold Joseph into Egypt."[18] Other common manifestations of envy are found among those who incur excessive consumer debt in an attempt to satisfy the pain of lack, or those who seek to pull down others through faultfinding, backbiting, and gossiping.

SAM WALTON—WAL-MART FOUNDER AND HUMBLE BILLIONAIRE

In 1962, Sam Walton opened the first Wal-Mart store at the age of 44 in Rogers, Arkansas. Five years later, in 1967, Wal-Mart had 24 stores doing more than $1 million per month in sales. In 1975, Wal-mart had 125 stores doing almost $1 million per day in sales. In 1979, Wal-Mart had 276 stores doing more than $100 million per month in sales, becoming the fastest company in history to reach a billion dollars a year in sales. Wal-Mart is now doing nearly a billion dollars a day. In 2005, Wal-Mart did $312 billion in sales from 6,200 facilities with 1.6 million employees and more than 138 million customers visiting the stores each week.[19]

Although his fame, power, and net worth grew over the years,[20] Sam Walton remained the same—a humble man focused on helping others. He "lived a clean Christian life . . . taught Sunday school . . . [and was] a man whose handshake you can rely on in any kind of deal."[21] Sam Walton saw an opportunity to bless the lives of those in small towns across America that were being overlooked by the big retail chains. He was driven by his mission "to provide a better shopping experience for everyday people living in small towns. He wanted to improve their standard of living by providing quality goods at low prices in a pleasant shopping environment."[22]

"Even though he was a billionaire many times over, you wouldn't know it if you met him on the street. He drove [an] old pick-up truck, and he lived in a humble house in Bentonville[23] that almost anyone with a job could have afforded"[24] and he purchased many of his clothes from Wal-Mart. "Bernard Marcus, chairman and co-founder of Home Depot, recalled going out to lunch with Walton after a meeting in Bentonville: 'I hopped into Sam's red pickup truck. No air-conditioning. Seats stained by coffee. And by the time I got to the restaurant, my shirt was soaked through and through. And that was Sam Walton—no airs [attempts to impress others], no pomposity [arrogance].'"[25]

An executive who joined Wal-Mart from Frito-Lay shared this story: "After I had joined the company, I still remember seeing Sam walk into the Home Office bathroom—the same bathroom used by everybody else ... multibillionaire Sam Walton didn't have a private executive washroom. He used the same facilities that everybody else used. This was quite a contrast for me from the executives I had known at Frito-Lay, who enjoyed a private underground parking area, private bathrooms, and an executive dining room."[26] "In the thirty years of Walton's leadership, Wal-Mart didn't authorize a penny for the decoration of executive offices."[27]

Don Soderquist, retired senior vice chairman of the board for Wal-Mart, shared the following experience while working with Sam Walton at a store grand opening: "Like most of the grand openings, we expected a big crowd, but in this one our productivity couldn't keep up with the traffic flow. Before long, Sam jumped in and began to bag merchandise. He handed out candy to the kids and did anything he could think of to help the customers feel more comfortable with the long lines ... I confess, as a former company president of a national retail chain and now an executive vice president for Wal-Mart, I had never served customers on the front lines like I did that day. You don't think I was going to stand around and watch my leader do you? Sam was a very humble man, and he taught me a valuable lesson that day. None of us are too good to do the little jobs. In fact, there are no little jobs. If the chairman of the board wasn't too high and mighty to hand out lollipops and bag goods—neither was I ... No matter how large we became, Sam always reminded us that we were no better than anyone else and should never become blinded by our own importance."[28]

Sam Walton valued Wal-Mart's employees and took the time to listen and learn from them. During his 30 years as Wal-Mart's CEO, he had a policy that any employee could contact him directly with a problem, comment, or idea. On several occasions, Sam took donuts to the Wal-Mart employees and talked to them during their breaks. He continually tried to improve the Wal-Mart experience for the customers and employees. After the company made a public stock offering in 1970, Sam implemented a profit-sharing plan for all employees to be paid in Wal-Mart stock. As a result, many managers and hourly employees retired from Wal-Mart as millionaires. Sam Walton loved each of his employees, calling them associates and treating them like family.

On April 5, 1992, at age 74, Sam Walton passed away from cancer. "The news was sent via satellite directly to the company's 1,960 stores; when the announcement played on the public address system at some stores, clerks started crying."[29] An executive of a competing store said of Sam Walton, "The way he lived his life reminded me that I had rather see a sermon than hear one anytime."[30]

Conclusion

"If anyone would like to acquire humility . . . the first step is to realize that one is proud . . . If you think you are not conceited, it means you are very conceited indeed."[31] "We come nearest to the great when we are great in humility."[32] We should choose to be humble for "Pride goeth before destruction."[33] May we each declare, "Lord, I have given up my pride and turned away from my arrogance."[34]

TRUTH 14

"He That Is Greatest Among You Shall Be Your Servant."[35]

CHOICE 3:
HYPOCRISY OR INTEGRITY

"The supreme quality for a leader is unquestionably integrity.
Without it, no real success is possible."
–Dwight D. Eisenhower

Truth Is Subjective and Relative

There are theories regarding truth that suggest truth is created by cultural and social processes—what is true for one society may be different than what is true for another society—that truth is merely a result of consensus by some specified group. The irrational nature of these ideas is illustrated by the following paraphrased dialog of the ancient Greek philosophers Protagoras and Socrates.

> PROTAGORAS: Truth is relative; it is only a mater of opinion.
>
> SOCRATES: You mean that truth is mere subjective opinion?
>
> PROTAGORAS: Exactly. What is true for you is true, and what is true for me, is true for me. Truth is subjective.
>
> SOCRATES: Do you really mean that? That my opinion is true by virtue of it being my opinion?
>
> PROTAGORAS: Indeed I do.
>
> SOCRATES: My opinion is: Truth is absolute, not opinion, and that you, Mr. Protagoras, are absolutely in error. Since this is my opinion, then you must grant that it is true according to your philosophy.
>
> PROTAGORAS: You are quite correct, Socrates.[1]

Just as there are truths that govern nature, such as gravity, so also are there truths that govern our happiness, peace, and prosperity. It is by learning and living by truth that we experience true joy and peace. The Savior said in relation to truth, "If ye know these things, happy are ye if ye do them."[2] If we are committed to anything but the principles of truth, we will ultimately be unsuccessful.

The Parable of the Ticket Agent—A Real Life Story

Tuesday September 11, 2001 began the same as many days. "Millions of men and women readied themselves for work. Some made their way to the Twin Towers . . . Others went to Arlington, Virginia, to the Pentagon. Across the Potomac River, the United Sates Congress was back in session. At the other end of Pennsylvania Avenue, people began to line up for a White House tour. In Sarasota, Florida, President George W. Bush went for an early morning run."[3] In Portland, Maine, Michael Tuohey, a ticket agent for U.S. Airways, went to work at the airport like he had for 37 years, arriving at 4:30 a.m.

"Tuohey was working the preferred customers line, where the frequent travelers and high-end flyers get quick service. The line was empty… Then he spotted two young men come in and motioned them to his station."[4] At 5:40, Atta and Omari approached Tuohey's counter. Tuohey pulled up their information in the computer. They had one-way, first-class tickets to Los Angeles. The first leg of the flight was U.S. Airways Flight 5930 from Portland, Maine, to Boston, and the second leg was American Airlines Flight 11, non-stop from Boston to Los Angeles. Tuohey noted that the flight left in 20 minutes and said to Atta, "You're cutting it close … Got any bags?"[5] Atta checked two bags. "Tuohey then checked their drivers' licenses … [and] his eyes locked on Atta…Then Tuohey went through an internal debate that still haunts him."[6]

Tuohey felt something was wrong. He recalled, "I got chills when I looked at [Atta]."[7] "I got an uncomfortable feeling… I said to myself, 'If this guy doesn't look like an Arab terrorist, then nothing does.'"[8] Tuohey had checked in thousands of Arabic people during the years and never had such thoughts or feelings. However, Tuohey began to rationalize away his instincts. He gave himself a politically correct "mental slap, because in this day and age, it's not nice to say things like this."[9] The two men were wearing ties and jackets so he thought to himself, "These are just a couple of Arab businessmen."[10] "Setting aside his gut reaction, Tuohey issued the boarding passes."[11]

Atta and Omari arrived in Boston at 6:45 a.m. and boarded American Airline Flight 11 bound for Los Angeles. The plane took off at 7:59 a.m. and the hijacking began at 8:14 a.m. The terrorists stabbed flight attendants and passengers and controlled the others by spraying Mace. The hijackers gained access to the cockpit and Atta—the only terrorist on board trained to fly a jet—took control of the aircraft. At 8:26 the plane was "flying erratically," and a minute later, Flight 11 turned south.[12]

At 8:46 American Airline Flight 11 "traveling at hundreds of miles per hour and carrying some 10,000 gallons of jet fuel plowed into the North Tower of the World Trade Center in Lower Manhattan. At 9:03, a second airliner hit the South Tower. Fire and smoke billowed upward. Steel, glass, ash, and bodies fell below. The Twin Towers, where up to 50,000 people worked each day, both collapsed less than 90 minutes later... More than 2,600 people died in the World Trade Center."[13]

Tuohey was told by a co-worker that American Airline Flight 11 had crashed into the World Trade Center and a few minutes later he heard of the second crash. In response, Tuohey said, "I checked in two guys for the flight, and I thought they were terrorists."[14] He now knew his instincts had been correct saying, "I was right. This guy was a terrorist."[15]

Since 9/11, Tuohey has been "wracked by guilt at the thought he could have done something to stop it"[16] and on CNN he stated, "I felt ashamed that I did not react to my instincts."[17]

"Tuohey says he just hopes that the next person chosen by chance to make that first contact with evil ... does what he did not, and reacts when his gut tells him to. [Tuohey stated,] 'I had the devil standing right in front of me, you know, and I ignored him.'"[18]

If the contents of the two bags Atta checked in more than 3 hours before the first attack had been searched, the story may have had a much different ending. "A mix-up in Boston prevented the luggage from connecting ... [and following the attacks it was] seized by FBI agents ... it contained Arab-language papers revealing the identities of all 19 hijackers involved in the four hijackings, as well as information on their plans, backgrounds, and motives ... a videocassette for a Boeing 757 flight simulator, folding knife, and pepper spray ... [and] papers amounting to Atta's last will and testament, along with instructions to the other hijackers to prepare themselves physically and spiritually for death."[19]

Following 9/11, Tuohey vehemently stated, "I will never ignore my instincts again." He "worked for three more years at the U.S Airways ticket counter before retiring ... [and] twice his inquires led to arrests."[20]

THE INTEGRITY MODEL™

Integrity is often defined as an undeviating commitment to a set of beliefs. By this definition, a terrorist who lives his beliefs—and thus carries out acts of murder and destruction—would be a person of great integrity, willing to even give his life for his beliefs. This definition is incomplete. Integrity is much more than just aligning our actions with our beliefs. It is aligning our actions and beliefs with truth. The Integrity Model illustrates the elements of integrity (see illustration). As we strive for a life of integrity, understanding each of the components of the model will increase our ability to believe and act in accordance with truth, thus living with integrity.

Truth

God is our source of truth. The more we know and live truth, the more we know God. Truth, like God, is eternal, absolute, unchangeable, spiritual, and perfect. Truth is not invented or created but discovered. "All truths are easy to understand once they are discovered; the point is to discover them."[21] In the words of Winston Churchill, "Truth is incontrovertible. Ignorance may attack it and malice may deride it, but in the end, there it is." Michael Tuohey had conflicting thoughts as he checked in Atta, but his rationalization that they were businessmen or his desire to be politically correct and unbiased did not change the truth that Atta was, in fact, a terrorist.

Beliefs

Beliefs are ideas such as "I am a child of God," "All men are created equal," and "I am saved by the grace of Christ." Our beliefs determine many of our actions. For example, Adolf Hitler believed "that the races were graded. There were, according to him, superior races and inferior races. The highest race, according to Adolf Hitler, was the Aryan race—the race destined to be masters. The lowest race were the Jews and blacks—those who, in Hitler's view, were the root of all of civilization's evils and ills."[22] From Hitler's belief in graded races, can we predict his behavior? Yes, and history documents the destruction his beliefs caused. Were Hitler's beliefs in accordance with truth? Of course not. The key to transforming Hitler's behaviors would have been to change his belief in graded races to a belief that all men are created equal. One of the great blessings in life is that we can change our whole outlook on life by changing our beliefs. The Bible says, "Let God transform you into a new person by changing the way you think."[23]

Beliefs are things that we know, not things that we do. With beliefs there are no "hows" to be learned. Some try to treat beliefs like skills, such as goal setting, prayer, or giving compliments, and then become frustrated when they can't apply them in daily life. They complain that beliefs are abstract and of no benefit. They want something they can *do*—not realizing that gaining knowledge (aligning beliefs with truth) is one of the most powerful ways to improve their attitudes and actions, which will lead to joy, peace, and prosperity.

For example, what if someone asked you, "How can I apply the grace of Christ in my everyday life?" The person may get frustrated when you can't give him or her a specific answer. It's not that there isn't a good answer; it's simply a bad question. You can't directly do things to apply Christ's grace in your life. You apply the grace of Christ by understanding it and believing it. You can *know* and *believe* the grace of Christ, but you can't *do* the grace of Christ. However, understanding and believing in Christ's grace will change your behavior. When a person understands and believes in Christ's grace, he or she is filled with hope, peace, and joy and relies on the merits of Christ, not his or her own.

The key to changing how we act and live is to change how we think and what we believe. The key to changing our financial situation is to change the way we think and believe about finances. Often people try to correct behavior when behavior is not the real problem. In the word of Henry David Thoreau, "There are a thousand hacking at the branches of evil to one who is striking at the root."[24] Our behaviors stem from our beliefs and thoughts. Thus, if we want to make lasting changes and improvements in our lives, we need to change the way we think and believe. The root of our actions is how we think and believe. Aligning our beliefs with truth is necessary to living with integrity.

Actions

When one's beliefs create actions that align with truth, this person has integrity. When beliefs create actions that align with truth under extreme opposition, this person has great integrity. There are numerous accounts of people of faith who acted in accordance with their beliefs in truth even when faced with great opposition. The story of Shadrach,

No Integrity

When our actions do not align with truth, we have no integrity. Even when our actions align with our belief, if they do not also align with truth we still have no integrity. Also, there is no integrity when our beliefs align with truth but our actions do not.

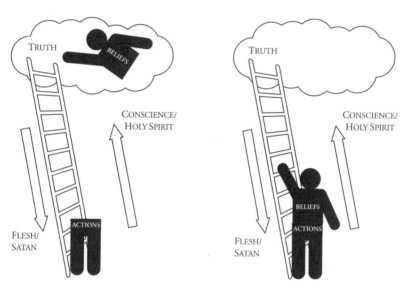

Integrity

The more our actions align with truth, the greater amount of integrity we possess.

Meshach, and Abednego recorded in the book of Daniel is one such example. A decree was sent to the people that all "nations, and languages . . . are to fall down and worship the golden image that King Nebuchadnezzar has set up. And whoever does not fall down and worship shall immediately be cast into a burning fiery furnace."[25] Most of the people adhered to the decree and worshipped the idol, but there where three men of integrity who refused. King Nebuchadnezzar had the three men brought to him and declared, "'If you do not worship, you shall immediately be cast into a burning fiery furnace . . . Shadrach, Meshach, and Abednego answered and said to the king, '. . . we will not serve your gods or worship the golden image that you have set up.'"[26]

A similar account is recorded when the prophet Daniel continued to pray to God daily, despite the new law to worship only King Darius. He refused to act contrary to what he believed to be true, even when threatened with being cast into the lion's den.[27]

Even though Job experienced all manner of suffering, affliction, and pain, he refused to compromise his faith and commitment to God. When tempted to curse God, Job said, "Until the day I die, I will refuse to do wrong"[28] " . . . I will not deny my integrity. I will maintain my righteousness and never let go of it; my conscience will not reproach me as long as I live."[29]

The book of Acts records the integrity of the apostles who were put into prison for preaching of Christ. "During the night an angel of the Lord opened the doors of the jail and brought them out. 'Go, stand in the temple courts,' he said, 'and tell the people the full message of this new life.' At daybreak they entered the temple courts, as they had been told, and began to teach the people."[30] The apostles were then brought to be questioned by the high priest who said, "We gave you strict orders not to teach in this name. Yet you have filled Jerusalem with your teaching . . . Peter and the other apostles replied: 'We must obey God rather than men!'"[31]

We should each strive to exemplify these examples of integrity. To achieve the highest level of integrity, truth must be more than something we know or do—it must be something we are. For example, consider the principle of service. You can't just know about service and believe it is a true principle. You must be a service-oriented person. It must be a part of you. Service must become more than an action you perform—it must be an attribute you possess. "To become divine is then the aim of life: [when truth] is no longer outside us, or even in us, but we are it, and it is we . . . the creature is one with its creator . . . It is what it ought to be; its education is finished, and its final happiness begins."[32]

Conscience/Holy Spirit vs. Flesh/Satan
"Conscience is a divine voice in the human soul." –Francis Bowen

Why is it that we believe in high and lofty principles yet do not live in accordance with them? Gandhi once said, "There are 999 who believe in honesty for every honest man." What makes integrity elusive to so many? What must we understand in order to live with integrity?

We need to realize that when we are faced with life's choices, we are influenced by two forces—our conscience and the Holy Spirit and our flesh and Satan. The key to developing integrity is to adhere to our conscience/Holy Spirit. Our conscience tells us what is right and wrong; what we should and should not do. As we adhere to the direction we receive from our conscience/Holy Spirit, we align our actions with truth. The ability to listen to and adhere to our conscience/Holy Spirit is a developed talent.

The flesh or our physical bodies do not seek to live in accordance with truths. Just as a smoke detector cannot detect carbon monoxide, the flesh cannot detect truth. The flesh only seeks pleasure and to avoid pain without distinguishing between right and wrong. If we follow the desire of the flesh, we will violate truth—for the desires of the flesh naturally serve Satan. To let our actions be directed by the flesh will be just as deadly to our spirits as using a smoke detector to protect against carbon monoxide. The apostle Paul taught, "But the natural man does not receive the things of the Spirit of God, for they are foolishness to him; nor can he know them, because they are spiritually discerned."[33]

The flesh will seek the way of the world and " . . . whoever wishes to be a friend of the world makes himself an enemy of God."[34]

Satan will try to lead us away from truth. "The Spirit clearly says that in later times some will abandon the faith and follow deceiving spirits and things taught by demons."[35] Satan will work to get us to ignore the promptings of our conscience/Holy Spirit. He will instead lead us to focus on the flesh's desire for pleasure or the desire to avoid pain. For example, imagine you make a mistake at work that costs the company thousands of dollars, which could never be traced to you, and then your boss asks you if you know anything about it. Your conscience tells you to tell the truth because it is the right thing to do. Your flesh tells you to lie to avoid the pain and punishment that may be associated with taking responsibility for the mistake.

Rationalization

"The voice of conscience is so delicate that it is easy to stifle it."
–Madame de Stael

The apostle Paul taught, "Some people have made a mess of their faith because they didn't listen to their consciences."[36] "When we hear the first whispering of conscience, we do one of two things—we either act in harmony with it, or we immediately begin to rationalize—tell ourselves 'rational lies'—as to why we should make some other choice. If we choose the first response, we feel peaceful. We create alignment with [truth]. We grow in our ability to recognize that inner voice and in our personal effectiveness. If we choose the second option, we feel disharmony and tension… The key to acting with integrity is to simply stop playing the game. Learn to listen—as well as to conscience, to our own response. The instant we feel ourselves saying, 'Yes, but' change it to, 'Yes, and.' No rationalizing. No justifying. Just do it. Look at every expression of conscience as an invitation to create greater alignment with the [truth]."[37]

When we receive a prompting from our conscience/Holy Spirit, Satan may try to use procrastination and indecision as tools to prevent us from acting with thoughts such as, "You can do that later" or "This is very important. You need more time to think about it before you act."

Satan will also use rational lies. For example, most people believe in the commandment, "Thou shalt not steal";[38] however, some rationalize stealing from creditors through bankruptcy saying, "Bankruptcy laws are good because they give a person, who is hopelessly burdened with debt, a fresh start by wiping out his or her debts," ignoring the words of the Bible, "The wicked borrows and does not pay back."[39]

Michael Tuohey received the prompting from the conscience/Holy Spirit that Atta and Omari were terrorists. Right away rational lies began, "They are just businessman" and "It is not politically correct to think an Arab is a terrorist." These rational lies prevented him from acting, causing him to have feelings of disharmony and tension. He described these feelings saying, "I don't know how to describe it . . . your stomach twists and turns. You get sick to your stomach."[40]

We all have been guilty at some time of not acting upon the prompting of the conscience/Holy Spirit. We must learn to hear and act upon these promptings without rationalization or delay. George Washington taught, "Labor to keep alive in your breast that little spark of celestial fire, called conscience." By listening and acting upon the prompting of the conscience/Holy Spirit, we build our lives upon the foundation of truth.

CONCLUSION

Often times we don't see or understand the full effects of following or not following the Spirit. However, we can be certain that failure to hear or failure to follow the Spirit when heard will be extremely damaging, while adhering to the Spirit will bring blessings. We all receive promptings from our conscience and direction from the Spirit. It is vital to our happiness and the happiness of others that we learn to hear and act on these promptings.

Following his experience on 9/11, Michael Tuohey was determined to follow the prompting of the Spirit no matter what, without question, and without rationalizing. He declared, "I will never ignore my instincts again." His experience clearly shows the effects of not following our conscience and the Holy Spirit. There is no reason great enough to justify not following the Spirit. May we each make a declaration similar to that of Michael Tuohey, "I will never ignore my conscience or the Holy Spirit again."

Truth 15

"The Godly Walk with Integrity."[41]

MYTH 16

IT'S NOT PERSONAL.
IT'S JUST BUSINESS.

In life, there seems to be two acceptable ethical standards. One applies to our personal life (religious ethics) and the other standard applies to sports or other competitive games (gaming ethics). Under religious ethics, "most of us would generally agree that it's wrong to deliberately mislead or deceive another person, or to steal. We also would agree that it's wrong to identify another person's weakness and then deliberately design a scheme to take advantage of that weakness for personal gain. . . In competitive games, the rules or ethics, are different than in personal life. . . In gaming ethics, deliberately misleading and deceiving others is not only allowed but is an essential skill for winning."[1] For example, a basketball player seeks to mislead and deceive his opponent with head fakes, screens, and misdirection plays. Also, "to take advantage of another's weakness is not only allowed but is expected of good players. If, in a competitive game of tennis, you discover your opponent has a weak backhand, it is ethical to drill the ball to that backhand as much as possible. . . In baseball, stealing bases is a good strategy for base runners; in football and basketball, stealing the ball is one of the objects of defense."[2]

Many believe that business is a game about profits with personal gain acting as the score. Many also believe that it is just as ethical to deceive another for personal gain while playing poker as it is to not keep one's word in a business transaction if it leads to personal advantage or gain. Much of the lack of integrity in business stems from the application of competitive gaming ethics to business situations. In business, you commonly hear the phrase "It's not personal. It's just business." This phrase of rationalization often signifies that they have applied gaming ethics to business to justify what they have done.

Competitive gaming ethics should not be applied to business. In fact, it should never leave the court, field, or playing table. The Lord did not create 10 commandments for personal life and a separate 10 commandments for business life. The Lord did not say, "Deception is ok if it helps make sales" or "It is ok to steal as long as the market is such that you can." The Lord has said, "Thou shalt not bear false witness"[3] and "Thou shalt not steal."[4] Followers of Christ will treat family, neighbors, employees, and business relations with religious ethics, caring for everyone as brothers and sisters.

Two Choices of Business Ethics

In the world of business, many view business as a game and leave their religious ethics at home. Business often relies on what is termed "industry standards," which has taken precedence over religious ethics regarding business decision making. Many very powerful and brilliant business owners, CEOs, and presidents have given in to applying "competitive gaming ethics," feeling they did not have a choice.

The truth is there is a choice. You can achieve financial success in business by applying competitive gaming ethics, but by so doing you will most likely violate the laws of God. Money acquired this way is never worth its cost. The Savior taught, "It is worth nothing for them to have the whole world if they lose their souls."[5] The other option: you can achieve financial abundance by applying religious ethics to business. The following looks at this dichotomy.

1. Industry Standard vs. The Lord's Standard

In one of my previous companies, the parent company began making decisions violating religious ethics. The excuse the executives often gave in the board meetings was it was "industry standard." Basically, they were saying, "We exploit employees, we manipulate our accounting and tax returns, we use some deceptive marketing strategies because other companies in the industry also do." I expressed my concerns and did my best to correct the wrongs. When it became clear they would not change their new business practices and continued to request that

Competitive Gaming Ethics	Religious Ethics
1. Industry Standard	1. The Lord's Standard
2. Deception	2. Honesty
3. Profit First	3. Integrity First
4. Is It Legal?	4. Is It Right?
5. Shrewd	5. Fair
6. Win	6. Serve
7. Stealing Is OK	7. Stealing Is Wrong
8. Circumstances Change	8. My Word Is My Bond
9. Loyal to Man	9. Loyal to God

I make similar changes, I left the company. Financially, leaving cost me millions of dollars, but I was not willing to violate the principles of Christ. Our standard should not be what others are doing but what God would have us do.

The argument that "everyone is doing it" has not and never will make it right. The CEO of AT&T Broadband issued a letter to explain why they sold and profited from the sale of pornography. The letter explains that "competitive pressures with companies like General Motors, which owned rival service DirectTV, was keeping AT&T in the business."[6] Basically, he was saying, "We sell pornography because DirectTV does."

"In Arthur Miller's play, 'All My Sons,' a son sees his father cheating in the business world. When confronted, his dad responds, 'Son everybody does it. You have to cheat to be successful.' The son replies, 'I know Dad, but I thought you were better than everyone else.'"[7]

While fudging the numbers, using deceptive tactics, profiting from immoral products, and exploiting employees may be the industry standard, there is a minority who have chosen to rise above the industry standard and adhere to religious and moral principles in their business affairs. Our challenge is to join this minority. The business world is full of deceit and immorality, but it will only get worse unless each of us becomes an example in our work of integrity and living the Lord's standard. "All noble attainments are as difficult as they are rare."[8] Give heed to the words of the apostle Paul who taught, "Continue to have faith and do what you know is right."[9]

2. Deception vs. Honesty

"The LORD detests lying lips, but he delights in men who are truthful."
—Proverbs 12:22, New International Version

In the past several years, we have seen the devastating effects of dishonest business leaders at Enron, WorldCom, Xerox, Qwest, Tyco, ImClone, Anderson, and others. Through competitive gaming ethics, they fraudulently gained short-term profits but in the end lost everything, with many going to prison. "If you plot and connive to deceive men, you may fool them for a while, and profit thereby, but you will without fail be visited by divine punishment. To be utterly honest may have the appearance of inflexibility and self-righteousness, but in the end, such a person will receive the blessings."[10] Honesty is key to long-term success. David Green, founder of the billion-dollar Hobby Lobby stores, wrote, "It's all part of our corporate commitment to follow biblical principles in everything we do. Some businesspeople think that's a noble claim but that it ties one hand behind your back. I disagree. Nothing taught in the Bible is harmful to business. Doing things God's way pays dividends—maybe not immediately, but in the long run."[11]

Jay Van Andel and Rich DeVos, founders of Amway, ran their company according to biblical principles. Jay Van Andel wrote in his biography, "Rich and I sought to run our . . . organization according to biblical principles of integrity, faithfulness, and truthfulness. . . Knowing that we were dependent upon God for the ability to do what was right, we bathed our activities in private prayer. All of our corporate meetings were opened with prayer. . . A business without integrity will be penalized in the marketplace. If a business's products don't meet the claims of its advertisers, or if product quality is inconsistent, the business will lose customers to its competitors. Skilled employees, frustrated with internal policies, depart for other jobs. On the other hand, a firm known for its integrity will be rewarded by increased demand for its products and greater customer and employee loyalty."[12] "Part of the genius of an open free market system is that integrity pays… In the end, customers, employees, and shareholders gravitate toward companies with stable leadership—those that are credible and have integrity."[13]

3. Profit First vs. Integrity First

Donald Trump is an advocate and example of running a business with competitive gaming ethics. He wrote, "Business is about making money. It's about the bottom line. The sooner you realize that, the sooner you'll make it to the top in the business world. I'm often surprised by people who think business is something else. They come in with lofty ideas and philanthropic purposes that have absolutely no place in a business meeting. It's a waste of everyone's time."[14] With this view, business would be outside the realm of morality. Business would be only about making profit and would not be directed or founded on any moral standard.

Donald Trump's beliefs about money and business have led him to pursue the immoral but profitable businesses of pornography and casinos. Companies such as Trump International, Hilton, Marriott, Comcast, and Time Warner are making millions selling pornography. A lobbyist who represents 900 companies in the porn business said, "Corporations are in business to make money. This is an extremely large business, and there's great opportunity for profits in it."[15] Donald Trump can teach you how to make money but so can a prostitute or a drug dealer. Business decisions should be based on morals and not solely driven by demand and profits.

The Omni hotels will not sell pornography despite the potential for substantial profit. "The pay-per-view pornography business has been a lucrative one for hotels. In 1996, hotel guests spent over $175 million to watch 'adult' movies in their rooms. Omni's decision will cost the chain $4 million a year. That's not the point, according to Omni's vice president of marketing, Peter Strebel. 'Money is not the issue in this matter,' he said. 'Not all business decisions should be fiscally driven. We believe that this is the right thing to do.'"[16]

I personally will not own the stock of a hotel or any company that sells pornography because I believe it violates God's laws, and I will not participate in any way with such a business. In the words of Henry Ford, "A business that makes nothing but money is a poor kind of business."[17]

4. Is It Legal? vs. Is It Right?

Kenneth Lay, former CEO of Enron, said of their unethical accounting practices, "We don't break the law."[18] Many companies use the shield of "It is legal" to justify their immoral practices. It is legal in some places to hire a prostitute, but that doesn't make it right.

I ended relations with a business because they failed to pay as agreed. I received a call from the law firm who represented the company and was told, "I have reviewed the information and legally we do not have to pay you." I responded, "There is sometimes a big difference between what is legal and what is right."

5. Shrewd vs. Fair

According to competitive gaming ethics, it's ok to take whatever you can get. When applied to business, this can mean that the more you can squeeze out of employees and customers the better—this is not only ethical but is shrewd and good business. Many practices that businesspeople call shrewd are unethical and dishonest. "Those who unjustly profit at the expense of others may gain a fortune, but they forfeit something more important, which is their own integrity. Taking advantage of others is a counterfeit form of true success and honor."[19]

No company should take unfair advantage or undercompensate their employees because they are in a position of power to do so or the market is such that they can. Those who use the free enterprise system to mistreat or take advantage of employees are classified by the Lord in the same category as adulterers and liars. As the Lord declared, "I will come near you for judgment; I will be a swift witness against sorcerers, against adulterers, against perjurers, [and] against those who exploit wage earners . . ."[20]

6. Win vs. Serve

Under competitive gaming ethics, the only goal is to win. A former general manager of an NBA franchise summed up this attitude saying, "All we reward is winning. We don't reward people who have high values, integrity, or character."[21]

Those who follow religious ethics "realize that self-respect is more important than winning, and that being a leader means putting the needs of others ahead of your own."[22] Chairman of the board of R.C. Willey Home Furnishings teaches, "Money should not be your driving force. . . The profit comes as a by-product of better serving our customers."[23]

7. Stealing Is Ok vs. Stealing Is Wrong

In many competitive sports, stealing is a part of the game. In baseball, it is a good strategy to steal bases, and in football and basketball the defense tries to steal the ball from the offense. Some who use competitive game ethics in business, view stealing as a part of the game of business. They view stealing not only as an acceptable strategy but as a skill needed to succeed.

This command "Thou shalt not steal"[24] applies to all aspects of life and is wrong regardless of the situation. The apostle Paul, speaking to the Ephesians, counsels, "He who has been stealing must no longer, but must work, doing something useful with his own hands . . ."[25]

8. Circumstances Change vs. My Word Is My Bond
"Let your 'yes' be 'yes' and your 'no' be 'no.'"
—James 5:12, English Standard Version

"A good measure of the value of a person's word is how much he or she is willing to give up to keep a promise or commitment."[26] A long time business partner and I had a successful and profitable relationship though years of mutual loyalty and trust. During this time, I worked for years to create a relationship with a large company and eventually secured a working partnership. A year into this partnership, the revenue and profits dramatically increased. Our dreams and hard work paid off when one transaction generated more than $2 million in revenue. Systems were in place for such transactions to occur on a regular basis and for business to continue to grow. Before and after this successful transaction, my partner and I talked about the exciting success and future potential. Just before I was to receive my share of the profits from this successful transaction, I received a report from accounting on the amount I was to be paid. I called accounting and questioned the amount. I was told that my partner requested that I not be paid on this transaction. I met with my partner, and he said, "I have always taken the high road (kept promises/commitments), but this time I can't." He cut me out of the relationship. I learned that his word or commitment was only good up to a certain dollar amount. Having worked with him for some time, I knew he wasn't willing to sell his integrity for smaller amounts, but he was for the now large amount. It wasn't until keeping his word would have cost him hundreds of thousands of dollars that money took priority over his honor and integrity.

Keeping commitments is vital to having a successful relationship. There is nothing more damaging to a relationship than making a promise that is important to someone and not keeping it. Breaking commitments destroys trust and reliability. To be successful with people, you must adopt a philosophy of never making a promise you cannot or will not keep.

Occasionally, despite all our best efforts, the unexpected and uncontrollable comes up, creating a situation where it would be unwise or impossible to keep a promise. In this case, you should either keep the promise anyway, or explain the situation to the person you committed to and ask to be released from the promise. You should never tell the person you can't keep the promise. You should ask to be released from your commitment. If they will not release you from your commitment, then you should follow through. A commitment is binding until it is fulfilled or until one is released from it.

Those who have genuine integrity do not just keep their word when it is to their advantage or when it is easy. For those with genuine integrity, their word is their bond. They keep their word even in the face of great challenges, opposition, and even when it is not to their advantage. "People who have genuine integrity . . . consider their word a sacred treasure."[27]

9. Loyal to Man vs. Loyal to God

Does your loyalty lie with God or with man? When faced with decisions that involve social pressure, we need to decide if we are going to follow the commands of the Lord or the counsel of men.

Often we seek to please those around us or participate in actions we know to be wrong because we don't want to offend or displease those around us. Are we like the accountant who, when asked by a CEO, "Tell me, what is two plus two?" replies, "What do you want it to be?" Or are we like the apostle Peter when he stood with boldness and strength before magistrates and rulers who could imprison him, flog him, and even take his life. On one occasion when brought before the high priest to be questioned why he had violated their command not to preach, "Peter and the other apostles answered and said, We ought to obey God rather than men."[28]

WHEN IS SUCCESS A FAILURE?

When competitive gaming ethics are used to succeed at business, success is a failure. One of Gandhi's seven sins that destroy society is "commerce without morality." It represents a moral end (commerce) achieved by an immoral means (without morality). Immoral means corrupt—a worthy end into a dishonorable achievement. You cannot achieve a moral end by immoral means. "Financial ends never justify unethical means."[29]

The son of a business executive shared this story: "I grew up in a brutal business environment. My father worked as the chief executive for one of the richest men in the world, Howard Hughes, and that world turned many lives upside down. I witnessed firsthand greed, deception, power struggles, and destruction of souls all for the sake of money. But perhaps what influenced me most is what I had seen in Mr. Hughes himself. For many years on Christmas Eve or Easter Sunday, this annual ritual was not what it appeared to be; Mr. Hughes invited my father to his home. When my father arrived, Mr. Hughes would simply say, 'Bill, I just wanted to talk.' Then after a couple of hours of friendly conversation he would say, 'It's Christmas. You better get back to your family.' And I remember thinking to myself: 'With all the money, with all the power, all the accomplishments, and even all the good he has done, he is both lonely and alone.'"[30]

DEFINING OUR VALUES

Establishing and committing to a set of values or principles is key to living with integrity. Making the decision before the situation arises helps us make the correct choices when the pressures of the moment arise. The following four steps may be helpful as you define your own values. First, write down the 5 people you most admire and respect. Second, next to each name write 4 to 5 attributes you most admire about each person. The attributes in your list that appear the most are your core values. Third, identify 5 people you don't admire and write down next to their names the attributes that come to mind to describe them. These are attributes you will want to avoid. Once you have written down your core values and the values to avoid, the fourth step is to review them daily. This will help to keep you focused on living and achieving your values and will guard against them being pushed aside in daily pursuits.

A dear friend and business associate of mine, G. Kent Mangelson, shared will me the following: "After nearly thirty years in the financial business and having associated with thousands of wealthy individuals, I have developed a firm philosophy about people and money. If an individual does not clearly establish personal values and goals before making financial goals, then wealth and the accumulation thereof will begin to take on a life of its own. Without clearly established values to keep the individual's direction in focus, money tends to distract the person, gradually moving him or her away from everything in life that means the most. Sadly, and all too often, when it is too late to repair the damage, the person discovers that he or she has lost those things that meant the most and that all the money in the world cannot buy nor replace that which is gone."

JON M. HUNTSMAN—A BILLIONAIRE THE RIGHT WAY

Jon M. Huntsman was born in 1937 in the small town of Blackfoot, Idaho, to a music teacher and a homemaker. Following high school, Huntsman enrolled at the Wharton School of Finance at the University of Pennsylvania. In 1961, Huntsman, age 24, graduated and went to work as a salesman for an egg-producing company and was later assigned to a team to develop a plastic egg carton. By 1967, Jon Huntsman, now age 30, was the president of Dolco Packing, a joint venture between the egg business and Dow Chemical. In 1970, Huntsman left Dolco Packing to start his own business, Huntsman Container, with his brother Blaine in Fullerton, California.

In 1971 and 1972, Huntsman worked as a special assistant to President Richard Nixon. Huntsman described an atmosphere that demanded blind loyalty to Nixon. Huntsman related the following experience, "I was asked by [H.R.] Haldeman [White House chief of staff] on one occasion to do something 'to help' the president. We were there to serve the president, after all. It seems a certain self-righteous congressman was questioning one of Nixon's nominations for agency head. There was some evidence the nominee had employed undocumented workers in her California business. Haldeman asked me to check out a factory previously owned by this congressman to see whether the report was true. The facility happened to be located close to my own manufacturing plant in Fullerton, California… The information would be used, of course, to embarrass the political adversary…There are times when we react too quickly to catch the rightness and wrongness of something immediately. We don't think it through. This was one of those times. It took about 15 minutes for my inner moral compass to … bring me to the point that I recognized this wasn't the right thing to do … Halfway through my conversation, I paused. 'Wait a minute, Jim,' I said deliberately to the general manager of Huntsman Container, 'Let's not do this. I don't want to play this game. Forget I called' … I informed Haldeman that I would not have my employees spy or do anything like it. To the second most powerful man in America, I was saying no. He didn't appreciate responses like that. He viewed them as a sign of disloyalty. I might as well have been saying farewell. So be it, and I did leave within six months of that incident … I was about the only West Wing staff member not eventually hauled before the congressional Watergate committee or grand jury."[31]

In 1974, Huntsman Container created the clamshell container for McDonald's Big Mac. Huntsman Container pioneered more than 80 innovative plastic packaging products. In 1976, Huntsman sold Huntsman container for $8 million ($28 million in 2006 dollars). As a part of the deal, Huntsman agreed to serve as CEO for four more years.

In 1982, Huntsman formed the Huntsman Chemical Corporation. Huntsman shared this story from the early years: "As our company was going through the embryonic startup years, it was necessary … to sell a portion of our company. I found an appropriate buyer and negotiated a price to sell… I agreed to sell him a 40 percent interest in our business at a fixed price. Over the next several months much delay occurred. During the process … our business activity quadrupled and our profits went up five-fold to the point that when it came time to sign the document, the value, instead of being $53 million was $250 million. The chairman of the company said, 'Jon, you have an important decision to make. You can either make a great deal of money from me since we have not signed anything, or you can go back to your original handshake'… without hesitation I was proud and honored to step up and say, 'Mr. Campan, I shook your hand. I made an agreement. The price will be $53 million. That's what we agreed to six months ago.' I must tell you that throughout the last twelve to fifteen years there have been many times I have wondered, 'What about that $200 million?' That's a fortune, a mammoth fortune. I let it slip away. And on the other hand I say, 'My children are all in the business. They know their father; they understand an agreement. If it was for $53 million or just $53, the principle is still the same. A deal is a deal. A handshake is a handshake. Integrity is integrity.'"[32]

Huntsman is an epic deal maker and powerful negotiator, but he never takes advantage of others and ensures a deal is mutually beneficial with both parties achieving their objectives. Huntsman realized that negotiating and creating deals in this manner was the right thing to do and resulted in second and third deals. Huntsman shared this example: "In 1999, I was in fierce negotiations with Charles Miller Smith, then president and CEO of Imperial Chemical Industries of Great Britain, one of that nation's largest companies. We wanted to acquire some of ICI's chemical divisions. It would be the largest deal of my life, a merger that would double the size of Huntsman Corp ... During the extended negotiations, Charles' wife was suffering from terminal cancer... When his wife passed away, he was distraught, as one can imagine. We still had not completed our negotiations. I decided the fine points of the last 20 percent of the deal would stand as they were proposed. I probably could have clawed another $200 million out of the deal, but it would have come at the expense of Charles' emotional state. The agreement as it stood was good enough. Each side came out a winner, and I made a lifelong friend."[33]

Huntsman was the first American to own controlling interest in a business in the former Soviet Union. He founded a box company to help this emerging economy. "Initially the company was told it would have to pay a certain tax rate on boxes sold to Russian customers and a much lower rate on boxes shipped for resale to other former republics. After the company started producing boxes, a tax administrator came and informed the company that the rates were being increased on the exported boxes—to a point that made the company completely unprofitable. However, the official said, if certain amounts could be paid under the table directly to the tax official, he could 'take care of them.' It is Jon Huntsman's policy never to pay a bribe. He never has; he never will. The official was insistent. Jon Huntsman decided to sell the factory to local management for $1 rather than pay a bribe. He lost his investment of millions of dollars, but he would not compromise his integrity for money."[34]

The first value of the Huntsman Corporation is: "We believe that ethical and moral standards are the foundation of good business policies, and we'll operate with integrity."[35] In 2005, Huntsman Corporation had 78 operations in 24 countries with 15,000 employees and company revenues of $13 billion. Huntsman is a living example that "nice guys really can and do finish first in life."[36]

CONCLUSION

The Lord appeared to Solomon in a dream and said, "Solomon, ask for anything you want, and I will give it to you."[37] Solomon replied, "Give your servant a discerning heart . . . to distinguish between right and wrong."[38] To live with integrity, we each must ask the Lord for wisdom to make right decisions in our professional and personal lives. As we ask the Lord for this, He will answer our request with wisdom and the reply, "I'm pleased that you asked for this."[39]

May we each declare the words of George Washington: "I hope that I shall always possess firmness and virtue enough to maintain what I consider the most enviable of all titles; the character of an honest man."[40]

TRUTH 16

Religious Ethics Are the Foundation for Lasting and Meaningful Business Success.

CHOICE 4:
IDLENESS OR INDUSTRY

"Satan selects his disciples when they are idle; Jesus selected his when they were busy at their work either mending their nets or casting them into the sea." —Farrenden

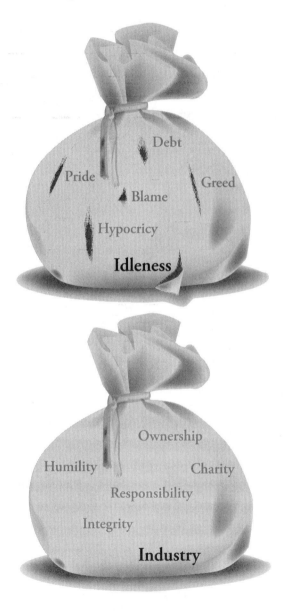

Debt

Pride

Greed

Blame

Hypocricy

Idleness

Ownership

Humility

Charity

Responsibility

Integrity

Industry

WHATEVER THE MIND OF MAN
CAN CONCEIVE AND BELIEVE, IT CAN ACHIEVE

A powerful real-life illustration of the long-term effects of various approaches to life can be found in the study of prison camps "… where everyday human nature, stripped bare, can be studied under a magnifying glass of accelerated time. Lessons spotlighted and absorbed in that laboratory sharpen one's eye for their abstruse but highly relevant applications in the 'real time' world of now."[1] After studying several prison camp experiences, I have categorized prisoners' approaches to life into three groups: vain optimists, pessimists, and true optimists. The majority of the vain optimists and pessimists died in the camps, but the true optimists survived. This discovery led me to search for a reason why this occurred.

THREE APPROACHES TO LIFE™
1. Vain Optimism
2. Pessimism
3. True Optimism

VAIN OPTIMISM

Admiral Stockdale was the highest ranking naval officer held as a prisoner of war in Vietnam. He was tortured more than 20 times during his 7 ½ years in the Hoa Lo prison ("Hoa Lo" means "fiery furnace" in Vietnamese). Stockdale is one of the most highly decorated officers in the history of the Navy, having received 26 combat decorations, including the Medal of Honor, the nation's highest medal for valor.

In his book *Good to Great*, Jim Collins shares a discussion he had with Admiral Stockdale on the campus of Stanford University. While they were walking to the faculty club, Jim Collins asked Admiral Stockdale, "Who didn't make it out?" "Oh that's easy," replied Admiral Stockdale. "The optimists." Jim replied, "The optimists? I don't understand." Admiral Stockdale answered, "The optimists. Oh, they were the ones who said, 'We're going to be out by Christmas.' And Christmas would come and Christmas would go. Then they'd say, 'We're going to be out by Easter.' And Easter would come, and Easter would go. And then Thanksgiving, and then it would be Christmas again. And they died of a broken heart."[2]

In February 1945, a prisoner in a Nazi prison camp and composer, fairly well-known throughout the camp, believed that on March 30th he would be liberated and his sufferings ended. He was "full of hope and convinced his dream would be right. But as the day drew nearer, the war news which reached our camp made it appear very unlikely that we would be free on the promised date. On March 29th, [the composer] became ill and ran a high temperature. On March 30th… he became delirious and lost consciousness. On March 31st, he was dead."[3]

The vain optimist ignores the facts and places hopes and expectations on things that are false. They create a world of fantasy and pretend bad things do not happen, or they dissociate from bad so they don't have to deal with it. The end result in the prison camp was repeated disappointment and eventual death. The result of vain optimism in everyday life situations is much the same, repeated disappointed and eventual death of our ambition.

In Myth 1, you read the story of the trader who went to an Indian tribe to sell them gunpowder. During his visit, the trader was able to convince the Indians that if they planted the gunpowder it would grow and produce more gunpowder. The Indians purchased the gunpowder, planted it, and tended the fields in anticipation of the gunpowder harvest. According to the myth, "Whatever the mind of man can conceive and believe, it can achieve," the Indians should have had a great gunpowder harvest. Their minds conceived the idea, and they believed the idea, but no gunpowder grew. Why not? Because thir beliefs were not based on truth. The story of the gunpowder trader and Indians continues that a couple years later a fellow Frenchman returned to the Indians and again tried to convince the Indians to plant gunpowder, telling them that gunpowder does grow in the soil of France.[4] Likewise, vain optimists continually preach that a positive mental attitude can achieve anything with no regard for truth.

To vain optimists, the truth is whatever you think it is. Their motto is, "I can do anything I want to do." Were the teachers of vain optimism to approach the Indians about growing gunpowder, they would hold a seminar and tell them to think more positively. They would teach the Indian that if they have more belief and hope, surely the plants will grow gunpowder. They would try to convince the Indians to try again—telling them that if they don't succeed at growing gunpowder, it is their fault for not having enough belief and hope or for not working hard enough.

The doctrine of vain optimism is dangerous because it will eventually break people. Vain optimism promotes the doing of things that are not based on truth, such as planting gunpowder, and then blames the person instead of the false teaching for the lack of success. Just as a false belief in the prison camps of a rescue by Christmas or Easter will eventually break and kill the prisoner when it doesn't come to pass, so also will the setting of goals and positive thinking not based on truth eventually break the goal setter when goals are not achieved.

Satan's Success Literature

Contained within some of the self-help and success literature are the teachings of vain optimism. These books falsely teach that success is solely a result of a person's thoughts with a disregard to truth. They use such phrases as, "Whatever the mind of man can conceive and believe, it can achieve," and "With a positive mental attitude, you can do anything." In addition, much of the new age literature is secular rather than religious. This literature teaches that Jesus was not God, that man is God, and that you can create your own destiny through the power of your own mind, with such comments as "Your mind is the Creator, " and "Every man prospers according to his genius."

We must be careful to avoid the allure of these false doctrines and anti-God teachings. These teachings of so-called success and new age literature are false, and the author is the devil. These teachings promote a vain optimistic approach to life and the result is not success, but misery. Vain optimism may provide temporary false hope and the illusion of happiness, but the end result is disappointment and despair. Vain optimism is a dangerous doctrine. It is Satan's counterfeit of true optimism. We must be careful to avoid the allure of vain optimism and its vicious cycle of false hope and the eventual breaking of body and spirit.

PESSIMISM

Pessimists had a very short life expectancy in the prison camps. The pessimists died because they saw a challenge or situation and concluded, "It can't be done, so why try?" Examples of this can be found in the book, *Man's Search for Meaning*, by Viktor E. Frankl. In his book, he describes his experiences and his observations as a psychiatrist in the concentration camps of Nazi Germany during World War II. He describes sad accounts of individuals who lost hope, viewed the tasks before them as impossible, and gave up. Once this occurred it was only a matter of hours or days until they were dead.

Overcoming Pessimism

Many people have been conditioned with thoughts of inadequacy. Studies have shown that within the first eighteen years of our lives, the average person is told "no" more than 148,000 times.[5] We are constantly being told by parents, friends, teachers, television, and co-workers what we cannot do. This conditioning causes many of us to achieve a small fraction of our potential. Having been conditioned this way, we often believe we can't achieve greatness, so we don't try. If we do try, we expect to fail. This result is a pessimistic approach to life. A pessimist approaches life with a statement of what can't be done instead of asking how it can be done.

To dispel the pessimist in each of us, we must transform our approach to life by finding solutions instead of excuses. I often hear people give the excuse, "I can't do it." Instead of giving an excuse, they should find a solution which begins by asking the question, "How can I do it?" Instead of saying "I can't afford it," or "It's impossible," begin asking the questions, "How can I afford it?" and "How is it possible?" This small change in our approach to life will produce great outcomes.

The Massage Chair

I was meeting with one of my business partners and financial mentors. At the time of this meeting, we were both founders and CEOs of multimillion dollar companies. During our meeting, two deliverymen came with a massage chair for my mentor's top floor office. The only access to the office was a narrow stairway that switched back and forth up to the office door. After a few minutes, the two deliverymen returned to let my mentor know that that the chair would not fit in the office. My mentor gave a quick reply of, "Find a way to get the chair in the office." The deliveryman responded that they had done measurements and the chair would not fit. My mentor again said, "Find a way to get the chair in the office," and we continued with our meeting. The deliverymen left to make another attempt. Another few minutes went by and the deliverymen again returned saying, "There is no way for the chair to fit into your office. It is impossible."

My mentor looked at me and asked, "Will you please get the massage chair into my office?" I replied, "Absolutely," and went to work. The deliverymen were not much help. As I began to consider options to get the chair up the stairs and through the door, they said to me, "The chair will not fit, we have already tried twice." I then did measurements, to which the deliverymen said, "We already measured. It is impossible."

I calculated that if we took off the door as well as the inside molding of the doorway and went in at the right angle that it would just barely fit through the door. The deliverymen commented that it would not fit because it was impossible to get it around the switchback corner in the stairs and to hold it at the angle required to enter the door. I told them that it was possible, but it would require 4 people. I asked if they would help. They declined saying, "It will not fit, and what you are going to attempt will damage the chair. If you want to try it, you are on your own." My business office was close to my mentor's office, so I called over to my company and asked 3 of the employees to come over and help me move the chair. Once they arrived, we lifted the chair and began to maneuver it up the stairs. As we were working, the deliverymen were looking on and telling each other that we would never get the chair into the office. In a couple minutes, we had the chair up the stairs, around the corner, through the door and into the office. We had done the impossible, and had done it without damaging the chair or walls.

I thanked the 3 employees from my office and returned to my meeting. I entered my mentor's office and told him, "The massage chair is in your office." He replied, "We can learn a valuable lesson from what has just happened. The deliverymen came up with excuses, you came up with solutions. They said it was impossible. You said, 'How do we do the impossible?'" Then my mentor looked me in the eyes and said, "That is why they make $8 an hour and you will be a millionaire."

TRUE OPTIMISM

Why did Admiral Stockdale survive the prison camp when the vain optimists did not? It was because he approached things differently. While the vain optimist put his faith and hope in the false idea of a rescue by Christmas, Admiral Stockdale saw the brutal facts of the situation and accepted that it could be years until his release. He then put his faith and hopes in the idea that he could deal with the pain and awful situation until it was over.

The true optimists base their hope on truth and the source of truth, which is God. To a true optimist, truth is to be found within God's law, not within one's mind. Instead of the vain optimist's thought of, "I can do anything I want to do," the true optimist's motto is, "I can do anything God wants me to do."

Finding Your God-Given Mission

Aligning with God is the start of the process to make sure your goals and attitudes are based on truth. This is how you can exhibit true optimism instead of vain optimism. We've all heard the familiar saying, "A journey of a thousand miles begins with but a single step," but a journey of a thousand miles is pointless unless we know where we are going and why we want to get there. We define where our journey is to take us and why we want to get there by setting goals and discovering our God-given missions.

Inspired Goal Setting

When setting goals, it is important that they be inspired. We begin the inspired goal setting process by asking the question, "What would God have me do?" Once we have our inspired goals and mission, we will be filled with energy and enthusiasm to work and accomplish the goals. We will wake up each day excited to go to work because we are filled will a sense of inspired vision and purpose.

One of the wealthiest men in the world was asked in an interview what drives him to continue to create and achieve when he has already achieved so much. He responded by saying, "I am not driven. I am drawn. Men are driven by the negative. I am drawn to a dream. I am drawn to the idea of how many lives I can improve and touch for good. When is a man so rich that he has to quit what he loves to do? When is a man so rich he has to stop helping people?"

Yale Study of Graduating Seniors

There is great power in having goals and dreams. "A study was done on Yale University's graduating class. It asked seniors a long list of questions about themselves, and three questions had to do with goals.

They were, 'Do you set goals?' 'Do you write them down?' and 'Do you have an action plan to accomplish them?' Only three percent of the class answered yes to those questions. Twenty years later, a follow-up study was done. It turned out that the three percent who had said yes to goals reported that they were more happily married, were more successful in the careers they had chosen, had a more satisfactory family life, and had better health. And listen to this: Ninety-seven percent of the net worth of that graduating class was in the hands of that three percent!"[6]

Three Steps to Goal Achievement

Numerous studies have been done in addition to the Yale study to find that 97 percent of people do not have written goals. 97 percent achieve little because they have never decided to achieve something. Make today the day you become one of the 3 percent with written goals, which is the first of three steps to goal achievement.

THREE STEPS TO GOAL ACHIEVEMENT	
Step 1	Write Down Your Inspired Goals
Step 2	Review and Visualize Your Inspired Goals Daily
Step 3	Create Inspired Action Plans to Achieve Your Inspired Goals

Step 1: Write Down Your Inspired Goals

All of us have goals, yet few of us have written goals. An unwritten goal is merely a wish. Many people achieve little in life simply because they never decided to achieve something. "It grieves me to watch individuals squander their lives because they have neglected the process of writing down their personal goals."[7] Studies show that when we write down our goals, we are significantly more likely to obtain them. Writing down our goals helps us clearly define what we want to accomplish.

Step 2: Review and Visualize Your Inspired Goals Daily

Review your written goals daily. To help you do this, place your goals in prominent places such as your bathroom mirror, the refrigerator, the headboard of your bed, and the dashboard of your car. Keeping your goals at the forefront of your thoughts will greatly enhance the likelihood of their achievement.

Visualization can also be used to help achieve goals. For example, let's say your goal is to get an "A" on an exam. What you visualize in relation to this goal can affect your performance. Many of us visualize the negative, so as we study, we think things such as, "I am going to forget this information" or "I am going to do poorly on the exam." Instead, visualize the positive, saying and visualizing such things as, "I will remember this information," and "I am going to do excellent on the exam." Visualization can greatly affect performance either positively or negatively. For example, "In the early 1950s, a study was done on the effectiveness of visualization. Researchers took 90 college students with no prior basketball experience and divided those students into three groups of 30 students. Then each group was told to shoot free throws and the results were recorded. For the next month, those in the first group went out and practiced shooting free throws every day. The second group was instructed to visualize shooting free throws every day, but to actually have nothing to do with a basketball. The third group was the control group and was directed to do nothing. After a month, they were again tested. The first group, as expected, had improved; they averaged a 20 percent increase in shooting accuracy. The third group, also as expected, displayed little or no improvement, shooting 1 percent better. The big surprise was the second group; those who had practiced only in their mind improved . . . their shooting accuracy by 19 percent."[8]

Step 3: Create Inspired Action Plans to Achieve Your Inspired Goals

During one of my presentations, I hold a $20 bill in the air and ask the audience, "Who wants this $20 bill?" Of course, all the hands in the room go up. I again ask, "Who wants this $20 bill?" The hands stretch a little higher and some will stand up. I continue to ask the question until someone comes up and takes the $20 from my hand. I then ask the question, "Everyone wanted the $20 bill, but who got it?" To which they reply, "The one who took action." It is the same with goals. You can write and visualize goals all you want, but if you do not take action, your goals will never become a reality. To obtain a goal you have never before achieved, will require tasks you have never before done.

Implementation

The Does Your Bag Have Holes? Foundation has developed a *Statement of Excellence Workbook* to help you discover, write down, and achieve your inspired goals and mission. This mind-enlarging, life-improving, and entertaining workbook takes you step-by-step through this process. Completing and implementing the exercises in the *Statement of Excellence Workbook*, will put you in the top 3 percent of achievers in the world. You can obtain a copy of the *Statement of Excellence Workbook* on our web site at www.DoesYourBagHaveHoles.org

CONCLUSION

Understanding that vain optimists need help being grounded to facts and that pessimists need to change negative thoughts to positive thoughts will aid in motivating ourselves and those we work with to succeed. The goal is to help everyone search for facts, and then set inspired, optimistic goals based on truth. Setting and acting upon inspired goals will lead to success in the work place and in life.

TRUTH 17

"I Can Do All Things Through Christ Who Strengthens Me."[9]

MYTH 18

EVERYTHING IS A RESULT OF LUCK

Many have the notion that those who are successful are blessed with luck and that the wealthy have achieved their wealth through the luck of inheritance or winning the lottery. When you study the wealthy, you will find that most did not achieve wealth by luck or by accident. One of my business partners who makes more than $1 million a year was approached by someone who said, "You are so lucky!" My partner smiled and replied, "I know, and the harder I work, the luckier I get." Thomas Edison stated, "I never did anything worth doing by accident, nor did any of my inventions come by accident; they came by work." "No one achieves anything without paying a price of hard work, integrity, emotion, and years of effort and sacrifice. It doesn't fall in your lap by luck."[1]

SUCCESS IS A PROCESS

If you want to make more money, it starts with your becoming more. Success is not a process that occurs overnight. Children follow the process of learning to crawl before they walk and learning to walk before they run. Great achievers are not simply born, they are developed. A concert pianist starts out learning to play "Chopssticks" and "Mary Had a Little Lamb." After years of practice and effort, they develop their skills to a point where they can play Beethoven's Fifth Symphony or Bach's Concertos.

Success takes time. I have never learned a principle, developed a skill, lost weight, or gained muscle in an instant. How do we go from where we are to where we want to be? In steps. "A house is built one brick at a time. Football games are won a play at a time. Every big accomplishment is a series of little accomplishments."[2] Success doesn't happen all at once. You should get better every year. Knowledge, skills, and prosperity are to be obtained by consistent and determined study and practice.

As you become more, you will make more. "He which soweth sparingly shall reap also sparingly; and he which soweth bountifully shall reap also bountifully."[3] There are no shortcuts to true success, so learn to work. God did not design us to be idle, but to be industrious.

Learning to Speed Read

I was accepted to a private university and set the goal to get a 4.0 my first semester. Many people began to tell me I wouldn't be able to do it. I had a friend who got a 35 on the ACT and had a 4.0 through high school who didn't get a 4.0 his first semester at this university. Many thought this would be impossible, but I set the goal. I was able to obtain a 4.0 my first semester; However, I spent 40 hours a week reading outside of class to do this. I achieved my goal, but it threw my life out of balance. I realized that I needed to find a way to learn faster and also adjusted my goal to maintain an average of a 3.9 GPA.

At the time, my reading speed was weak. I had a reading speed of 200 words per minute and in high school, I received a very poor score of 13 on the reading portion of the ACT. One day, I saw an advertisement on TV for a speed reading course. I thought this was the answer. The commercial claimed that by using their program, a person could learn to read thousands of words per minute and they had testimonials of people who learned to speed read. I thought in my mind, "If they can do it, then I can do it. If they have done it, then it is possible. The only difference between me and them is learning, time, and effort." So I ordered the program and began practicing the skills and techniques in my studies. I purchased several other programs and books on speed reading and attended workshops the university provided. I practiced and practiced and my reading speed and comprehension continually improved. By my senior year, I could read 3,000 words per minute, with a very high level of comprehension.

During my senior year, I spent only four hours a week reading and still maintained my high GPA. I took just as many credits as I did my first year but was able to do in four hours a week what it used to take me 40 hours. My senior year, I was able to spend a lot of time writing books, golfing, and waterskiing, while still graduating with a 3.9 GPA.

As I saw friends studying long hours and struggling to get good grades, I would share with them what I had learned and suggest they also learn to speed read. Most of them responded with answers such as, "I could never do that," "You are gifted. You are a born genius. I could never do what you do," or "It's not possible to read that fast." I would explain that 3 years ago, I could only read 200 words a minute, and if I was a born genius, where was my genius 3 years ago? I also explained that speed reading was a skill everyone could learn and develop.

Other friends responded to my speed reading story by saying, "You only read 4 hours a week and you're an 'A' student? I've got a test next week. Teach me." To them I explained that it took me three years to go from a reading speed of 200 words a minute to 3,000 words a minute, and they wouldn't be able to do that in a week. Expecting to learn how to read 3,000 words a minute in a week is as impossible as expecting to dramatically increase the amount you could bench press by spending a week in the gym. However, you can begin the process and at least double your reading speed in one week.

Mentorship

*"He that walketh with wise men shall be wise:
but a companion of fools shall be destroyed."*
–Proverbs 13:20, King James Version

When someone is successful, whether it be at speed reading, sales, or business, don't view them as being lucky. Find out how they did it so you can achieve the same success by duplicating what they did. The quickest way to find the process to success in any field (athletics, music, reading, finances, and marriage) is to find someone who has already achieved this success and learn how they did it. Talk to people who are already where you want to be and then do what they did. If you had to walk through a minefield, would you rather follow a person who had been through the field, or learn by trial and error? Find a mentor whose footsteps you can follow to your dreams. Successful people are accessible. You simply have to seek them out. So make it a rule to get advice from people who have done what you want to do.

Anyone can be successful because everything it takes to be successful can be learned. The only thing that stands between where you are and where you want to be is time and effort. Mahatma Gandhi taught, "I claim to be no more than an average man with below average capabilities. I have not the shadow of a doubt that any man or woman can achieve what I have if he or she would put forth the same effort and cultivate the same hope and faith."

Christopher Columbus

The Italian Historian Benzoni related the following story about Christopher Columbus. After Columbus' discovery of the Americas, he was invited to a banquet where he was assigned the most honorable place at the table. He was served with ceremonials which were observed toward kings. From across the table, a shallow courtier, a man who was extremely jealous of columbus, abruptly asked, "If you had not discovered the Americas, would there not have been other men in Spain who would have been capable of the enterprise?" Columbus made no reply but took an egg and invited the company to make it stand on end. They all attempted the task unsuccessfully and lamented that it was impossible. He then struck the egg upon the table so as to break one end and left it standing on the broken part, illustrating that once he had shown the way to the new world, nothing was easier than to follow it. Following someone who has achieved what you want to achieve is the simplest and quickest way to get where you want to be.

Chocolate Cake Metaphor

"If someone makes the greatest chocolate cake in the world, can you produce the same quality results? Of course you can, if you have the person's recipe. A recipe is nothing but a strategy, a specific plan of what resources to use and how to use them to produce a specific result. If you believe that we all have the same neurology, then you believe we all have the same potential resources available to us. . . So what do you need to produce the same quality cake as the expert baker? You need the recipe, and you need to follow it explicitly. If you follow the recipe to the letter, you will produce the same results, even though you may never have baked such a cake before in your life. The baker may have worked through years of trial and error before finally developing the ultimate recipe. You can save years by following his recipe, by modeling what he did. There are strategies for financial success, for creating and maintaining vibrant health, for feeling happy and loved throughout your life. If you find people who already have financial success or fulfilling relationships, you just have to discover their strategy and apply it to produce similar results and save tremendous amounts of time and effort."[4]

Warren Buffett Finds a Mentor

In seeking to learn how to invest in the stock market, Warren Buffett read a book by Benjamin Graham called *The Intelligent Investor*. In this book, he found an investment philosophy and system which he could learn and apply. Warren sought Benjamin Graham as a mentor and began taking the classes Professor Graham taught at Columbia University. He even offered to work for the professor for free. In 1954, Warren Buffett was hired by Benjamin Graham to work at his New York investment firm, Graham-Newman for $12,000 per year ($87,000 per year in 2006 dollars). Two years later, Graham retired and closed his investment firm. In 1957, Warren started his own investment partnership. His business began with 7 family members and friends who invested $105,000 ($729,000 in 2006 dollars) with Warren Buffett only investing $100 ($694 in 2006 dollars) of his own money. Eleven years later, in 1968 his investment partnership business was worth $104 million ($553 million in 2006 dollars). Warren Buffett continued to apply his investment strategies and in 2006, Forbes estimated Warren Buffett's net worth to be $40 billion.

Don't Take Financial Advice from Those Who Struggle Financially

It amazes me how much confidence people put in their family members' advice on financial matters when their family members have struggled financially all their lives. Your family members cannot teach you how to make more money than they have made, because they cannot teach what they do not know.

I remember one man being hesitant to join with me as a business partner because his father told him the business would distract him from his schoolwork. I asked for the financial background of his father. He told me his dad was heavily in debt. His dad was in his fifties, and both he and his wife had to work full time to simply get by. I asked this man if he wanted to duplicate his father's financial pattern. He answered, "No, I don't what to be struggling financially in my fifties." "Then why are you seeking his financial advice?" I asked. I told my friend that he needed to find a mentor—that he needed to listen to those who were where he wanted to be.

A person with a $30,000 a year income can only teach you how to make $30,000 a year. On the other hand, a millionaire can teach you how he made his millions. When I was in college, I never listened to the financial advice of my school counselors or professors. The counselors were only making around $30,000 and the professors were only making between $40,000 and $70,000. They were able to teach me some principles, which are true and helpful, but they could not teach me how to achieve a six or seven figure income. You wouldn't consult your parents, friends, or professors if you needed brain surgery, would you? Unless these people were neurosurgeons, you would not seek their advice. Are financial matters any different? You need to look at a person's history, achievements, income, and lifestyle before you ask them to help shape your financial future.

Advisor vs. Salesman

Another problem is that many people get their financial advice from salesmen, not advisors. The poor and middle class hire those who call on them (salesmen) as advisors. The rich interview, scrutinize, check credentials and performance before they hire advisors. I am called on all the time by people who want to sell me insurance, investments, or help me with a financial plan. In response, I simply ask to see their tax returns and the performance of their investments for the past three years, as well as a statement of their net worth. I let them know that based on my evaluation of these documents, I can tell if they qualify to be one of my advisors. I have interviewed and checked the net worth of each of my advisors before hiring them. All of my accounting, legal, and investments advisors have net worths in the millions.

CONCLUSION: CHRIST—THE PERFECT MENTOR

Jesus Christ is the perfect example to follow. We must strive to emulate the Savior by fulfilling his directive to ". . . always act like your Father in heaven."[5] If we are to become truly successful and prosperous, Christ is our pattern. All the enabling and perfect virtues are to be found in the Master Jesus Christ. As we follow the example of the Savior, we become like the wise man who has built his house upon a rock.[6] As we make Christ our foundation, we will avoid the great fall of foolish men who have built upon the shifting sands of business ethics and the marshlands of the philosophies of man.[7] Much of the world seeks not the Lord as their guide but the blind ". . . and if the blind lead the blind, both shall fall into the ditch."[8] We should seek our mentors among those who can say as the apostle Paul, "Follow my example, as I follow the example of Christ."[9]

TRUTH 18

Success Is a Process of Learning and Industry.

MYTH 19

FAILURE IS BAD

There are a few things not included in my bio at the conclusion of the book that I would like to include here. I have never lost a marathon. I have never had an unprofitable day in the restaurant business. I have never been cut from a basketball team in college or professionally. I have never lost a chess tournament or national spelling bee, and I have never lost an election running for public office.

This all may sound quite impressive until you realize that I have never failed at any of the above mentioned tasks because I have never attempted them. Success and accomplishment are not defined by a lack of failure. However, much of our society believes that failure is bad. A correct understanding of the role failure plays in life is necessary to obtaining prosperity.

FAILURE IS A PART OF LIFE AND LEARNING

Even the greatest baseball players in the world fail more than they succeed. They fail to get a hit 7 times for every 3 times they do get one.

Does a baseball player think about quitting the game every time he gets out? Is he afraid to go to bat because he might fail? No. He knows he will probably fail 7 out of the 10 times he goes to the plate. He knows that failing is a part of the game. We, too, must learn that failure is part of the game of life. Babe Ruth holds the record for the most strikeouts, but he is considered to be one of the greatest athletes of all time because of the home runs he hit. He struck out 1,330 times and hit 714 home runs during his career.

A $10 Million Dollar Lesson

Tom Watson, Sr., IBM's founder, called into his office an executive whose mistake had lost the company $10 million. The nervous executive entered the office and said, "I guess you want my resignation?" Watson replied, "You can't be serious. We've just spent $10 million educating you!"[1] We must come to view mistakes not as failure but as learning. "Bill Gates, the founder of Microsoft, has said, 'I like to hire people who have made mistakes. It shows that they take risks.'"[2]

Pay the Price

Some seek to eliminate the chance for failure and by default eliminate the possibility of success. One of the reasons so few people have written goals is because they are afraid to fail. In an attempt to avoid failure, they have no goals. Those who seek to avoid the pain of failing live a life of constant failure, because they never learn, grow, or improve. If you don't pay the price for success, you will live in mediocrity. What is more painful: the pain it takes to achieve success or the pain of being average and never achieving your potential? Don't be afraid of failure, be afraid of being average.

THREE APPROACHES TO FAILURE

Myth 17 compared the approach to life of the vain optimist, the pessimist, and the true optimist. In this chapter, I would like to reflect on how each responds to failure.

Vain Optimists

Vain optimists in the prison camps set the goal to be out by Christmas. When the goal was not achieved, a new goal was set to be out by Easter. When this goal was not achieved, they set another goal to be out by Thanksgiving. Each time the goal was set without considering the brutal facts or truth. They created a false hope, which sets them up for failure. Because vain optimists consider failure to be bad, they will ignore that a failure took place. They will not evaluate the negative and as a result will not learn from previous failures. Vain optimists will do the exact same thing over and over again and will expect success from a process that has not proven successful. Eventually, vain optimists break and either become pessimists and quit or become true optimists with goals based on reality and truth.

Pessimists

When the pessimist tries and fails, he or she determines it will not work and quits. The extreme pessimists say, "It can't be done," and don't even try. The extreme pessimists may avoid mistakes but they make the biggest mistake of all—doing nothing.

True Optimists

The true optimists have learned that failure is a part of learning and growing. Their desire and commitment to achieve their goals is stronger than their dislike of failure and rejection. True optimists never quit and have goals based on reality and truth. They learn from mistakes and try different approaches until they find one that works.

In the prison camp, the true optimists had a goal to go home but also had a goal to survive every day until it was over. Each day they did not go home could have been considered both a failure and a victory, for, although they did not get to go home, they had survived another day. The true optimists continued to endure and survive each horrible day until the goal of going home was achieved. On September 9, 1965 during a mission in the Vietnam War, Admiral Stockdale was taken as a prisoner of war. He endured and survived 2,712 days (7 years, 5 months) of torture and deprivation and was released on February 12, 1973. While in prison, Admiral Stockdale was kept in solitary confinement for four years, in leg irons for two years, malnourished, and physically tortured more than 20 times, having his shoulders wrenched from their sockets, his leg shattered, and his back broken, but he never quit.

PERSISTENCE

A lesson every man must learn is that he must persist even when it is difficult. When we experience defeat and rejection, the easiest and most logical thing to do is to quit. However, if you give up during the struggle, you will never experience the victory. The formula for success is trying until you succeed. With this view there are no failures, only those who quit before success. How many tries do you give a baby to learn to walk? Do you give him five tries or fifty tries and after that say you're done? "You failed fifty times, no more trying to walk for you." Is that how we do it? No. We encourage the baby to try until he or she walks. It is a formula that works and so everyone learns to walk.

Sylvester Stallone—The Real Life Rocky [3]

When Sylvester Stallone was first trying to launch his acting career, failure seemed to be the one thing he had success with. By 1973, he had been rejected by every casting agency in New York City, with more than 600 rejections total. In order to keep his days open so he could circulate among casting agents, he worked an assortment of odd jobs, including fish-head cutter, lion cage cleaner, usher, and bouncer. Also, in an attempt to make ends meet, he began writing screenplays.

Stallone recalled of his first screenplay, "I had written one hundred and eighty pages of garbage . . . but even though the script was bad, it gave me a sense of accomplishment . . . I did sit down and I did complete a story from beginning to end. For better or worse, it's there. This was something new for me because I was a man who had never passed an English course." During the next year and a half, Stallone wrote 8 screenplays but was unable to sell any of them. Stallone decided to move to Hollywood and try his luck there, but he still had no success in selling his scripts.

In 1975, Stallone had $106 ($398 in 2006 dollars) in the bank. His beat-up car had just blown up, so the struggling actor/writer had to hitchhike. To make matters worse, his wife was pregnant with their first child. Even though he'd managed to pay off four month's rent with the $700 ($2,600 in 2006 dollars) he'd earned on *Death Race 2000*, things were looking bleak—so bleak, if fact, that he was forced to sell his dog and best friend, Butkus, a 135-pound bullmastiff.

He stood outside a store and tried to sell his beloved dog to strangers for $50. Finally, someone bought the dog for $25. Stallone cried as he walked home from the store. The day he had to sell his dog was one of the lowest days of his life. Stallone recalls that day saying, "It was either the dog or us. Trust me. I thought it was over."

Shortly after selling his dog, Stallone saw a fight between Muhammad Ali and Chuck Wepner in which Wepner was a 30:1 underdog. Inspired by this fight, Stallone began developing the Rocky screenplay. For the next three and a half days straight (without sleeping), Stallone and his wife, Sasha, wrote the first draft of Rocky.

Stallone took the finished script to his agent and received an offer of $75,000 ($281,000 in 2006 dollars) from United Artists. This was a huge sum of money to Stallone who had no money and a baby on the way. Stallone wanted to play the role of Rocky, however, and United Artists wanted a well-known actor such as Burt Reynolds, Paul Newman, or Al Pacino to play the lead role. United Artists came back with an offer of $200,000 ($750,000 in 2006 dollars) for the script, without Stallone in the leading role. Stallone refused. The offer went up as high as $340,000 ($1.3 million in 2006 dollars), to which Stallone said, "I would sooner burn the script . . . than to have anyone else play Rocky. Even if the price goes up to a million, no sale."

The producers at United Artists finally gave in and allowed Stallone to play Rocky. However, they also lowered the budget for the film from $2 million to $1 million ($7.5 million to $3.75 million in 2006 dollars). Stallone received $20,000 ($75,000 in 2006 dollars) for the script and the SAG minimum of $350 ($1,300 in 2006 dollars) per week for his acting duties. Stallone also negotiated to receive 8 percent of the film's net profits.

After Stallone received the $20,000 for the script, he returned to the store, hoping the stranger he sold his dog to would return. After three days the man did return and Stallone offered to buy the dog back for $100. The man refused, saying he loved the dog and would never sell him. Stallone then offered him $1,000 for the dog, to which the man replied, "No amount of money is going to buy you this dog." Stallone, determined to get his dog back, eventually paid the man $15,000 ($56,000 in 2006 dollars) and also gave him a part in Rocky for the return of his dog. In the movie, Rocky's dog is played by Stallone's real-life dog, Butkus.

Rocky opened in theaters on November 21, 1976 and took in $117 million ($389 million in 2006 dollars) in U.S. box office sales, with Stallone making more than $5 million ($16.6 million in 2006 dollars).

Christopher Columbus

Christopher Columbus had an inspired dream of crossing the ocean. He petitioned many people to find somebody to invest in this inspired dream. Finally, after 20 years, Queen Isabella and King Ferdinand agreed to support his venture. Columbus wrote of his struggle, "Our Lord unlocked my mind, sent me upon the sea, and gave me fire for the deed. Those who heard of my [adventurous enterprise] called it foolish, mocked me, and laughed. But who can doubt but that the Holy Ghost inspired me?"[4]

On the evening of August 3, 1492, Columbus left from Spain with three ships, the Niña, Pinta, and Santa Maria. On October 10, 1492, 68 days after leaving Spain, Columbus' crew began to lose hope of ever reaching their destination. The crew expressed fear that the nearly continuous winds blowing from east to west might make it impossible to return home. Frightened that they would die at sea, his officers and crew demanded that they turn back and return to Spain. Columbus could only answer that God had given them the weather to take them this far, and He would give them proper weather to get back home. Unconvinced that the matter should be left entirely in God's hands, Columbus's crew threatened to kill him if he did not consent to their request. Columbus urged them to reconsider and proposed a compromise. Columbus suggested that if land was not found after two more days, they would turn back. The officers and crew accepted the compromise. That night in his cabin, Columbus, "prayed mightily to the Lord."[5]

On October 11, they spotted land birds and other signs of nearing land and at 2 a.m. ". . . on October 12th, with the Pinta sailing ahead, the weather cleared. In the moonlight one of the sailors on the Pinta, Juan Rodriquez Bermejo, saw a white sand beach and land beyond it. After his shout of 'Land! Land!' the Pinta's crew raised a flag on its highest mast and fired a cannon."[6] They had arrived at an island which Columbus called San Salvador (holy Savior), which today is an island in the Bahamas. Columbus wrote of naming the island, "I named the first of these islands San Salvador, thus bestowing upon it the name of our holy Saviour under whose protection I

made the discovery." Columbus had achieved his inspired dream of sailing the Atlantic and the world was changed forever because one man refused to quit. Columbus wrote of his journey, "God gave me the faith, and afterwards the courage so that I was quite willing to undertake the journey." Columbus achieved a grand victory because he had the courage to press forward when all others had lost faith.

Conclusion

In seeking to achieve prosperity there will be failures along the way. We must come to view mistakes not as failure, but as learning. God designed us to learn by making mistakes. In the Old Testament, the word "sin" is translated from the word "hattat" which literally means "to fail or miss." In the New Testament, the word "sin" is translated from the Greek word "hamartia" which literally means "miss the mark", derived from the sport of archery. When an archer missed his target it was called "sin." Although the archer missed the mark or target with that arrow, he or she can attempt again and again until the mark is hit. So in life, there will be times we miss our target, but this is not the end. We can learn from our mistakes and attempt again and again until we hit our target. Achieving prosperity is a not a single event but a process. What matters more than where you are is the direction you are heading.

TRUTH 19

Failure Is a Part of Learning. The Formula for Success Is Trying Until You Succeed.

CHOICE 5:
DEBT OR OWNERSHIP

"There is a God, and He's not averse to business. He's not just a 'Sunday deity.' He understands margins and spreadsheets, competition and profits. I appreciate the open door to discuss all those things with Him."
—David Green, founder of Hobby Lobby

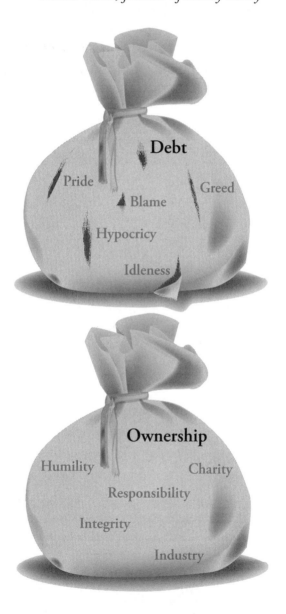

MYTH 20

IF I CAN MAKE THE PAYMENTS, I CAN AFFORD IT

Many of the products we consider purchasing are no longer listed by their total costs but by their monthly payments. We can buy iPods for $25 a month, engagement rings for $50 a month, and cars for $500 a month. This "monthly payment" purchasing ability has resulted in a buy now pay later mentality. More and more people make purchases based on whether or not they can make the monthly payments. This approach is contrary to building wealth. To build wealth, the approach must be save now and buy later.

TEN HABITS OF THE PROSPEROUS™

The poor and the prosperous have much different habits in relation to money. You will want to learn and develop the 10 habits of the prosperous so you to can achieve prosperity.

TEN HABITS OF THE POOR™	TEN HABITS OF THE PROSPEROUS™
1. Vague Unmonitored Financial Goals	1. Clear Monitored Financial Goals
2. Instant Gratification	2. Delayed Gratification
3. Value Social Status	3. Value Financial Independence
4. Live Beyond Income	4. Live Below Income
5. Spend Tomorrow's Money Today	5. Save Money for Tomorrow
6. Pay Interest	6. Earn Interest
7. Pay Themselves Last	7. Pay Themselves First
8. Buy Retail	8. Buy Wholesale
9. Kill Gold-Laying Goose	9. Create Gold-Laying Goose
10. Slave of Money	10. Master of Money

1. Vague Unmonitored Financial Goals vs. Clear Monitored Financial Goals

"If you put one hundred people in a room and ask them how many would like to be financially independent, all the hands will go up. If you then ask them how many have a personal financial statement detailing assets, liabilities, and net worth that is current in the last ninety days … ninety of those hundred people will not raise their hands. If you ask those remaining ten people how many have that financial statement laid out in a pro forma goals format for one, three, five, ten, and twenty year periods, nine of the people will sit down. The one still standing will be a millionaire."[1]

"Only three percent of Americans are independently wealthy: they can live off the income from their investment capital."[2] Most people have not joined this group not because it is difficult or complicated, but because they simply have never created the goals and action plans that lead to independent wealth. Most Americans earn enough throughout their working life to become financially independent, but few create and follow a financial plan that leads to freedom.

Four Steps to Financial Freedom™
I. **Know** Your Current Financial Status

You must know your current financial status in order to organize your finances and future goals. First, calculate your cash flow. You need to know exactly how much money you have coming in, where it is coming from, how much you are spending, and what you are spending it on. Subtract your expenses from your incomes and you will have your cash flow. Second, you need to determine your current net worth. This is done by adding up your assets and subtracting your liabilities. Third, evaluate and determine your progress toward financial independence. Passive income is an important factor when striving for financial independence. An example of passive income is earning interest from a savings bond (i.e. $100,000 in a savings bond at 7 percent interest would create $7,000 in passive income each year). Financial independence is achieved when your passive income exceeds your expenses. When this occurs you will no longer have to work for money—you can choose whether or not to go to work.

II. **Identify** and Set Your Financial Goals

Once you know your current financial status, decide where you would like to be financially as well as how you are going to get there. Decide today to be financially free. To achieve the ultimate goal of financial freedom, you will need to set specific goals to increase passive and active incomes, decrease expenses, increase assets, and reduce liabilities.

III. Create an **Action** Plan to Reach Your Goals

A specific action plan must be created to achieve your goals. For example, the goal to increase passive income may be achieved by buying and renting a commercial or residential property, writing a book to create royalties, or dividends from stocks. A goal to increase active income may be achieved by starting a part-time business, working more hours, making more sales calls, or getting a promotion and/or raise.

IV. **Track** Your Progress

If you do not track your progress, you will not know if you are on the road toward your goals or if you've unknowingly taken a detour. You will be able to track your progress toward financial freedom by keeping current and regularly reviewing three reports:

1. Cash Flow Statement = Total Income – Expenses
2. Net Worth Statement = Assets – Liabilities
3. Financial Independence Statement =
   Passive Income – Expenses

There are many products available to help you track your expenses. However, I couldn't find one that tracked progress including the above reports. There were paper forms of some of the components and software that contained some of the functionality but none that were simple and automated and contained all 4 steps to achieve financial freedom. As a result, The Does Your Bag Have Holes? Foundation has spent thousands and thousands of dollars on the top programming minds to create *The Ten Habits of the Prosperous Software System.*™ With this program, you simply enter your financial information, set goals as prompted by the program, and it will create your Cash Flow Statement, Net Worth Statement, and Financial Independence Statement with easy-to-read charts and graphs. With these statements, you will easily see areas you are succeeding in and areas that need additional focus. To learn more about this program, go to page 303 in this book, visit our website at www.DoesYourBagHaveHoles.org, or call 1-877-No-Holes (664-6537).

2. Instant Gratification vs. Delayed Gratification

Professor Michael Mischel wanted to see the long-term effect of being able to delay gratification. "To find out, Mischel developed a simple experiment . . . a researcher met with a child and established a reward that the child would like such as a marshmallow. Children were then offered two of the treats instead of one if they could wait for the researcher to leave and then re-enter the room before eating the treat. The researchers then ran follow-up interviews every five years... It turned out, says Mischel, that one's ability to delay gratification 'is quite a significant predictor of a variety of important long-term outcomes'... Learning to delay gratification gives children an edge in coping with life's challenges—an edge that lasts into adulthood."[3]

Many people have not learned to delay gratification and want in their twenties what it took their parents 40 years to earn and acquire. Many fall into the trap of focusing on what they want now instead of what matters most long term. A tragic example of this tendency is found in the book of Genesis. "Once when Jacob was cooking some stew, Esau came in from the open country, famished. He said to Jacob, 'Quick, let me have some of that red stew! I'm famished!' Jacob replied, 'First sell me your birthright.' So [Esau] swore an oath to him, selling his birthright to Jacob. Then Jacob gave Esau some bread and some lentil stew.'[4] One of the biggest mistakes we make in life is that we give up what we want most for what we want right now. The prosperous have learned to resist the temptation to lose what matters most long-term for the short-term pleasure of something now.

3. Value Social Status vs. Value Financial Independence

There is a common misconception that the wealthy drive Ferraris, have multimillion dollar houses, and wear extremely expensive clothes. Typically, those who drive expensive cars and wear expensive jewelry have a low net worth. Those with a high net worth are often unconcerned about how they are viewed by others. The prosperous value their financial independence much more than displaying high social status.

In 2006, Forbes researched the 10 richest people to find out what kind of cars they drive. The results are interesting. "You won't find a Bugatti, Ferrari, or BMW driven by these billionaires. But you will find a Lincoln, a Mazda, even a Dodge and a Ford. It seems that for the super-rich, a vehicle is seen not as a status symbol but a means to an end in which to get from point A to point B. Status is something that these billionaires need not prove to others. In many cases, the people on our list prefer to live inconspicuously."[5] On average, the cars they drive are 6 years old.

Often times those who display the highest social status (big house, fancy cars, expensive clothes, jewelry) actually have the least in terms of net worth and financial independence. They create the illusion of wealth by greatly leveraging their income to purchase items on credit. A great deal of their money goes toward paying interest, and nothing they have is really theirs—it is the bank's. The prosperous enjoy the security and independence of owning their possessions more than social praise and status. This paradox is similar to the Indian proverb, "A mango tree loaded with fruit bends to the ground; the one without fruit stands tall."

Those who value social status more than self-reliance will spend money they don't have to purchase things on credit for the purpose of impressing others. On average, the most credit you can acquire is about 10 times your income. If someone values social status a great deal more than financial independence, they will leverage themselves as far as possible and thus will have 10 times more debt than their annual income. Those who highly value financial independence, on the other hand, will have zero debt. To figure out where you are on the Social Status/Financial Independence Continuum, take your total consumer debt (house mortgage, cars, credit cards, etc.) and divide it by your annual income. For example, someone who makes $30,000 a year and has $300,000 in total consumer debt would have a score of 10 ($300,000/$30,000)—indicating they value social status a great deal more than financial independence. Someone who highly values financial independence will have a low income to debt ratio. For example, someone making $50,000 per year with $100,000 in consumer debt would have a score of 2 ($100,000/$50,000)—indicating they value financial independence more than social status. Both the numerical score and the direction you are headed indicate what you value more.

SOCIAL STATUS / FINANCIAL INDEPENDENCE CONTINUUM ™

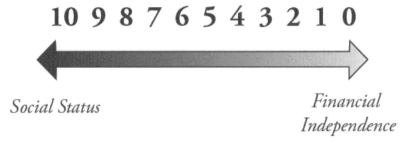

10 9 8 7 6 5 4 3 2 1 0

Social Status

Financial Independence

4. Live Beyond Income vs. Live Below Income

The poor typically spend more than they earn. They will buy homes and cars on credit and will make payments over a long period of time. They think, "If I can make the payment, I can afford it." The prosperous, on the other hand, typically spend less than they earn and will buy cars they can pay cash for and homes they can pay off quickly. The prosperous think, "If I can't pay cash for it, I won't buy it."

In 2002, my wife and I were looking to buy a house. We were not looking at what payment we could afford but for a house we could pay for in a short period of time. It took some time but we finally purchased a beautiful 5,000-square-foot home on a half acre lot for $284,000. We made average monthly payments of approximately $8,000 (representing about 20–25 percent of our monthly income) and paid off the house in just more than 3 years. Having paid $312,000 total, we now own our home and have no mortgage payment. Had we bought a home on a 30-year mortgage, with a monthly payment of $8,000, we could have purchased a $1.33 million house, which would have been larger and newer. However, if we had purchased a $1.33 million house, we would have paid the same $312,000, after the three years, but instead of owning the home we would have paid $255,000 in interest[pn] and only $57,000 toward the principle and would still have 27 more years of $8,000 per month mortgage payments.

One major difference between the prosperous and the poor is simply this: For every $10 the prosperous make they spend $7. For every $10 dollars the poor make, they spend $13.

5. Spend Tomorrow's Money Today vs. Save Money for Tomorrow

Many spend tomorrow's resources for today's pleasures. They spend all the money they earn and then borrow more money and, as a result, commit a portion of their future income to interest payments. This creates an insecure financial foundation.

What if your earned income stopped? How long could you survive? One who spends tomorrow's money today would typically have no way to make their payments. Depending on how much they have leveraged their incomes with debt, they would only be able to survive months before creditors would take their cars, home, furniture, etc. The financially independent who saves and invests today's money for tomorrow, however, could answer this question saying, "For the rest of my life." This is security and financial peace of mind.

We should seek to follow the example of Joseph in Egypt found in the Old Testament. During the 7 years of plenty, he saved and stored resources to sustain the country during 7 years of famine.[7] The Savior has told us that great calamities will precede His second coming. Now is the time to prepare and save for when the prophesied days of great wars, famine, pestilence, and natural disasters will plague the earth.[8] The Savior likened the day of His second coming to 10 virgins with lamps. The 5 wise virgins had oil in their lamps at his coming and went to meet him. The foolish virgins who had not oil for their lamps "said unto the wise, 'Give us of your oil; for our lamps are gone out.' But the wise answered, saying, 'Not so; lest there be not enough for us and you.'"[9] The wise virgins went in unto the Lord and the door was shut. The foolish virgins came to the door saying, "'Open the door for us!' But he replied, 'I tell you the truth, I don't know you.'"[10] The 5 foolish virgins were unprepared and lost their opportunity. At the time of His coming, they could not borrow what another had, and they were not rescued by saying, "The Lord will provide." We must each prepare for the needs of tomorrow and be prepared for the day of His coming. At the time of His coming, it will be too late. Now is the time to prepare to meet God "for ye know neither the day nor the hour wherein the Son of man cometh."[11]

6. Pay Interest vs. Earn Interest

Interest is a very powerful tool that either builds or diminishes wealth. "Interest never sleeps nor sickens nor dies; it never goes to the hospital; it works on Sundays and holidays; it never takes a vacation; it never visits nor travels; it takes no pleasure; it is never laid off work nor discharged from employment; it never works on reduced hours; ... it has no love, no sympathy; it is as hard and soulless as a granite cliff ... interest is your companion every minute of the day and night."[12] Another simple difference between the prosperous and the poor is that the prosperous earn interest while the poor pay interest.

For example, while I was in college, I paid $1,200 cash for a 17-year-old Ford pickup. One of my neighbors purchased a new Ford pickup for $24,000. I was curious as to how he could afford such a truck, and he told me he could make the $400-a-month payment. He had a 6-year loan at 7 percent interest, so the total payments for the truck were $29,500. Had he purchased an old Ford pickup like I did, and invested[13] the $400 a month, at the end of the 6 years he would have had $40,000. Instead, he had a 6-year old truck worth $12,000. Those who understand interest earn it and those who don't understand interest pay it.

Many spend beyond their income during Christmas putting their purchases on credit cards. A $1,000 Christmas shopping spree—with a credit card that charges 18 percent interest and requires a minimum payment of interest plus 1 percent of the balance—will take 13 years to pay off. With interest, the $1,000 shopping spree will cost $2,129. Again, those who understand interest earn it and those who don't pay it.

Here is a simple plan or outline for investing in real estate that will offer prosperity in the long run. First, let's look at the traditional situation. A home for $262,000 (2005 national average house price) with a traditional 30-year mortgage fixed at 6 percent interest would have the monthly payments of $1,571, with the house costing you a total of $565,000 over 30 years of payments. Now consider a second option. With the purchase of a slightly less expensive house for $200,000 on a 15-year mortgage at 5.75 percent (interest rates are lower on 15-year mortgages than 30-year mortgages), the monthly payment would be $1,660 a month. This house would cost you $299,000 ($133,000 less than if you paid for the house over 30 years).

At the end of 15 years, the $200,000 house is paid for so you now have the $1,660 payment freed up. Instead of spending this money on consumer products, use the $1,660 a month toward the purchase of a second house for $200,000, which you rent for $1,500 per month. By putting your $1,660 payment and the $1,500 collected from rent toward the purchase of the rental home, it will be paid for in 6 years and 4 months. After the second house is paid for, do it again. Take your $1,660 a month, the $1,500 rent from the first rental (which now has no mortgage) and purchase a second rental for $200,000, which you also rent for $1,500. This totals $4,660 going toward the purchase of the second rental. With this payment, this home will be paid for in 4 years. You then purchase a third rental for $200,000 and put the original house payment of $1,660 a month and the new income of $4,500 (rent from the three rental properties) for a total monthly payment of $6,160. This third rental home will be paid for in 3 years. In summary, in just more than 28 years, you will own your home and 3 rental properties producing $4,500 a month income. With appreciation over the 28 years, the total value of the four properties would be millions of dollars.

Now compare the above example with what you can get with the conventional 30-year loan. At the end of 30 years, you simply own a single personal residence. Both options cost you $565,000, but at the end of option 2 you are financially independent. Which option are you going to choose? Is having a slightly more expensive home worth millions in future income?

OPTION 1 SUMMARY: 30-YEAR MORTGAGE						
Property	Purchase Price	Interest Rate	Total Cost	Amount Paid by You	Amount Paid by Renter	Cash Flow
Personal Residence	$262,000	6.0%	$565,000	$565,000	$0	$0

OPTION 2 SUMMARY: 15-YEAR MORTGAGE AND RENTALS						
Property	Purchase Price	Interest Rate	Total Cost	Amount Paid by You	Amount Paid by Renter	Cash Flow
Personal Residence	$200,000	5.75%	$299,000	$299,000	$0	$0
Rental # 1	$200,000	5.75%	$240,000	$126,000	$114,000	$1,500
Rental # 2	$200,000	5.75%	$224,000	$80,000	$144,000	$3,000
Rental # 3	$200,000	5.75%	$222,000	$60,000	$162,000	$4,500
Total	$800,000	5.75%	$985,000	$565,500	$420,000	$4,500

7. Pay Themselves Last vs. Pay Themselves First

According to the 2003 U.S. Census Bureau, the average household income was $45,000—that is $1.8 million over 40 years. Most people earn enough money during their lifetime to become millionaires. Those who develop the habit of paying them themselves first do become millionaires. However, most people pay themselves last—they pay their bills, spend money on food, clothing and entertainment, and only save if anything is left over. With the pay yourself last approach, there is typically nothing left because of the natural tendency for our expenses to rise to the amount of our income.

You can become financially independent simply by paying 10 percent of your income to savings and investments first, and then living on the rest. Using the average household income of $45,000, $4,500 could be saved and invested each year and $41,500 would be available to live on. At the end of 40 years, you would have saved $180,000 (10 percent of $1.8 million) and earned more than $2 million in interest for a total of $2.2 million.[14]

From Security Guard to Millionaire—A Real Life Case Study

I wanted to find someone who had done this in real life. I found such a person and he provided me with 30 years of detailed information on his income, savings, and investments.[15] For privacy purposes, I will call him Alan. In 1978, Alan worked as a security guard making $15,195 a year and began paying himself first. He had money automatically taken from each paycheck and put into a retirement account. He invested the money in his retirement account in the stock market. As a result of his industry and hard work, he received raises and promotions. His raises were 6.4 percent a year on average. During the 30 years, his total earned income equaled $1.6 million and he had $135,000 (8.4 percent of $1.6 million) put into his retirement account. His best annual return on his money in the stock market investments was 56.9 percent in 1989. In Alan's worst year, he lost 15.6 percent in 2001. Overall, he received an average annual return of 18.9 percent. After 30 years, his retirement account is worth more than $1 million ($1,054,631). He paid himself first, invested, and became a millionaire, and you can too.

8. *Buy Retail vs. Buy Wholesale*

The prosperous have developed the habit of buying things wholesale, where as the poor buy things retail. I am wearing a nice long-sleeve Hathaway Golf® shirt which would cost $50 at a golf shop; however I would never buy clothes at a golf shop. I purchased this shirt new for $2 at a Salvation Army thrift store. When my wife and I were looking to purchase a home, we searched for a home we could buy below its value. The home we purchased for $284,000 in 2002 had been valued at $386,000 by the tax assessor, and this was the amount the seller paid property tax on the previous year. I was able to purchase a house at more than $100,000 below its value. The house is now valued at approximately $500,000.

By the habit of asking for or searching out a discount on everything you buy can save you thousands of dollars each year. It is helpful to learn the profit margins on various items and then ask for the appropriate discount. They can always give you at least 10 percent off the price, and for some products they can give you up to 50 percent off the price. I enjoy purchasing fine art for my home and offices. When I first was looking at buying art, I had to learn how the industry worked. I spoke to a few gallery owners and found out that galleries buy their art from the publishers for 50 percent of retail price. I saw a piece of art in the home of a friend of mine that I loved. I asked how much he paid for it and where he bought it. He paid $4,800—the retail price for this limited edition giclée print. I went to the same gallery and offered to buy the same picture for $2,800, which was $400 above the gallery's purchase price, and he agreed. I saved $2,000 simply by knowing the industry and asking for a discount.

You can do the same thing with tires, cars, boats, medical expenses, etc. You can greatly decrease your expenses by learning how to buy items at wholesale and by always asking for a discount.

9. Kill Gold-Laying Goose vs. Create Gold-Laying Goose

"A man and his wife had the good fortune to possess a goose which laid a golden egg every day. Lucky though they were, they soon began to think they were not getting rich fast enough and imagining the bird must be made of gold inside, they decide to kill it in order to secure the whole store of precious metal at once. But when they cut it open they found it was just like any other goose. Thus they neither got rich all at once, as they had hoped, nor enjoyed any longer the daily addition to their wealth."[16]

Lottery winners are a great example of killing the gold-egg-laying goose. William "Bud" Post won $16 million in the Pennsylvania lottery. Among his purchases were a mansion, a twin–engine plane, 5 cars and trucks, 2 Harley-Davidson motorcycles, two 62-inch Sony televisions, a luxury camper, and a $260,000 sailboat. As a result of his spending, he eventually declared bankruptcy and lost everything. Mr. Post now lives on food stamps and a Social Security check of $450 a month.[17] Mr. Post had a $16 million-dollar goose that could have produced an abundance of gold eggs. Had he simply put the $16 million into a CD and lived on the 6 percent interest it produced, he would have received a golden egg of $80,000 every month forever without ever touching the $16 million. Instead, he wanted the riches all at once and spent his gold-egg-laying goose, which resulted in a life of poverty.

Benjamin Franklin died in 1790 at the age of 84. As part of his will, he gave 1,000 pounds (approximately $4,400) to the city of Boston and another 1,000 pounds to the city of Philadelphia. To prevent the cities from killing the gold-egg-laying-goose by spending the money, Franklin required that the money be place in a trust fund and then invested and used to provide loans to "married tradesman under the age of 26" to get them started in business. During the two hundred years of the trust, money was loaned to hundreds of individuals. The trust fund in Philadelphia grew to $2.25 million, and the trust fund in Boston grew to $5 million.[18] They received very modest average annual returns of 3.1 percent and 3.5 percent respectively. A slightly higher average rate of return of .4 percent yielded the city of Boston $2.75

million more than the city of Philadelphia. If the cities had received 7 percent average annual returns, after 200 years the funds would have each been worth $5 billion. Benjamin Franklin understood the value of creating a gold-egg-laying goose and the power of compounding interest. Hopefully, the trusts will continue for another 200 years. If the city of Boston now simply puts the $5 million in a savings bond at 5 percent interest, they would receive interest payments of $250,000 a year—$50 million over the next 200 years.

To become financially independent, you need passive income to exceed your monthly expenses. The prosperous create a gold-egg-laying goose (assets with passive income) and then live on the eggs. The poor only receive income from their work and if they don't put some of this money toward buying assets and investments, they will never join the ranks of the financially independent. The average American makes $1.8 million during a 40-year working career, yet most never create a gold-egg-laying goose. Like many of the lottery winners, Americans spend all of their $1.8 million and often even more on credit to buy homes, cars, boats, etc. They spend their golden goose and thus remain in the poor and middle class.

Those who have reached the ranks of prosperity have learned "that money is of a prolific generating nature. Money can beget money, and its offspring can beget more, and so on."[19] In summary, the prosperous buy assets—things that create money—and the poor buy liabilities—things that cost money.

10. Slave of Money vs. Master of Money
"If money be not thy servant, it will be thy master." –17th Century Proverb

The prosperous have their money work for them, while the poor work for money. The prosperous have achieved financial security and peace of mind by becoming the master of their financial resources. They realize that financial independence cannot be obtained when they are in debt, because debt puts them in bondage and obligation to others. The prosperous follow the counsel of the apostle Paul and prophet Elisha to "Let no debt remain outstanding"[20] and to "pay thy debt, and live."[21]

The poor put themselves in bondage by living on credit and thus obligate themselves to a lifetime of monthly payments. "The borrower is the slave of the lender."[22] "Someone bound in the slavery of debt is just as helpless as the slave who is bound by ignorance, or by actual chains."[23] The Savior rebuked the Pharisees for being servants of money saying, "No servant can serve two masters, for either he will hate the one and love the other, or he will be devoted to the one and despise the other. You cannot serve God and money."[24] Debt results in money being our master and we its servant. Are you a master of money or a slave to money?

You cannot be completely free without economic freedom. Financial independence releases us from the bondage of debt and financial obligations, freeing us to fully serve God. The world teaches that you want to be financially free so you can live a life of luxury and leisure. The truly prosperous want to be financially free so they have obligations to no one but the Lord and the moving forth of His work.

CONCLUSION

Benjamin Franklin gave this advice to a young tradesman in 1748: "The way to wealth, if you desire it, is as plain as the way to market. It depends chiefly on two words, industry and frugality; that is waste neither time nor money, but make the best use of both … I will acquaint you with the true secret of money-catching, the certain way to fill empty purses, and how to keep them always full. Two simple rules, well observed, will do the business. First, let honesty and industry be thy constant companions; and secondly, spend less than you earn . . . then shalt thou reach the point of happiness, and independence."[25]

TRUTH 20

The Habits of Saving and Investing Create a Life of Freedom, Security, and Peace.

Myth 21

9 Out of 10 Businesses Fail in the First Year

"If you believe that 90 percent of small businesses fail in their first year, you probably also believe that Bill Gates will send you cash for forwarding an e-mail message. Neither story is true, yet neither will go away."[1] The myth often continues that 9 out of 10 of the businesses left after 1 year will fail within 5 years—that is only a 1 percent success rate for new businesses. This myth creates a fear that being an entrepreneur is much harder and riskier than it really is. In reality, businesses succeed at a much higher percent. A study of 212,182 businesses started in 1998 found that 81 percent were still in business after their first year and 44 percent were in business after the fourth year.[2] "And according to a studies conducted by the U.S. Commerce Department from 1971 to 1987, less than 5 percent of franchises have been terminated on an annual basis."[3] Starting a business is not free of risk, but success as a business owner is not as far-fetched as many believe.

Employee vs. Entrepreneur

There are basically two ways in which people accumulate wealth. One is through a job and the other is through developing a business. A job brings you money immediately. You make money your first day of work. A career as an employee is typically a 40-year plan of working at least 8 hours a day to reach retirement. A job typically has limitations on the amount of money you can make, while there is unlimited income potential with a business. However, when building a business, the money is delayed and you may not see significant profit for years. It typically takes 3 to 7 years to build an income generating business system. Once this system is in place and can continuously run without you, you can retire if you choose.

While giving a seminar at a university I asked, "How many of you are planning on becoming teachers?" Several hands went up. I then asked, "How many of you with your hands raised plan to struggle financially your entire lives?" All the hands stayed up. They all thought that if you wanted to be a teacher, you had to teach for the government and be poor. In the current government education system, there are limits to what teachers can earn, how far they can advance, and how they can use and develop their talents. Teaching, however, does not have to have these limitations.

People often narrow their vision and think that a job is the only way to fulfill their passion. There is a second option, and that is starting a business. If your passion is teaching, that does not mean you have to teach in the limited and restricted government education system. You could start your own business teaching and then the potential in earnings and in blessing lives is endless. I know many teachers who make millions every year. One of my mentors has two PhDs and was a university professor for about 20 years before he started his own business. Within 11 months, his business generated more income than his salary. He currently gets paid $15,000 for one lecture. Another former university professor currently gets paid around $75,000 per lecture. He teaches the same principles that he did at the university, but now makes more in a day than he used to in a year. What is the difference? He created his own business.

Most people have been taught to go to school, get good grades, and get a good job. In school, we learn the skills and habits that will make us successful as employees, but rarely do schools teach the skills and habits to succeed at creating a business. To succeed as an entrepreneur requires a completely different set of habits and skills. It is not any harder to succeed as a business owner than to succeed as an employee—it only takes developing different habits.

As many have not been taught about or considered the opportunity and option of starting their own business, I will discuss the 6 habits of successful entrepreneurs.

6 Habits of Succesful Entreprenuers™

1. Work for Profits

2. Value Independence

3. Paid for Ideas

4. Skills of Organizing Resources and Efforts to Seize Business Oportunities

5. Create Systems

6. Build Ownership

Habit 1. Work for Profits

Your compensation for hours worked will depend greatly on whether you are working for a salary or working for profits. All working people will do enough work during their lifetimes to become multimillionaires; however, most will not reach this financial status. Most become employees of businesses instead of owners of businesses—they work for a salary instead of working for profits. Most business owners are just regular people who choose to work differently. I graduated with a bachelor's degree in business management. There were 400 in my graduating class, and the average starting salary was $36,300 per year. I interviewed at a couple of companies and had job offers, but I declined the offers. Most of my classmates chose to work for a salary. I chose to focus my time on developing a business. The 7 years following graduation, I earned an average of $99.81 per hour, while my classmates earned on average $21.02 per hour. During the seven years following graduation, I earned a total of $1.6 million, and my classmates earned on average a total of $344,384. My classmates and I both worked hard to earn our college degrees, and we both worked hard after we graduated. What did I do differently? I chose to work hard building a business and they chose to work hard at a job.

Job vs. Business Case Study

Cameron C. Taylor—Working for Profits

Year	Hours Worked Per Week	Hours Worked Per Year	Dollars Per Hour	Annual Income*
1999	40	2,080	$0.00	$0
2000	40	2,080	$0.00	$0
2001	40	2,080	$8.65	$18,000
2002	40	2,080	$52.88	$110,000
2003	55	2,860	$97.90	$280,000
2004	45	2,340	$191.03	$447,000
2005	45	2,340	$311.11	$728,000
Totals	**43.6 Average**	**15,860**	**$99.81**	**$1,583,000**

*2005 income includes income from the sale of my interest in one of my businesses at the start of 2006.

Classmates—Working for a Salary

Year	Hours Worked Per Week	Hours Worked Per Year	Dollars Per Hour	Annual Income*
1999	45	2,340	$15.51	$36,300
2000	45	2,340	$17.06	$39,930
2001	45	2,340	$18.77	$43,923
2002	45	2,340	$20.65	$48,315
2003	45	2,340	$22.71	$53,147
2004	45	2,340	$24.98	$58,462
2005	45	2,340	$27.48	$64,308
Totals	**45 Average**	**16,380**	**$21.02 Average**	**$344,384**

*1999 income is the actual average starting salary of my graduating class, 2001-2005 Incomes are estimated based on a 10 % a year raise.

Habit 2. Value Independence

At the beginning phases of his entrepreneurial efforts, Jay Van Andel was offered a high-paying executive job. He was tempted by the offer but turned it down. He wrote of the experience, "There before me was a secure, steady income … The loss of independence was too much for me to accept, however. It was important to Rich [business partner] and to me to be self-employed, to set our own courses and make decisions that would truly be our own. Even in a high-level position . . . I would be an employee, limited in my ability to do what I thought was best and at the mercy of someone else's decisions."[4] Jay Van Andel went on to earn billions from his businesses.

Why, in a land of freedom and opportunity, do most Americans voluntarily choose to work for companies instead of starting their own company? The need for security is one major factor. The employee will give up his or her independence and accept lower compensation for a guaranteed place to work. The paycheck may not be large, but it is defined and comes every two weeks. While a job does give a sense of security, it also takes away your independence and control. The more security you have the less freedom you have. The people with maximum security in prison have the least amount of freedom.

Fear of losing money is another factor that drives many to remain employees. The employee responds to fear by playing it safe. In the parable of the talents found in the New Testament, the servant who received one talent ($300,000 in 2006 dollars)[5] said at his accounting, "I was afraid, and went and hid thy talent in the earth."[4] It was fear that kept him from doing anything with the money. To ensure he didn't lose the money, he buried it. Likewise, the fear of losing money keeps many Americans from winning. The entrepreneur responds to fear by managing risk. The entrepreneur learns, plans, and then takes calculated and educated risks. The entrepreneur plays to win, while the employee plays not to lose.

When Moses freed the children of Israel from slavery, they rejoiced in their deliverance and sang praises to Moses and the Lord.[7] Just six weeks following their freedom and independence from Egypt, the children of

Israel longed to return to the security of slavery in Egypt saying, "When we lived there, we could at least sit down and eat."[8] They feared they would starve in the desert and complained to Moses saying, "You have brought us out here into this desert, where we are going to starve."[9] Just as the children of Israel quickly desired to give up their independence and freedom for a secure meal in slavery, many Americans prefer the guaranteed meal provided by a job over the independence and freedom of business ownership. When the road became rough, the children of Israel were willing to abandon the journey to the promise land and freedom. Likewise, many Americans are not willing to take risks and go through the initial struggles and lean years of a business startup to reach the promised land of business ownership flowing with the milk and honey of independence and financial abundance.

Habit 3. Paid for Ideas

Employees are paid by the hour for completing a task. Entrepreneurs, on the other hand, are paid for ideas. "Physical labor as such can extend no further than the range of the moment. The man who does no more than physical labor, consumes the material value-equivalent of his own contribution to the process of production, and leaves no further value, neither for himself nor others. But the man who produces an idea … is the permanent benefactor of humanity… It is only the value of an idea that can be shared with unlimited numbers of men, making all sharers richer at no one's sacrifice or loss, raising the productive capacity of whatever labor they perform."[10] You can sell a task or your time only once. You can sell an idea over and over again. For example, writing a book is the creation of ideas. Once the ideas are created and published, it can be sold over and over again. On the other hand, a transcriptionist also writes words but simply sells a skill. They get paid once to transcribe something. If they want to get paid again, they must transcribe something else.

For labor or task completion, you are limited to earning an hourly fee for your time—from minimum wage for washing dishes up to $300 per hour for legal work. For this type of work you can only get paid when you work. If you stop working, your income stops. Doctors, lawyers, and employees all have temporary limited income as the result of their income coming from the renting of their time and skills.

Compensation for an idea is only limited to the number of people who can benefit from it. You can get paid over and over again for the same idea. A good idea is worth years of labor. In the words of Henry Ford, "Thinking is the hardest work there is, which is the probable reason why so few engage in it."[11] You are one good idea away from financial independence. Here are a couple of examples.

1-800 CONTACTS

"1-800 CONTACTS was founded in 1995 by two entrepreneurs who sought to address contact lens wearers' basic frustrations. Wearing contacts themselves, they understood that contact lenses could be expensive and inconvenient to replace. With that in mind, they set out to offer low prices, convenient ordering, and fast delivery to their customers. Their plan to accomplish this centered on buying contact lenses in large quantities to get the best prices and housing a large contact lens inventory so customers' prescriptions would be in stock and ready to ship. . . Contact lens wearers have recognized the advantages 1-800 CONTACTS has to offer and sales have grown rapidly from $4 million in 1996 to $212 million in 2004. The company's growth is a testament to the benefits it offers to contact lens wearers seeking a hassle-free, quick, and affordable way to replace their contact lenses."[12]

Post-It® Notes

"The idea of a low-tack adhesive note was conceived in 1974 by Arthur Fry as a way of retaining bookmarks in his hymnal while singing in his church choir. Fry's markers had fallen from his hymn book on multiple occasions. He was aware of an adhesive developed in 1968 by Spencer Silver, a 3M researcher, who, while attempting to design a strong adhesive, had instead developed one that was very weak. No immediate application was apparent and the adhesive remained unused until Fry's idea."[13] Millions of Post-It® Notes are now sold each year.

Habit 4. Skills of Organizing Resources and Efforts to Seize Business Opportunities

The employee looks for a job and someone to tell them what to do. They seek someone who can direct their activities and duties. The entrepreneur directs the activities and duties of others. One who can direct others will receive a much higher compensation than the person who can do a job. The employee looks for a company he can sell his skill to and develops a good resume. The entrepreneur looks for business opportunities and creates a good business plan. The employee looks for a job. The entrepreneur creates jobs.

A certain amount is paid for developing the skill of flipping hamburgers; much more is paid for the skills of flying a plane or performing a surgery. To increase income, the employee must either work more hours or develop and perfect a skill to get paid more per hour. The entrepreneur develops the skills of organizing and directing resources to increase profits. As a result of seizing more opportunities as well as organizing and directing more resources and people, the entrepreneur increases his income.

Thomas Edison developed more than the skill of inventing. He was also an amazing entrepreneur. One of his greatest inventions was the creation of the first company with the specific purpose of producing commercially marketable inventions. He organized and directed the work of numerous employees, resulting in the more than 1,500 patents for his inventions worldwide. He is the founder of General Electric, which today is the world's second largest company with 2006 revenues of $163 billion. He realized his real skill was not that of a technical nature but of organizing and directing the technical skills of others, saying, "I am not a mathematician . . . I can always hire mathematicians, but they can't hire me."[14] The job of entrepreneur is not something you apply and interview for, it is something you create.

Habit 5. Create Systems

The entrepreneur creates a business system that the employee is a part of. In April 2001, I started a company and began developing a database and marketing system to seize an opportunity. In my thirteenth month of business, my company earned $294,420 in revenue with a very high profit margin. I knew my systems worked well. It was now time to expand. I worked to perfect and develop the system so it could be used by someone else. I now needed someone to work the expanded portion of the system. I had created my first job. I hired my first employee, a 20-year-old college student, for $8.50 per hour and taught her the system. My business partners were skeptical and thought I would not be able to teach someone else what I had done. They did not think a 20-year-old college student could generate hundreds of thousand of dollars in revenues as I had done. My first employee worked full time for 3 months before transferring to a new school and moving away. She generated more than $500,000 in revenue from the work she did in those 3 months, for which she was paid $4,400. When I presented this report to my business partners, they asked me to hire as many people as I could to expand the reach of the business system I had created. My system enabled college students to produce amazing results time and time again. The system enables each employee to generate hundreds of thousands in revenue each year.

If I was not able to create a system that could be run by others, I would have simply been self-employed and would have created a job for myself. I was not interested in developing a system that was dependant upon me. I was working to develop a business system that could be run and managed by others, which is the unique skill of an entrepreneur. A business is to work for you, not the other way around.

Ray Kroc, founder of McDonald's, is a great example of an entrepreneur developing a system. The genius of McDonald's was the business system behind the burger. Ray Kroc said of the early days of McDonalds's, "We wanted to build a restaurant system that would be known for food of consistently high quality and uniform methods of preparation. Our aim, of course, was to ensure repeat business based on the system's reputation rather than on the quality of a single store or operator. . . I knew in my bones that the key to uniformity would be in our ability to provide techniques of preparation that operators would accept because they were superior to methods they could dream up for themselves."[15] He created a system that was not people dependant—a system where the majority of the work could be done by employees under the age of 20. Once the system was created, it was then duplicated and expanded. Ray Kroc opened his first McDonald's in 1955 with first day revenues of $366. The duplication and expansion then began.

Year	Number of Restaurants
1955	1
1958	100
1968	1,000
1988	10,000
1999	25,000

Today, McDonald's is the world's largest foodservice retailer with more than 30,000 restaurants serving nearly 50 million people in more than 119 countries each day with revenue exceeding $20 billion a year. It all began with one restaurant and a proven duplicatable system. Once an entrepreneur creates a successful system, he expands the size and reach of his system.

There are six ways to benefit from a business system:
I. Corporation—Build your own system
II. Franchise—Buy a system
III. Network Marketing—Buy and sell a system
IV. Write a Book—Create an educational system
V. Patent—Create an idea to sell to a business system
VI. Investor—Buy ownership in a system

I. Corporation

To build a traditional corporation, you develop your own system. It requires startup capital, buildings, employees, insurance, and manufacturing.

II. Franchise

With a franchise, you buy a system someone else has created. A franchise provides you with "all the elements required to make a business work. It transforms a business into a machine, or more accurately, because it is so alive, into an organism, driven by the integrity of its parts, all working in concert toward a realized objective."[16]

The start-up cost for a franchise varies from industry to industry. Here are a few:

Commercial cleaning:	$8,400+
Real estate:	$21,000+
Frozen yogurt:	$25,000+
Postal and business service:	$115,000+
Hamburger restaurant:	$413,000+

III. Network Marketing

Network marketing is like buying a personal franchise for a few hundred dollars. The only difference between network marketing and franchising is that in network marketing you can not only utilize the business system, but you can also sell the business system to others. With franchising you can utilize the business system, but you can't sell the business system to anyone else. For example, if you were to buy a McDonald's franchise you would have the rights to use their business system to sell their Big Macs and fries, but you would not be able to sell a McDonald's business system and franchise to someone else. If McDonald's was set up as a network marketing business system, you would buy a McDonald's business system and have the right to sell

Big Macs and fries as well as be able to sell the McDonald's business system to others and profit from their use of the McDonald's business system.

IV. Write a Book

When writing a book, you create a story or education that can be shared over and over again with no additional effort on your part. Once you find a publisher and use their business system to print and market your book, you will collect a royalty payment for each book sold.

While working as an advertising executive, Richard Paul Evans wrote a book for his children in his spare time called *The Christmas Box*. He sold the rights to this book to the publisher Simon & Schuster for $4.2 million.

While living in a small basement apartment as a housewife, Stephanie Ashcraft was looking for a way to increase their family income as her husband went to school. She developed a cookbook called *101 Things to Do With a Cake Mix*. She found a publisher and has now sold more than 1 million books in her cookbook series.

V. Patent

Todd Moses has earned millions from one simple idea he patented. In April 2003, Moses, age 29, created several reports for an important meeting. As he went to staple his 19-page report, the staple went only halfway through. On the next stack, the stapler completely jammed. In panic mode, Moses tried to pull out the staples that had partly penetrated his papers, only to cut his finger. In frustration, he threw the stapler against the wall. Most have experienced this but Moses turned his experience into millions by solving the problems with staplers. He wondered if the technology in a staple gun could be applied to an office desktop stapler. He did some research online at retailers such as Staples and Office Depot to find that no such product existed. He then contacted the engineer, Joel Marks, who designed the spring loaded shooting mechanism in the Black and Decker staple gun. Marks agreed to help build the prototype in exchange for the promise of equity if the idea took off. Together they created the PaperPro® Stapler. Moses patented the idea to ensure that each time a stapler was sold with this technology he would get paid. Millions of these staplers are now sold each year in more than 100 countries with total sales well into the eight figures.[17] One good patent idea sold to a business system can produce thousands of dollars in royalties.

VI. Investor

Investing is the purchase of ownership in a system. For example, through interviewing and studying various investors, I learned how to invest in the exploration and discovery of oil and natural gas. Each well typically costs millions of dollars, and investors are sought to put up the money for the drilling costs. In return, the investor is given a percent of all the proceeds from the sale of the oil and natural gas produced by the well. I have purchased ownership in several oil/natural gas wells, and I receive a check each month for my percent of the oil and natural gas sold.

You can also invest in companies through the stock market. As the value of the company increases so does your stock. Also, many companies pay a share of the profits to stock holders through dividends. For example, in 1971, Wal-Mart had 51 stores that did $78 million in revenue and $2.9 million in profit.[18] A $1,000 worth of Wal-Mart stock at the start of 1972 would grow in value at an average rate of 23 percent per year to $1.1 million at the start of 2006. Wal-Mart expanded its system from 51 stores at the end of 1971 to more than 6,200 stores with sales of $312 billion.[19]

In 1965, McDonald's offered its stock for the first time to the public. "A hundred shares of stock costing $2,250 dollars would [have been] worth over $1.8 million on December 31, 2003."[20] During this time period, McDonald's expanded its system from a few hundred restaurants to more than 25,000 restaurants.

Habit 6. Build Ownership

Business owners and employees are paid very differently. For example,

Paul Allen was one of the original founders and owners of Microsoft. In 1983, he left his full-time employment position after being diagnosed with Hodgkin's disease. Had he simply been an employee and quit his job, his income would have stopped, but this was not the case for Paul Allen. As an owner, he continued to receive profit from Microsoft, even after he resigned. Since his resignation in 1983, he has collected billions of dollars as a result of his ownership in Microsoft, and he continues to receive millions in profit each year.

The differences in compensation for owners and employees can be compared to owning or renting a house. Let's say you rent a $100,000 house paying $700 per month for 10 years (120 months). At the end of the 10 years, the owner sells the house for $200,000. The renter had paid $70,000 in rent and the property appreciated $100,000 in value during the 10 years to $200,000. How much money does the renter get when the house is sold? $0. How much does the owner receive? The owner received payments of $70,000 over the ten years and the capital gain of $100,000 from the sale of the property. When you rent a home or work as an employee, you are building equity for the owner of the property or business. By becoming an owner, you can start building equity for yourself instead of for others.

CONCLUSION

Developing the habits of successful entrepreneurs can dramatically increase your income and net worth. Studies of millionaires have found that "the business owner category is the largest group in the millionaire population."[21] The average individual income in America in 2005 was $36,286 [22] while the national average income for a business owner was $258,400.[23] "Success in business requires training and discipline and hard work. But if you're not frightened by these things, the opportunities are just as great today as they ever were."[24]

You must be wise in developing the required entrepreneurial skills and business plan before beginning a business. Seek the counsel of successful business owners. Remember the counsel of the Savior, "For which of you, intending to build a tower [or business], does not sit down first and count the cost, whether he has enough to finish it."[25] After developing a plan, you should pray for guidance. Once you have received an inward assurance that you should begin your own business, do it.

TRUTH 21

You Can Succeed at Creating a Successful Business.

MYTH 22

I Do Not Need Corporations or Trusts

Many legal and financial advisors, practicing outside their realm of expertise, falsely teach that corporations are only for big business and trusts are only for those who are very wealthy. There are more than 1 million practicing lawyers in America, and less than 1 percent claim asset protection as one of their specialties. As a result of so few asset protection attorneys, many do not know the benefits corporation and trusts offer and that these benefits can be used by practically anyone.

Working with America's top asset protection experts, I have helped thousands of clients achieve financial peace of mind through properly structuring their assets for tax reduction, lawsuit protection, and estate planning. It is vital to learn how to keep and protect the assets you work hard to accumulate. I am currently under contract to not teach these principles. Once my contract expires, this chapter will be available as a special report called "How to Achieve Financial Peace of Mind Through Asset Protection." From this special report, you will learn strategies most advisors are unaware of including:

- How to legally save up to 40 percent in income taxes each year.
- How to protect 100 percent of your professional and personal assets from a lawsuit.
- Legal strategies that eliminate 100 percent of capital gains tax on the sale of real estate, a business, or other assets.
- Tools you can use to pass assets to your heirs taxfree.
- How to use asset protection entities (C-Corporations, S-Corporations, LLCs, Trusts, Limited Partnerships) to achieve your financial goals.

To receive this chapter at no charge, go to
www.DoesYourBagHaveHoles.org
and click on the Free Special Reports link.

TRUTH 22

Proper Use of Corporations and Trusts Can Dramatically Increase Your Income and Net Worth.

CHOICE 6:
GREED OR CHARITY

"Money is like manure. If you spread it around it does a lot of good.
But if you pile it up in one place it stinks like hell."
–Junior Murchison

Money Is Bad

Many people believe that money is bad. The truth is money, in and of itself, is not good or evil. You could put a billion dollars into a room and it would never do anything good or bad. Money is good or bad depending on the person who possesses it. A person's personality and character are magnified by their use of money. C.S. Lewis taught, "Surely what a man does when he is taken off his guard is the best evidence for what sort of a man he is? Surely what pops out before the man has time to put on a disguise is the truth? If there are rats in a cellar you are most likely to see them if you go in very suddenly. But the suddenness does not create the rats; it only prevents them from hiding. In the same way the suddenness of the provocation does not make me an ill-tempered man: it only shows me what an ill-tempered man I am."[1] Likewise, money does not create greed, pride, or any other negative trait. It simply magnifies a person's character to a point where their strengths and weakness cannot be hidden.

Thus, it is not virtuous to be poor, nor is it virtuous to be rich. It is virtuous to be virtuous. Money is a tool that expands our ability to do both good and evil in the world. For example, the invention of the printing press has enabled us to mass produce positive materials such as the Bible. On the other hand, it has also increased the availability of pornography. The printing press by itself is neither good nor evil. Good people utilize the printing press to improve society. Bad people use the printing press to degrade society. This same analogy can be applied to the television, radio, telephone, Internet, and other advances in technology. With each advance, our ability to do both good and evil increases. Money, like all tools, is good or bad as a result of how it is utilized.

What Makes Money Good or Bad?

"A hammer is a tool. If one learns to use it well, a house can be built. If one doesn't use it well there will be many broken and bruised and very painful thumbs." –Lloyd Porter

If having wealth increases our power to do evil, is the solution to not be rich? Of course not. This solution would be as silly as doing away with the printing press and Internet because of pornography. Some are concerned about obtaining wealth, fearing that it will corrupt them. This would be similar to saying, "I am not going to get married, because I don't want to commit adultery." While it is true if no one were to get married, there would not be any adultery. The solution to adultery is not to eliminate marriage. The solution is for people to be faithful to their marriage covenants. The same applies to money. The solution is not to eliminate wealth and abundance but for people to faithfully fulfill their financial stewardships. It is not the amount of money we have but our attitudes toward it and use of it that makes it good or bad.

Money is A Bad Tool When...	Money is A Good Tool When...
1. Trust in Money	1. Trust in God
2. Money First	2. God First
3. Do It for Yourself	3. Do It for God
4. Greed/Selfish	4. Charity/Sharing
5. Achieved by Immoral Means	5. Achieved by Honorable Means
6. My Money	6. God's Money

1. Trust in Money vs. Trust in God

One source often used to support the myth that money is bad comes from misunderstanding the following New Testament story: "And a certain ruler asked him, saying, Good Master, what shall I do to inherit eternal life? And Jesus said unto him …. sell all that thou hast, and distribute unto the poor, and thou shalt have treasure in heaven: and come, follow me. And when he heard this, he was very sorrowful: for he was very rich. And when Jesus saw that he was very sorrowful, he said, How hardly shall they that have riches enter into the kingdom of God! For it is easier for a camel to go through a needle's eye, than for a rich man to enter into the kingdom of God."[2]

Many have misunderstood this, believing that it is hard for rich people to go to heaven. This is not the case. In answer to the apostles' question, "Who then can be saved?"[3] Jesus clarifies what he meant by saying, "How hard is it for them that **trust in riches** to enter into the kingdom of God!"[4] Christ was not teaching that riches are bad but that trusting in riches is bad. The Bible also says, "Blessed be ye poor, for yours is the kingdom of God."[5] Does this mean people are going to heaven simply because of small bank accounts? Of course not. To say it is hard for the rich to go to heaven would be as silly as saying it is easy for the poor to go to heaven. Our admittance to heaven is not dependant on our net worth. Whether you are rich or poor, you must "trust … in the living God"[6] to go to heaven.

God is not going to keep anyone out of heaven because he or she had wealth. The Bible teaches, "Thou shalt remember the LORD thy God: for it is he that giveth thee power to get wealth."[7] Many men of God have been rich. The Bible tells us Abraham "was very rich in cattle, silver, and in gold"[8] and that Isaac "became rich, and gained more and more until he became very wealthy. He had possessions of flocks and herds and many servants."[9] The Bible also tells us of one of Jesus' rich disciplines saying, "A rich man of Arimathaea, named Joseph, who also himself was Jesus' disciple."[10] Riches are a righteous desire when we trust in God.

2. Money First vs. God First

Near the end of my junior year in college, I received two job offers. Both required one year commitments and were full-time during the summer and part-time positions during the school year. The first job was to write and teach about Christ-centered leadership at the university I was attending. The second was a corporate management and training job, which paid $48,000 more per year than the offer from the university. My family and friends suggested I would be crazy not to take the higher paying job. If the decision was only based on money, the corporate job would have been an easy choice.

I went to the Lord in prayer and asked which job He would like me to take. The answer came to take the job with the university and the scripture came to my mind, "Seek ye first the kingdom of God, and his righteousness; and all these things [earthly possessions] shall be added unto you."[11] Exercising faith and an attitude of "What would God have me do?" I took the job at the university.

Whether we realize it or not, we each have a top priority in our life. Some of the things people center their lives around are God, family, money, work, possessions, friends, church, and self. What we make our top priority affects how we live, act, and see the world. True prosperity, success, and happiness come when God is at the center of our lives—when He is our number one priority. The Lord said, "If any man come to me, and hate not his father, and mother, and wife, and children, and brethren and sisters, yea, and his own life also, he cannot be my disciple."[12] Is the Lord teaching us that families are bad and that anyone who loves his family cannot be his disciple? Of course not. In this scripture, the Lord teaches an important principle: we must always put God first. "If you let important responsibilities like family, work, and money become the center of your attention instead of God—if you concentrate on them too much or too long—you will soon lose your ability to relate to God, and life will become meaningless."[13]

Our families, our jobs, and the numerous pleasures of life are all good things when we put God first. However, if anything other than God becomes the center our lives, we have lost the focus that will bring us true happiness, joy, and prosperity. Having a family is good unless it replaces God as the center of our lives. Money is good unless it replaces God as our number one priority. To say that having money is bad would be as foolish as saying having a family, attending church, or working are bad. The scriptures do not say, "Money is the root of all evil." They say, "The **love** of money is the root of all evil."[14] When you put money first—when it becomes your center and motive for what you do—then money will produce negative results. When God is at the center of our lives, money is good and desirable. When we put God first, wealth will not have a negative impact on us.

3. Do It for Yourself vs. Do It for God

Many have compartmentalized God and money as two unrelated portions of their lives, believing that God and money are unrelated and not to be discussed in the same context. I have seen this in my businesses as good Christian employees are uncomfortable when I start company meetings with prayer or seek divine guidance for answers to business problems and challenges. I also receive complaints when I give sermons on topics related to money receiving such comments as, "We should not talk about money at church." "The relative absence of sermons about money—which the Bible mentions several thousands times—is one of the more stunning omissions in American religion… There has long been a taboo on talking candidly about money."[15]

Many have taken God out of their jobs and the portions of their life related to money. The truly prosperous have learned to include God in all their actions, even those involving money. In the eyes of God, the world is not compartmentalized into temporal and spiritual for all things are spiritual to Him. "There is one God and Father of everything. He rules everything and is everywhere and is in everything."[16]

We must learn to involve God in everything we do. The Lord has commanded us to work and provide for ourselves and our families. The Lord said to Adam, "In the sweat of your face you shall eat bread, till you return to the ground."[17] The apostle Paul taught, "But if any provide not for his own, and specially for those of his own house, he hath denied the faith, and is worse than an infidel."[18] We should do all our work for the love of God, and He will guide and strengthen our performance.

A 17th century cook learned to do his work not for himself but for God. He began each day with this prayer, "'O my God, since Thou art with me, and I must now, in obedience to Thy commands, apply my mind to these outward things, I beseech Thee to grant me the grace to continue in Thy presence; and to this end do Thou prosper me with Thy assistance.'. . . In his business in the kitchen (to which he had naturally a great aversion), having accustomed himself to do everything there for the love of God, and with prayer . . . to do his work well, he found everything easy, during fifteen years that he had been employed there."[19] He said of his work as a cook, "'The time of business does not with me differ from the time of prayer; and in the noise and clutter of my kitchen, while several persons are at the same time calling for different things, I possess God in as great tranquility as if I were upon my knees at the blessed sacrament'. . . The foundation of the spiritual life in him had been . . . that he might perform all his actions for the love of God."[20]

As Sam Walton, founder of Wal-Mart, neared the end of his life, dying of cancer, he reflected on his life's work and wondered if he should have spent his time doing something else to improve the world.

He wondered if he made the right choice to invest so much time in building Wal-Mart. After much thought, he concluded that his work at Wal-Mart was his life ministry—that through his retail business, he was able to improve and bless the lives of others. He wrote, "Preachers are put here to minister to our souls; doctors to heal our diseases; teachers to open up our minds; and so on. Everybody has their role to play. The thing is, I am absolutely convinced that the only way we can improve one another's quality of life … is through what we call free enterprise—practiced correctly and morally… We've improved the standard of living of our customers, whom we've saved billions of dollars, and of our associates, who have been able to share profits … those companies out there who aren't… focusing on the customers' interest are just going to get lost… Those who get greedy are going to be left in the dust. [Business must] benefit the workers, the stockholders, the communities, and of course, management, which must adopt a philosophy of servant leadership."[21]

"Today we often feel we must 'get away' from our daily routine in order to worship God, but … worship [is] not an event to attend, but a perpetual attitude."[22] Our jobs and businesses should be driven by service and viewed as an ever-unfolding and expanding ministry. What we do, we should do for God. The apostle Paul taught, "Do your work heartily, as for the Lord rather than for men."[23]

4. Greed/Selfish vs. Charity/Sharing

Greed and selfishness are things each of us must guard against. The Savior has warned us saying, "Watch out! Be on your guard against all kinds of greed."[24] Greed is an unsatisfiable desire. The Bible teaches that, "Greedy dogs … can never have enough"[25] and "Whoever loves money never has money enough; whoever loves wealth is never satisfied with his income."[26] No matter how much a greedy person has it will never be enough.

The Savior gave two parables warning against greed and the hoarding of our possessions: "And he told them this parable: The ground of a certain rich man produced a good crop. He thought to himself, 'What shall I do? I have no place to store my crops.' Then he said, 'This is what I'll do. I will tear down my barns and build bigger ones, and there I will store all my grain and my goods. . . But God said to him, 'You fool! This very night your life will be demanded from you.'"[27] The Savior also told the following parable. "There was a rich man who was dressed in purple and fine linen and lived in luxury every day. At his gate was laid a beggar named Lazarus, covered with sores and longing to eat what fell from the rich man's table. . . The time came when the beggar died and the angels carried him to Abraham's side. The rich man also died [and was taken to hell]."[28]

Is the message from these parables that rich people go to hell? Of course not. If this was the case, Abraham would not have been in heaven, for he was a very rich man on earth. The rich man was sent to hell not for being rich, but for denying the beggar food and not giving of his money. The message is not that riches are bad, but that greed and selfishness are bad. Wealth and riches are good when they are used to build the kingdom of God and care for His children. Wealth allows you to cloth the naked, feed the hungry, and nourish the sick. As disciples of Christ, we should be filled with a love that will motivate us to use our riches to care for the needs of our fellowman.

5. Achieved by Immoral Means vs. Achieved by Honorable Means

If we violate a law of God to obtain money, that money is bad. Money obtained by theft, bribery, false advertising, excessive charges, exploiting employees,[29] or from the sale of gambling, pornography, harmful drugs, or other sinful practices is what the Bible calls filthy lucre.[30] Money acquired through the violation of divine law is never worth its cost. The Savior taught, "For what is a man profited, if he shall gain the whole world, and lose his own soul? Or what shall a man give in exchange for his soul?"[31]

The Lord expects us to be honest and treat others fairly in our work and financial duties. The Bible teaches that as we follow the laws of God, we will be blessed. "Do not let this Book of the Law depart from your mouth; meditate on it day and night, so that you may be careful to do everything written in it. Then you will be prosperous and successful."[32]

6. My Money vs. God's Money

"Always remember that your lives, your ability, the food you eat, the water you drink, the clothes you wear, the earth you tread, the air you breathe, are all the Lord's. . . Then, whether you are rich or poor will make no difference. . . You will look upon yourselves as stewards, and if you have a hundred dollars in your hands, you will say, this is the Lord's, and if He wants it, He can have it. If you have a million dollars, you will feel the same. And where people have this feeling, riches cannot hurt them."[33]

We are often caught up in the "mine, mine, mine" mentality, allowing greed and selfishness into our hearts. Once we can say, "It is the Lord's" instead of, "It is mine," we are freed from the attachment to treasures which can be corrupted by rust or taken by thieves.[34]

MONEY IS IMPORTANT

Some say that money is not important at all. Money is not most important in our lives, but it is important. Money enables the fulfillment of needs, the needs of others, and to fulfill life's missions. We all have the following six needs of life, and money plays a key role in fulfilling each of these needs.

THE 6 NEEDS OF LIFE
1. Survival
2. Security
3. Family and Friends
4. Personal Growth
5. Charity and Service
6. Recreation

1. Survival

Food, water, clothes, and shelter are necessary to stay alive. Each of these needs cost money.

2. Security

Our need for security can be fulfilled with money. A person who is without debt and has money set a side for emergencies will feel much more security than the person who has debt, can barely pay the bills, and has no extra funds for possible expenditures that might arise, such as car repairs or medical expenses.

3. Family and Friends

Money can assist us in fulfilling our need for family and friends by enabling us to spend more time with them instead of having to work all the time. Money certainly matters when your children have sporting events or music recitals you have to miss because you can't take off work due to financial obligations.

4. Personal Growth

My son began preschool at the age of 4 and his learning and growth has been amazing to watch. It requires money each month for me to pay for his tuition. As I have taken on the challenge of writing this book, I have attended seminars and purchased books about writing and publishing to help me learn and grow. If I did not have money, these options would not have been available.

5. Charity and Service

"Most of us would like to make a positive impact on the lives of others and on our world. If we do not feel that this is in some way happening, we tend to experience a sense of emptiness, low self-worth, futility, and sometimes even depression."[35] We each have been given special gifts and talents from God, which only we possess. There are specific ways in which each of us are to contribute to society. To help people discover their mission I have them answer this question: "If you had unlimited time and money, what would you do?" Before you read on, answer this question for yourself.

I believe everyone is born with a God-given mission they are to perform. Many people do not fulfill their mission because they never have the time or money to do so. These people are too busy making a living to make a difference. They work their entire lives just to meet their survival needs and then die without fulfilling their missions. Talents are not developed and utilized to improve the world because they were too busy focusing on surviving. God did not send us to earth to be born, pay the bills, and die. God sent us here for a purpose. Don't die with your mission still in you. Leave a legacy.

6. Recreation

Life is best enjoyed when we take time for recreation. Thomas Jefferson taught, "Leave all the afternoon for exercise and recreation, which are as necessary as . . . learning." "People who cannot find time for recreation are obliged sooner or later to find time for illness."[36] Recreation is a source of renewal and rejuvenation that will increase our efficiency and productivity on other tasks. One of my favorite recreational activities is golf—golf clubs and green fees come with an expense. Family vacations are a great form of recreation, which many are unable to enjoy because they don't have the money.

Can Money Buy Happiness?

I often hear people say, "Money can't buy happiness." This is a bad argument. It is like saying, "Money can't buy modesty" or "Money can't buy wisdom." Ultimately, these statements are true because modesty, wisdom, and happiness are not purchasable items. So it is true that money can't buy modesty, but it can buy clothes. Money can't buy wisdom, but it can buy books and education. Money can't buy happiness, but it can help you fulfill your life's needs, bringing you increased happiness. Research has shown that "financially independent people are happier than those in their same income/age cohort who are not financially secure."[37]

Someone once said to me, "We don't have a lot of money, but we are happy. You have a lot of money, so remember that money can't buy happiness." This person was worried that my money was going to make me unhappy. I responded by saying, "I understand what you are saying, but poverty won't buy happiness either." Happiness is not a result of riches or poverty, and there are varying degrees of happiness. Happiness comes as needs are fulfilled and by simply making the personal decision to be happy. I was happy when I was poor, and I am still happy now that my income has increased. With increased income, I have been able to fulfill more personal and family needs, which have resulted in increased degrees of happiness.

Money Gives You Options

Around each of us is a financial cage. This cage determines what we can and cannot do or buy. One person may have a $30,000 a year cage, another may have a $100,000 a year cage, and another may have a $10 million a year cage. Each cage has limitations. The larger the cage, the more options a person has. A person may want to go and spend a week in Australia, but if he or she can't afford it, it is not an option. A dad may want to spend time during the day with his children, but if he can't afford time off, then it is not an option. A person may want to retire to do missionary work, but if he or she can't afford it, then it is not an option. Money gives you options. If you have little money, your decisions as to what to eat, where to live, and the vacations to take will all be greatly influenced by cost. Decisions will not necessarily be based on what is best, but on what you can afford.

Money is important and allows us to fulfill our needs and bless the lives of others. Increased options and freedoms are available because of money. Money offers the option and freedom to spend time with family and provide your children with high-quality education. It is freedom to live in the home of your dreams and to take the vacations of your dreams. You will be able to give volunteer service in your church and community and to donate to causes that improve humanity.

One of my millionaire mentors shared with me the following story:

A while ago I was in the process of adopting a baby. The mother had been located, and we were set to adopt the baby as soon as it was born. The mother had some complications, and the baby was born prematurely. The adoption agency gave me the option of canceling my deal with them. They said, "We promised you a healthy baby, so if you want to back out, that will be ok. Don't feel guilty if you want to walk away." I responded, "What are you talking about? How could I walk away from my baby?"

At the same time, there was another couple adopting, and their baby was born early as well. They were given the same option to cancel the deal. Much to my surprise, they cancelled the deal and walked away. I remember thinking, "Why would they walk away from this baby? When the going gets tough, they simply leave. What cowards."

My thinking suddenly changed when I saw the couple crying. I quickly repented for my hasty judgment. They desperately wanted the baby. However, they simply could not pay the increased insurance premiums, the deductible, or the 20 percent co-pay. They could not afford the additional cost associated with a premature baby and had to walk away. As I watched this couple, there was no doubt that if they had more money, they would have taken the baby. With God as my witness, I never once thought about the money when I was making my decision. Because I had the needed money available, my decision was based on what was best for the baby, what was best for the birth mom, and what was best for my wife and children. I could focus on doing what was right in the sight of God, not in doing what I could afford. Money never entered into the picture as I considered my options. However, the options available to this other couple were extremely limited, because they lacked the needed money.

It is not riches that make a person greedy but the motives for and use of the riches. We should each strive to cultivate the proper attitudes toward the creation and management of earthly riches. The Lord said, "If you have not been faithful with riches of this world, who will trust you with true riches?"[38] A faithful steward is one who uses his or her time, talents, and resources to produce the greatest amount of good for his family, fellowman, and the kingdom of God.

TRUTH 23

Money Is Good When Obtained by Honorable Means and Used to Build the Kingdom of God.

MYTH 24

THAT'S THEIR BUSINESS, NOT MINE

In 1955, Emmett Till, a 14-year-old African American boy from Chicago, went to visit his relatives in the small town of Money, Mississippi. The racial climate in Chicago was much different from that in Mississippi, where racial tension was high and racial hate crimes were common. On August 27, Emmett was kidnapped by two white men who brutally beat him, breaking his wrists, legs, and skull. The two men eventually shot Emmett in the head and threw him into the Tallahatchie River with a seventy-five pound cotton gin fan tied to his neck with barbed wire. Emmett's body was found three days later by two fishermen. Emmett's mother, Mamie, requested that the body be returned to Chicago. The State of Mississippi carried out Mamie's request and sent her son's body, with orders that the Chicago funeral home was not to open the sealed casket. Mamie insisted on seeing her son and collapsed at the sight of his severely damaged body. Emmett was buried September 6th in the Burr Oak Cemetery outside of Chicago. The same day Roy Bryant and J.W. Milam were indicted for his murder.

Shortly after his death, Emmett's mother said, "Two months ago I had a nice apartment in Chicago. I had a good job. I had a son. When something happened to the Negroes in the South I said, 'That's their business, not mine.' Now I know how wrong I was. The murder of my son has shown me that what happens to any of us, anywhere in the world, had better be the business of us all."[1]

CIRCLE OF RESPONSIBILITY

In a Bible study class I teach, I offer a reward for the person who comes closest to the population of the world. The answers received are written on the board, and I instruct the audience that none of them are even close and ask them to open their New Testament and read the following parable of the sheep and the goats:

> And before him shall be gathered all nations: and he shall separate them one from another, as a shepherd divideth his sheep from the goats: And he shall set the sheep on his right hand, but the goats on the left. Then shall the King say unto them on his right hand, Come, ye blessed of my Father, inherit the kingdom prepared for you from the foundation of the world: For I was an hungred, and ye gave me meat: I was thirsty, and ye gave me drink: I was a stranger, and ye took me in: Naked, and ye clothed me: I was sick, and ye visited me: I was in prison, and ye came unto me. Then shall the righteous answer him, saying, Lord, when saw we thee an hungred, and fed thee? or thirsty, and gave thee drink? When saw we thee a stranger, and took thee in? or naked, and clothed thee? Or when saw we thee sick, or in prison, and came unto thee? And the King shall answer and say unto them, Verily I say unto you, Inasmuch as ye have done it unto one of the least of these my brethren, ye have done it unto me. Then shall he say also unto them on the left hand, Depart from me, ye cursed, into everlasting fire, prepared for the devil and his angels: For I was an hungred, and ye gave me no meat: I was thirsty, and ye gave me no drink: I was a stranger, and ye took me not in: naked, and ye clothed me not: sick, and in prison, and ye visited me not. Then shall they also answer him, saying, Lord, when saw we thee an hungred, or athirst, or a stranger, or naked, or sick, or in prison, and did not minister unto thee? Then shall he answer them, saying, Verily I say unto you, Inasmuch as ye did it not to one of the least of these, ye did it not to me.[2]

After reading these passages, I again ask, "What is the population of the world?" The answer eventually comes back as two. The population of the world is not 6.6 billion but two—Christ and you. The parable of the goats and the sheep is given to inspire us to live as if there were only Christ and you in the world. We must work to feed the hungry, cloth the naked, and bring comfort to the sick, lonely, and imprisoned.

If Christ was the victim of a natural disaster, would you help Him? If Christ was in a public school which destroyed moral values, would you help Him? If Christ was living in a neighborhood that was unsafe or unhealthy, would you help him? If Christ was starving in a foreign country, would you help him? Our circle of responsibility increases as we recognize the spiritual reality that we are our brothers' keeper. When we serve our fellowman, we are in the direct service of God. When we do not help our fellowman, we have directly neglected God.

If you are to be found as sheep on the right hand of God, you must be vigorously engaged in the improvement of your family, communities, country, and world. If there is a violation of biblical principles at work, you should do what you can to correct them. If your town is polluted with drugs or pornography, you should work to eliminate them. If there are politicians violating the constitution, you must labor to bring about change.

History has provided numerous examples showing the power of people who were engaged in a good cause. For example, Edward Jenner and Benjamin Jesty were involved with the creation and use of the smallpox vaccination. Before vaccination, "smallpox was responsible for an estimated 300–500 million deaths in the 20th century. As recently as 1967, the World Health Organization estimated that 15 million people contracted the disease and that 2 million died in that year. After successful vaccination campaigns throughout the 19th and 20th centuries, the World Health Organization certified the eradication of smallpox in 1979."[3]

In 1952, there were 3,145 Americans who died of polio. In 1955, a doctor named Jonas Salk invented a vaccine for polio. "By 1993 the number of U.S. cases of polio—not deaths, but cases—was three.

Moreover, typhoid fever, small pox, tuberculosis, and many other diseases have either disappeared or occur far less frequently than they did even 50 years ago."[5]

Smallpox used to wipe out whole communities. It is now a thing of the past. It was not that long ago that polio took thousands of lives. It is now a thing of the past. It used to be legal for one person to own another person. Slavery is now a thing of the past. If we can eliminate the devastating effects of polio, smallpox, and slavery, surely through an inspired, energetic effort we can eliminate the current diseases of poverty, hunger, pornography, drugs and child abuse that plague our world. What will you do to make these diseases a thing of the past?

Application Ideas for Circle of Responsibility

Hopefully, these ideas and questions have sparked a desire to improve your family, neighborhood, community, nation, and the world. Fill out the following table to identify what concerns you have and what you can do to make a difference.

CIRCLE OF RESPONSIBILITY TABLE™		
CIRCLES OF RESPONSIBILITY	WHAT IS YOUR CONCERN?	WHAT WILL YOU DO?
Family		
Neighborhood		
Community		
Nation		
World		

Since all things belong to the Lord, we are not owners of our wealth, possessions, and property but are stewards for the Lord. "We are the mere trustees of what funds we are temporarily given on this earth."[5] We will be accountable to the Lord for how we manage this stewardship.

Businessman and philanthropist Andrew Carnegie stated, "This, then, is held to be the duty of the man of wealth: First, to set an example of modesty, unostentatious living, shunning display, or extravagance; to provide moderately for the legitimate wants of those dependent upon him; and after doing so to consider all surplus revenues which come to him simply as trust funds, which he is called upon to administer, and strictly bound as a matter of duty to administer in the manner which, in his judgment, is best calculated to produce the most beneficial results for the community."[6]

Thomas Jefferson said, "I deem it the duty of every man to devote a certain portion of his income for charitable purposes; and that it is his further duty to see it so applied as to do the most good of which it is capable."[7] "Charity is the salt which keeps wealth from corruption."[8]

Jon Huntsman, founder of Huntsman Chemical, showed that he understands the stewardship of money when he said, "The Lord has tapped me on the shoulder and said, 'To you, my son, I am entrusting large amounts of money. You determine best how you can redeploy these assets into the community of humankind around you.'. . . Over the years we've spent a lot of money on homelessness and feeding the poor. . . I received a letter recently . . . all it said was Homeless Shelter. The letter read: 'Dear Mr. Huntsman. I am warm and dry and out of the cold of last night, and I had a real bed to sleep on. I know you sent some money to keep this shelter, where I am staying, alive. I arose knowing I would shower with warm water and have soap and shampoo and a clean towel to use. Maybe this humble letter does not, or will not mean much within the vastness of the universe, but for this moment in time I just wanted to say with all my heart, thank you. For it means to me a great deal, to this homeless woman a great deal indeed. Thank you.' I've had that letter framed, not because it's important to receive recognition for gifts, but because it's important to know the feeling in the hearts of people when they are down and out and receive help."[9]

We are to give a percent of our income each year to care for those in need, such as feeding the hungry, clothing the naked, administering to the sick, and "to look after orphans and widows."[10] What percent should we give for these purposes? Jon Huntsman suggests, "There is no set formula, but I would hold that the excess over and above one's guidelines for a comfortable standard of living is a reasonable starting point. . . We don't need millions of dollars to live comfortably."[11] C.S. Lewis provided this insight: "If our expenditure on comforts, luxuries, amusements, etc., is up to the standard common among those with the same income as our own, we are probably giving away too little. If our charities do not at all pinch or hamper us, I should say they are too small. There ought to be things we should like to do and cannot do because our charitable expenditure excludes them."[12] In the words of St. Augustine, "Find out how much God has given you and from it take what you need: the remainder is needed by others."

Parable of Greater Barns

Jesus spoke to the people saying, "'Take care, and be on your guard against all covetousness, for one's life does not consist in the abundance of his possessions.' And he told them a parable, saying, 'The land of a rich man produced plentifully, and he thought to himself, 'What shall I do, for I have nowhere to store my crops?' And he said, 'I will do this: I will tear down my barns and build larger ones, and there I will store all my grain and my goods. And I will say to my soul, Soul, you have ample goods laid up for many years; relax, eat, drink, be merry.' But God said to him, 'Fool! This night your soul is required of you, and the things you have prepared, whose will they be?' So is the one who lays up treasure for himself and is not rich toward God."[13]

The foolish rich man made two mistakes. One, he didn't give of his abundance to lift others, and two, he didn't produce all he could. Once he had enough for himself, he became idle, saying, "I have enough. I will now relax and eat, drink, and be merry." In doing God's work, you never retire. We must always work to move forth the kingdom of God. Abundance is about production, not consumption. We are not to simply produce as much as we need, but we are to produce as much as we can and use the excess to lift our fellow man and build the Kingdom of God. The gospel of Christ moves us past the focus of only providing for our needs to becoming abundantly productive so that we have surplus to serve others.

Jon Huntsman continued to work even after he became a billionaire. He wrote, "For the past 20 years, we concentrated on making money so we could give it away."[14] David Green, founder of Hobby Lobby, continues to work even with companies doing more than $2 billion in annual sales. He wrote, "God didn't put any of us here to sit on a yacht... In order to keep giving, we need to keep growing Hobby Lobby and its affiliate companies. This is what energizes my day-to-day work in retailing now—the knowledge that if we can add stores and thereby boost profits, we can give away that much more to make a difference eternally."[15]

The goal of producing is not to lift ourselves above others but to lift all to a higher level. The Lord doesn't want a few of His children to live in abundance; he wants all His children to live in abundance. We should strive to work toward the state found among the followers of Christ in the New Testament where "all the believers were one in heart and mind. No one claimed that any of his possessions was his own, but they shared everything they had. . . There were no needy persons among them."[16]

GIVE MORE AND YOU'LL HAVE MORE

"We make a living by what we earn—we make a life by what we give."
—Winston Churchill

"Giving does not cause you to have less, but in fact guarantees that ultimately you will have more."[17] For example, the Old Testament

-263-

prophet Elijah found a widow who was gathering sticks to prepare her family's final meal, possessing only a handful of flour and a small amount of oil. Elijah said to the widow, "'First make me a little cake of it and bring it to me, and afterward make something for yourself and your son. For thus says the LORD the God of Israel, 'The jar of flour shall not be spent, and the jug of oil shall not be empty, until the day that the LORD sends rain upon the earth.' And she went and did as Elijah said. And she and he and her household ate for many days. The jar of flour was not spent, neither did the jug of oil become empty, according to the word of the LORD that he spoke by Elijah."[18]

The Lord has promised that if we give to Him, he will pour upon us blessings saying, "All who have given up home . . . or land for me will be given a hundred times as much."[19] "If we will share what we have, many peoples' lives can be blessed, and what we have left will grow at a geometric rate."[20] "Whatever you want more of, give some of it away."[21] "If you give to others, you will be given . . . in return."[22]

Tithing
"Honor the LORD by giving him your money and the first part of all your crops. Then you will have more grain and grapes than you will ever need."
—Proverbs 3:9–10, Contemporary English Version

We are to give 10 percent of our annual income as a tithe to the Lord. The book of Genesis tells of Abraham paying tithing to Melchizedek: "Then Abram gave Melchizedek a tenth of everything."[23] Jacob promised the Lord he would pay tithing saying, "Of all that you give me I will give you a tenth."[24] Moses received the following command to tithe while on Mount Sinai: "A tithe of everything from the land . . . belongs to the LORD. . . Thou shalt truly tithe all the increase of thy seed, that the field bringeth forth year by year."[25]

The Lord promises to pour upon us His blessings as we pay our tithe saying, "'Bring the whole tithe into the storehouse, that there may be food in my house. Test me in this,' says the LORD Almighty, 'and see if I will not throw open the floodgates of heaven and pour out so much blessing that you will not have room enough for it. I will prevent pests from devouring your crops . . .' says the LORD Almighty."[26]

One of my mentors related to me the following story of a young widow of meager means with a large family to care for who went to her pastor to pay tithing. The pastor said to the widow, "It is not necessary for you to pay tithing; there are those who have an abundance that can support the work of the church." The widow replied to the pastor, "You ought to be ashamed of yourself. Would you deny me a blessing? If I did not pay my tithing, I should expect the Lord to withhold his blessings from me. I pay my tithing, not only because it is a law of God, but because I expect a blessing by doing it. By keeping this and other laws, I expect to prosper, and to be able to provide for my family."

Some argue that they can't afford to pay tithing. Those who understand the blessings that come from the payments of tithing say, "I can't afford not to pay tithing."

CONCLUSION

The Lord has poured upon us many blessings. We have a responsibility to bless and care for others. We must be among the engaged, not among the apathetic. Martin Niemoeller, a Lutheran pastor who was imprisoned in a Nazi concentration camp, wrote, "In Germany they came first for the Communists, and I didn't speak up because I wasn't a Communist. Then they came for the Jews, and I didn't speak up because I wasn't a Jew. Then they came for the trade unionists, and I didn't speak up because I wasn't a trade unionist. Then they came for the Catholics, and I didn't speak up because I was a Protestant. Then they came for me, and by that time no one was left to speak up."

When you stand before the judgment bar of Christ, He may ask: Did you bear the burdens of your neighbor? Did you heal and provide comfort to the sick and lonely? Did you instill virtue in your home, community, and nation? Did you use your time and money to lift and build others? Did you strive to build the kingdom of God? What joy will fill your heart and soul as you answer yes and hear the Lord say to you, "Well done, thou good and faithful servant . . . enter into my rest."[27]

Truth 24
"God Loves a Cheerful Giver."[28]

CONCLUSION

24 TRUTHS THAT LEAD TO FINANCIAL AND SPIRITUAL FREEDOM™

Mark Twain wrote, "It isn't what we don't know that kills us, it's everything we know that ain't so." "The great enemy of the truth is very often not the lie—deliberate, contrived, and dishonest—but the myth—persistent, persuasive, and unrealistic."[1] Many myths distort our views of money, life, and God. Hopefully this book has helped you replace such myths with truth. As you live the truths in this book, you will experience the joy of financial and spiritual freedom. The Savior taught, "And you shall know the truth, and the truth shall make you free."[2]

TRUTH 1

Faith is the moving cause of all action in intelligent beings and the process by which we gain power and knowledge.

TRUTH 2

If you put God last, you will go nowhere fast.

TRUTH 3

You are a child of God. Your Father in Heaven wants you to experience the joys of prosperity.

TRUTH 4

If each person produced to his or her potential, the world's needs would be satisfied with a great abundance.

TRUTH 5
Pain is inevitable and misery is optional.

TRUTH 6
We can choose our actions, but we cannot choose the consequences.

TRUTH 7
America was built on the foundation of divine law by wise and noble men inspired by the Almighty.

TRUTH 8
The U.S. constitution was founded upon the just and holy principles of the Almighty.

TRUTH 9
Government welfare violates the U.S. Constitution and the Lord's way of caring for those in need.

TRUTH 10
Free enterprise is the only economic system that recognizes our God-given rights of life, liberty, and the pursuit of happiness.

TRUTH 11
Happiness is a choice. Happiness does not depend on outward conditions but on inward decisions.

TRUTH 12
The blessings of prosperity are poured upon those capable of independent action—those who take the initiative.

Truth 13

Life should be a never-ending quest for improvement.

Truth 14

"He that is greatest among you shall be your servant."[3]

Truth 15

"The Godly walk with integrity."[4]

Truth 16

Religious ethics are the foundation for lasting and meaningful business success.

Truth 17

"I can do all things through Christ who strengthens me."[5]

Truth 18

Success is a process of learning and industry.

Truth 19

Failure is a part of learning. The formula for success is trying until you succeed.

Truth 20

The habits of saving and investing create a life of freedom, security, and peace.

Truth 21

You can succeed at creating a successful business.

Truth 22
Proper use of corporations and trusts can dramatically increase your income and net worth.

Truth 23
Money is good when obtained by honorable means and used to build the kingdom of God.

Truth 24
"God loves a cheerful giver."[6]

I will leave you will these final words. You are a child of God and as such the seeds of greatness are within you. The only thing that stands between where you are and where you want to be is time and effort. You decide what your life will be like. It doesn't matter what your past has been because you have the power to choose your future. Choose now to learn, change, and take the necessary actions to make your ideal a reality.

Now is the time to live a life of excellence by living the principles of prosperity. Now is the time to be responsible, humble, honest, industrious, thrifty, and charitable. Now is the time to live by these words from the Bible, "I can do all things through Christ who strengthens me."[7]

Your Father in Heaven wants you to experience the joys of prosperity and as you seek His help, God will give you inspiration and strength to achieve a life of financial and spiritual freedom. As you live God's truths, you will achieve happiness, independence, and peace. You will be prosperous.

True success and happiness are found in the teaching of the Bible and the Master Jesus Christ. I witness that the Bible is the inspired word of God and echo the words of John Adams who wrote, "I have examined all as well as ... my busy life would allow me and the result is that the Bible is the best book in the world. It contains more ...than all the libraries I have seen ..."[8]

Prosperity can be achieved with Christ as our pattern. All the perfect and beautiful qualities of maturity, strength, and courage are found in the Master Jesus Christ. He is the light and the life of the world and the foundation upon which if men and women will build they shall never fall. May God always be with you.

It is my prayer and hope that this book has been enjoyable and helpful to you. I would love to hear from you. Please tell me what you enjoyed about the book and how it has impacted your life.

Cameron C. Taylor
428 E. Thunderbird Road #504
Phoenix, AZ 85022
CameronTaylor@DoesYourBagHaveHoles.org

ENDNOTES

PREFACE

1 Psalm 119:105, King James Version

OVERVIEW

1 Deuteronomy 8:18, King James Version
2 Jon M. Huntsman, *Winners Never Cheat*, (Upper Saddle River, NJ: Wharton School Publishing, 2005) p. 12
3 Haggai 1:5–6, King James Version
4 C.S. Lewis, *Mere Christianity*, (New York: Simon & Schuster, 1996) p. 110
5 Matthew 23:28, King James Version
6 James 5:12, English Standard Version
7 Haggai 1:6, New International Version
8 Hyrum Smith, *The 10 Natural Laws of Successful Time and Life Management*, (New York: Warner Books, 1994) p. 203

MYTH 1

1 Acts 6:8, King James Version
2 Matthew 17:20, King James Version
3 Romans 10:17, King James Version
4 Hebrews 11:1, King James Version
5 Hebrews 11:1, King James Version
6 James 2:18, King James Version
7 1 Corinthians 15:17, King James Version
8 John 7:17, King James Version
9 Leon J. Cole, *The Delta of the St. Clair River*, (Lansing, MI: Robert Smith Printing Company, 1903) p. 196
10 Leon J. Cole, *The Delta of the St. Clair River*, (Lansing, MI: Robert Smith Printing Company, 1903) p. 197
11 Norman Wood, *Lives of Famous Indian Chiefs*, (Aurora, IL: American Indian Historical Publishing Company, 1906) p. 704–706
12 Matthew 9:2,6, bold added, King James Version
13 Matthew 9:20–22, bold added, King James Version
14 Matthew 9:27–30, bold added, King James Version
15 Matthew 7:7, King James Version
16 Steve Young, *Steve Young's Hall of Fame Send Off*, July 30, 2005

MYTH 2

1 St. Augustine; James Nichols, *The Works of James Arminius, D.D., Volume One*, (Auburn and Buffalo, NY: Derby, Miller and Orton, 1853) p. 526
2 Christopher Columbus, *Letter of Christopher Columbus to Rafael Sanchez*, (Chicago: W.H. Lowdermilk Co., 1893) p. 13–14
3 Matthew 6:11, King James Version
4 Matthew 6:12,14–15, King James Version

[5] David Noel Freedman, *The Anchor Bible Dictionary, Volume 6*, (New York: Double Day, 1992) p. 907
Walter A. Elwell, *Baker Encyclopedia of the Bible, Volume 1*, (Grand Rapids, MI: Baker Book House, 1988) p. 491 During the time of the New Testament, a talent was approximately 750 ounces of silver. A pence was approximately 1/8 of an ounce of silver. Thus, one talent equaled 6,000 pence (750 divided by 1/8). 10,000 talents were 60 million pence (10,000 multiplied by 6,000). One pence was the day wage of a laborer. To calculate the 2006 dollar value equivalents, I estimated the wage of a 2006 laborer at $50 per day ($6.25/hour for 8 hours) and multiplied that by the number of pence. Thus, 10,000 talents in the New Testament is equal to $3 billion in 2006 US currency (60,000,000 multiplied by $50) and 100 pence equals $5,000 in 2006 US currency (100 multiplied by $50).
[6] Matthew 18:28–30, King James Version
[7] Matthew 6:19
[8] Viktor E. Frankl, *Man's Search for Meaning*, (New York: Pocket Books, 1984) p. 163
[9] Matthew 10:39, King James Version
[10] Daniel Gross, *Forbes Greatest Business Stories of All Times*, (New York: John Wiley & Sons, 1996) p. 83
[11] Daniel Gross, *Forbes Greatest Business Stories of All Times*, (New York: John Wiley & Sons, 1996) p. 83–84

MYTH 3

[1] Luke 10:30–35
[2] James 4:2, King James Version
[3] Romans 8:26, King James Version
[4] James 4:3, King James Version
[5] Matthew 17:14–21, King James Version
[6] Matthew 7:9–11, King James Version
[7] Mathew 7:7, King James Version

MYTH 4

[1] The overall story is fictional but is based on several true stories.
[2] Genesis 1:20–21, 28, Genesis 9:7
[3] Stephen Budiansky, "10 Billion for Dinner, Please," *U.S. News & World Report*, 12 September 1994, p. 57–62
[4] Paul Pilzer, *God Wants You to Be Rich*, (New York: Simon & Schuster, 1995) p. 18–19
[5] Matthew 21:12–13, King James Version
[6] John 10:10, King James Version
[7] Stephen R. Covey, *Principle-Centered Leadership*, (New York: Simon & Schuster, 1991) p. 159
[8] Hyrum Smith, *The 10 Natural Laws of Successful Time and Life Management*, (New York: Warner Books, 1994) p. 201–202
[9] Harold C. Livesay, *American Made*, (New York: Pearson Longman, 2007) p. 269

[10] Bureau of Economic Analysis, U.S. Department of Commerce, Regional Economic Accounts, State Quarterly Personal Income, SQ1-Personal Income

[11] U.S. Department of Transportation, Federal Highway Administration, Exhibit 1.1 National Summary Statistics: 1960–2000

MYTH 5

[1] Job 1:1, King James Version

[2] Job 22:5, King James Version

[3] John 9:1–3, King James Version

[4] Harold S. Kushner, *When Bad Things Happen to Good People*, (New York: Avon Books, 1981) p. 58

[5] Matthew 5:45, Contemporary English Version

[6] C.S Lewis, *Mere Christianity*, (New York: Simon & Schuster, 1996) p. 176

[7] C.S. Lewis, *The Problem of Pain*, (New York: HarperCollins, 2001) p. 25

[8] John 15:2, New King James Version

[9] C.S. Lewis, *Mere Christianity*, (New York: Simon & Schuster, 1996) p. 176

[10] Philippians 1:6, New Century Version

[11] Hebrews 12:10, New International Version

[12] Hebrews 12:6, English Standard Version

[13] C.S. Lewis, *The Problem of Pain*, (New York: Macmillan, 1977) p. 93

[14] 2 Corinthians 11:24–26, Contemporary English Version

[15] Abraham Lincoln, Address at a Sanitary Fair, Baltimore, Maryland, April 18, 1864

[16] Matthew 5:10–11, Contemporary English Version

[17] Matthew 5:12, King James Version

[18] John McCain, *Why Courage Matters*, (New York: Random House, 2004) p. 91

[19] *Brother Lawrence*, (New York: Fleming H. Revell, 1895) p. 43

[20] Harold S. Kushner, *When Bad Things Happen to Good People*, (New York: Avon Books, 1981) p. 8–9

[21] Matthew 5:12

[22] John McCain, *Why Courage Matters*, (New York: Random House, 2004) p. 206

[23] Matthew 11:28–30, King James Version

[24] 2 Chronicles 32:7, New International Version

[25] 2 Timothy 4:7–8, King James Version

[26] Matthew 25:21, King James Version

MYTH 6

[1] The story from the beginning to the start of the conversion with the prison guard is an account from my memory of an experience I had teaching at a prison. The conversation with the prison guard to the end of the story are based on two true stories from the lives of two of my mentors. I felt the principles taught by these stories could best be told in the context of the prison encounter. Thus, from the prison guard to the conclusion of the story is fictional but is based on two true stories.

[2] Matthew 4:5–7, King James Version

³ Matthew 4:7, King James Version
⁴ John 8:34, New King James Version
⁵ Charles Hockema
⁶ Deuteronomy 11:26–28, King James Version

MYTH 7

¹ United States Constitution, Bill of Rights, Amendment I
² *Engel v. Board of Education*, 330 U.S. 1, 18 (1947); *Abington v. Schempp*, 374 U.S. 421 (1962); *Commissioner of Education v. School Committee of Leyden*, 267 N.E. 2d 226 (Mass. 1971), *cert. denied*, 404 U.S. 849
³ *Stone v. Graham*, 449 U.S. 39 (1980); *Ring v. Grand Forks Public School District*, 483 F. Sup. 272 (D.C. ND 1980); *Lanner v. Wimmer*, 662 F. 2d 1349 (10ᵗʰ Cir. 1991)
⁴ *McCreary County v. American Civil Liberties Union*; Forced removal of Ten Commandment display from the McCreary County, KY, courthouse
⁵ *Warsaw v. Tehachapi*, CV F-90-404 EDP (E.D. Ca. 1990)
⁶ *Roberts v. Madigan*, 702 F. Supp. 1505 (D. Colo. 1989), 921 F. 2d 1047 (10ᵗʰ Cir. 1990), *cert. denied*, 505 U.S. 1218 (1992)
⁷ *Allegheny v. American Civil Liberties Union*, 492 U.S. 573, 614 (1989)
⁸ *Iverson v. Forbes*, 93-3-232 (Or. Cir. Ct. 1993)
⁹ *Reidenback v. Pethtel*, 3:93CV632 (E.D. Va. 1993)
¹⁰ *Bebout v. Leimbaugh*, 93-C-1079 J (C.D. Ut. 1993)
¹¹ David Barton, *Original Intent*, (Aledo, TX: Wallbuilder Press, 2000) p. 16
¹² Message to the Knights of Columbus at a meeting held in Louisville, KY, on August 17, 1954
¹³ Melvin Ballard, Jr., "Religion in a Free Society," lecture delivered July 5, 1992, at America's Freedom Festival
¹⁴ E. B. Williston, *Eloquence of the United States, Volume II*, (Middletown, CT: E. & H. Clark, 1827) p. 414
¹⁵ Benjamin Franklin, *The Works of Benjamin Franklin, Volume XI*, (New York and London: G. P. Putnam's Sons, The Knickerbocker Press, 1904) p. 377
¹⁶ As I completed my writing on Washington, I was filled with the spirit testifying of the great and noble man of God he was. Words cannot do justice to describe one of the greatest men to walk the earth. I said a prayer of thanks. Thanking God for the inspiration and direction as I wrote about Washington and thanks for sending such a man to secure for me and all of this great country our liberty and freedom. What gratitude and honor should fill our hearts as we speak of and learn of the founders of our country. And what duty should fill our souls to diligently work to protect and preserve our liberty and freedom. We each should each pledge our lives and sacred honor to the work of freedom.
¹⁷ William H. Wilbur, *The Making of George Washington*, (DeLand, FL: Patriotic Education) p. 71
¹⁸ David Barton, *The Bulletproof George Washington*, (Aledo, TX: Wall Builders, 2003) p. 42

[19] John Frederick, *Life and Times of Washington, Volume I*, (Albany, NY: M. M. Belcher Publishing Co., 1903) p. 247–248

[20] Washington Irving, *Life of George Washington, Volume I*, (New York: G. P. Putnam and Son, 1869) p. 218

[21] John Warner Barber, *Thrilling Incidents in American History*, (New York: James Miller, 1868) p. 90

[22] Samuel Kercheval, *A History of the Valley of Virginia*, (Woodstock, VA: John Gatewood, 1850) p. 320

[23] Eugene Parsons, *George Washington: A Character Sketch*, Chicago: University Association, 1898) p. 30–31

[24] Matthew 23:11, King James Version

[25] *Orations of American Orators*, (New York: Colonial Press, 1900) p. 40

[26] *Orations of American Orators*, (New York: Colonial Press, 1900) p. 249–250

[27] Washington's daughter, Nelly Custis–Lewis, wrote in a letter dated February 26, 1833 that her father's mottos were, "Deeds, not words" and "For God and my country"; Jared Sparks, *The Writings of George Washington, Volume XII*, (Boston: American Stationers' Company, 1837) p. 407

[28] See Donald S. Lutz, "The Relative Influence of European Writers on Late Eighteenth-Century American Political Thought," *American Political Science Review*, LXXVIII (1984) p. 189–197

[29] Donald S. Lutz, *The Origins of American Constitutionalism*, (Baton Rouge, LA: Louisiana State University Press, 1988) p. 140–142

[30] Russ Walton, *Biblical Principles of Importance to Godly Christians*, (New Hampshire: Plymouth Foundation, 1984) p. 361

[31] Alan E. Sears, "Banning the Ten Commandments," Alliance Defense Fund, 2006

[32] Samuel W. Bailey, *Homage of Eminent Persons to THE BOOK*, (New York: 1871) p.12

[33] Samuel W. Bailey, *Homage of Eminent Persons to THE BOOK*, (New York: 1871) p. 13

[34] Ezra Benson, United States Secretary of Agriculture from January 21, 1953 to January 20, 1961

[35] Attributed to Alexis de Tocqueville but not found in his works.

MYTH 8

[1] U.S. Constitution Article 4, Section 4

[2] Jared Sparks, *The Writings of George Washington, Volume IX*, (Boston: Russel, Odiorne, and Metcalf and Hilliard, Gray, and Co., 1835) p. 317

[3] James Madison, *The Papers of James Madison, Volume II*, (Washington: Langtree & O'Sullivan, 1840) p. 718–719

[4] *A Collection of Essays by Alexander Hamilton John Jay and James Madison Interpreting the Constitution of the United States and Agreed Upon by the Federal Convention, September 17, 1787*, (New York: The Colonial Press, 1901) p. 195

[5] Paul Leicester Ford, *Essays on the Constitution of the United States*, (Brooklyn, NY: Historical Printing Club, 1892) p. 288

⁶ Paul Leicester Ford, *Essays on the Constitution of the United States*, (Brooklyn, NY: Historical Printing Club, 1892) p. 412

⁷ Constitution of the United States, article 6, section 2

⁸ United States Declaration of Independence

⁹ Ezra Benson, United States Secretary of Agriculture from January 21, 1953 to January 20, 1961

¹⁰ B. L. Rayner, *Life of Thomas Jefferson*, (Boston: Lilly, Wait, Colman & Holden, 1834) p. 37

¹¹ Alabama Constitution, Article 1, Section 35

¹² Upton Sinclair, Jack London, *The Cry for Justice*, (New York: Upton Sinclair, 1915) p. 305

¹³ From speech delivered by Woodrow Wilson on May 9, 1912

¹⁴ Ezra Benson, United States Secretary of Agriculture from January 21, 1953 to January 20, 1961

¹⁵ Thomas Jefferson, Albert Ellery Bergh, *The Writings of Thomas Jefferson Volume III*, (Washington, D.C.: Thomas Jefferson Memorial Association, 1903) p. 320–321

¹⁶ Bruce Smith, *Liberty and Liberalism*, (London: Longmans, Green and Co., 1887) p. 430

¹⁷ S. E. (Samuel Eagle) Forman, *The Life and Writings of Thomas Jefferson*, (Indianapolis: The Bowen-Merrill Company, 1900) p. 408–409

¹⁸ Isaiah 14:12–14, King James Version

¹⁹ C.S. Lewis, *Mere Christianity*, (New York: Simon & Schuster, 1996) p. 53–54

²⁰ From speech delivered by Ezra Benson on October 25, 1966

²¹ Ezra Benson, United States Secretary of Agriculture from January 21, 1953 to January 20, 1961

²² Benjamin Franklin, *The Works of Dr. Benjamin Franklin*, (New York: W. Van Norden, 1825) p. 87

²³ Thomas Jefferson, John P. Foley, *The Jeffersonian Cyclopedia*, (London: Funk & Wagnalls Company, 1900) p. 605

²⁴ William J. Federer, *America's God and Country Encyclopedia of Quotations*, (St. Louis, MO: Amerisearch, Inc, 2000) p. 392

²⁵ James Russell Lowell , *The Writings of James Russell Lowell, Vol. 6*, (Boston and New York: Houghton, Mifflin and Co., 1893) p. 207

Myth 9

¹ See Genesis 41:54–56; Genesis 47:13–26

² Norman Vincent Peale

³ Jonathan Elliot, James Madison, *The Debates in the Several State Conventions on the Adoption of the Federal Constitution Volume IV*, (Washington, DC, Taylor & Maury, 1863) p. 429

⁴ Thomas Jefferson, Albert Ellery Bergh, *The Writings of Thomas Jefferson Volume III*, (Washington, D.C.: Thomas Jefferson Memorial Association, 1903) p. 320–321

⁵ Thomas Jefferson, *The Writings of Thomas Jefferson, Volume VI*, (New York: Derby & Jackson, 1859) p. 574–575

⁶ Frederic Bastiat, *The Law*, (Whitefish, MT: Kessinger Publishing, 2004) p. 21; *The Law* was originally published as a pamphlet in 1850.

⁷ Frederic Bastiat, *The Law*, (Whitefish, MT: Kessinger Publishing, 2004) p. 18, 14; *The Law* was originally published as a pamphlet in 1850.

⁸ Frederic Bastiat, *The Law*, (Whitefish, MT: Kessinger Publishing, 2004) p. 8; *The Law* was originally published as a pamphlet in 1850.

⁹ The inscription on Davy Crockett's tombstone reads, "Davy Crockett, Pioneer, Patriot, Soldier, Trapper, Explorer, State Legislator, Congressman, Martyred at The Alamo. 1786–1836"

¹⁰ David Crockett, *Life of Col. David Crockett*, (Philadelphia: G.G. Evans, 1860) p. 20–21

¹¹ Oath of Office in place in 1826. The current oath taken by congressman is, "I do solemnly swear (or affirm) that I will support and defend the Constitution of the United States against all enemies, foreign and domestic; that I will bear true faith and allegiance to the same; that I take this obligation freely, without any mental reservation or purpose of evasion; and that I will well and faithfully discharge the duties of the office on which I am about to enter: So help me God."

¹² Edward S. Ellis, *The Life of Colonel David Crockett*, (Philadelphia: Poter & Coates, 1884) p. 141

¹³ Edward S. Ellis, *The Life of Colonel David Crockett*, (Philadelphia: Poter & Coates, 1884) p. 142

¹⁴ Edward S. Ellis, *The Life of Colonel David Crockett*, (Philadelphia: Poter & Coates, 1884) p. 143

¹⁵ Edward S. Ellis, *The Life of Colonel David Crockett*, (Philadelphia: Poter & Coates, 1884) p. 143–144

¹⁶ Edward S. Ellis, *The Life of Colonel David Crockett*, (Philadelphia: Poter & Coates, 1884) p. 144

¹⁷ Edward S. Ellis, *The Life of Colonel David Crockett*, (Philadelphia: Poter & Coates, 1884) p. 145

¹⁸ Edward S. Ellis, *The Life of Colonel David Crockett*, (Philadelphia: Poter & Coates, 1884) p. 145

¹⁹ Edward S. Ellis, *The Life of Colonel David Crockett*, (Philadelphia: Poter & Coates, 1884) p. 145–147

²⁰ Edward S. Ellis, *The Life of Colonel David Crockett*, (Philadelphia: Poter & Coates, 1884) p. 148

²¹ Edward S. Ellis, *The Life of Colonel David Crockett*, (Philadelphia: Poter & Coates, 1884) p. 138–139

²² David Crockett, Introduction by Paul Andrew Hutton, *A Narrative of the Life of David Crockett of the State of Tennessee*, (Lincoln: University of Nebraska Press, 1987) p. XXIX

²³ Nathaniel Wright Stephenson, *Texas and the Mexican War*, (New Haven: Yale University Press, 1921) p. 71

²⁴ Henry Grady Weaver, *The Mainspring of Human Progress*, (Irvington-on-Hudson, NY: Foundation for Economic Education, 1953) p. 40–41

25 Genesis 3:19, New King James Version

26 Exodus 20:15, King James Version

27 Seven social sins identified by Gandhi are wealth without work, pleasure without conscience, knowledge without character, commerce without morality, science without humanity, religion without sacrifice, and politics without principle.

28 1 Timothy 5:8, King James Version

29 "Fable of the Gullible Gull," *Reader's Digest*, October 1950, p. 32

30 Thomas Paine, *Life and Writings of Thomas Paine, Volume IV*, (New York: Vincent Parke and Company, 1908) p. 233

31 Social Security Administration, Office of Research, Evaluation and Statistics, "Social Security Programs in the United States," SSA Publication No. 13–11758, July 1997, p. 108

32 David M. Walker, "The Challenges & Opportunities of Public Service," *Marriott Alumni Magazine*, Fall 2006, p. 24–25

33 The numbers in this table have not been adjusted for inflation because inflation is a hidden tax used by the federal government to fund the welfare programs. In the words of Alan Greenspan, chairman of the Board of Governors of the Federal Reserve of the United States from 1987–2006, "The welfare state is nothing more than a mechanism by which governments confiscate the wealth of the productive members of a society to support a wide variety of welfare schemes. A substantial part of the confiscation is affected by taxation. But the welfare statists were quick to recognize that if they wished to retain political power, the amount of taxation had to be limited and they had to resort to programs of massive deficit spending … to finance welfare expenditures on a large scale… The financial policy of the welfare state requires that there be no way for the owners of wealth to protect themselves. This is the shabby secret of the welfare statists … Deficit spending is simply a scheme for the 'hidden' confiscation of wealth" (Ayn Rand, *Capitalism*, (New York: Signet, 1967) p. 100–101). The value of the American dollar declined in its purchasing power from 100 cents in 1901 to approximately 5 cents in the year 2000. From 1901–2000, the value of the dollar has been devalued by inflation 95 percent—in effect a 95 percent tax. In the words of Ezra Benson, United States Secretary of Agriculture from 1953–1961, "There is one and only one cause of inflation—expansion of the money supply faster than the growth of the nation's material assets. Whether those assets are gold and silver, or food, machines and structures, the creation of money more rapidly than the creation of tangible items of value which people may want to purchase, floods the market place with more dollars than goods and dilutes the accepted value of money already in existence. In America, only the federal government can increase the money supply. Only government can create inflation. The most common method of increasing the money supply today is by spending more than is in the treasury, and then merely printing extra money to make up the difference. Technically this is called 'deficit spending.' Ethically, it is counterfeiting. Morally, it is wrong. Deficit spending, and the inflation it produces, constitutes a hidden tax against all Americans—especially those who own insurance policies, have savings accounts, or who are retired on fixed incomes. Every time the dollar drops another penny in value, it is the same

as if the government had counted up all the money that you and I had in our pockets, in savings, or investments, and then taxed us one cent on each dollar. The tax in this case, however, does not show up on our W-2 forms. It is hidden from view in the nature of higher and still higher prices for all that we buy." Even if the numbers in the table were adjusted for inflation it does not change the trend of increased government spending and cost per household. Adjusted for inflation, from 1901–2000 the spending of the federal government increased by 174 times while population grew by 6.5 times. Thus, the yearly cost per household increased from $627 ($32 adjusted for inflation to 2000 equivalent) in 1901 to $16,949 in 2000—a 27 time increase in cost per household.

[34] Executive Office of the President of the United States, Office of Management and Budget, "Budget of the United States Government, Fiscal Year 2004, Historical Tables," Table 1.1: Summary of Receipts, Outlays and Surpluses or Deficits: 1789–2008, p. 21–22

[35] U.S. Bureau of the Census, "Historical Statistics of the United States, Colonial Time to 1970," (Washington, DC, 1975) p. 43; U.S. Department of Transportation, Federal Highway Administration, Exhibit 1.1 National Summary Statistics: 1960–2000

[36] *Orations of American Orators*, (New York: Colonial Press, 1900) p. 59

[37] Jared Sparks, *The Writings of George Washington, Volume IV*, (Boston: Ferdinand Andrews, 1838) p. 38

MYTH 10

[1] Stanley Lebergott, *The American Economy*, (Princeton, NJ: Princeton University Press, 1976) p. 169–170; $1 million dollars in 1892 is the equivalent of $21 million dollars in 2006.

[2] Thomas J. Stanley, William D. Danko, *The Millionaire Next Door*, (New York: Simon & Schuster, 1996) p. 212, 16

[3] U.S. Department of Treasury, Office of Tax Analysis, "Household Income mobility During the 1980s: A Statistical Assessment Based on Tax Return Data," June 1, 1992

[4] The myth that the rich get richer and the poor get poorer is perpetuated by flawed studies, data, and reports. For example, during the same time period of the Urban Institute study, according to the census data, the income of the bottom fifth of families declined 2.8 percent and the average income of the top fifth rose 16.4 percent. (Cited in: Dick Armey, Joint Economic Committee, "Family Income Growth and Income Equality: Progress or Punishment?", July 1992) This data is inaccurate because it is comparing two samples of income earners which do not consist of the same people. The U.S. Treasury Department found that the median age of the 1st quintile was 21, rising to age 37 in the 3rd and reaching age 61 in the 90th percentile. (U.S. Department of Treasury, Office of Tax Analysis, "Household Income Mobility During the 1980s: A Statistical Assessment Based on Tax Return Data," June 1, 1992) So the census data in 1977 of the bottom income earners would include people who on average were 21 years of age and the comparison sample ten years later from the census data of the bottom income earners would

include people who were on average 11 years old at the time of the first sample who were now on average 21 years old and earning income. To draw conclusion about the income of bottom income earners on such census data would be like a college analyzing how much its graduated students are making by sampling the current students. To get accurate data you have to follow the same group of people over time, which is what the U.S. Treasury Department and Urban Institute studies did.

5   Isabel Sawhill and Mark Condon, "Is U.S. Inequality Really Growing?", *Policy Bites*, June 1992, Washington, D.C., cited in U.S. Department of Treasury, Office of Tax Analysis, "Household Income Mobility During the 1980s: A Statistical Assessment Based on Tax Return Data," June 1, 1992

6   2 Corinthians 9:6, King James Version

7   Robert Rector and Rea Hederman, Jr., "Two Americas: One Rich, One Poor? Understanding Income Inequality in the United States," August 24, 2004

8   U.S. Census Bureau

9   World Bank, World Development Indicators Database, Table: Total GDP 2005, July 1, 2006

10 Central Intelligence Agency, *The World Fact Book*, 2006

11 World Bank, World Development Indicators Database, Table: Total GDP 2005, July 1, 2006

12 Central Intelligence Agency, *The World Fact Book*, 2006

13 Stanley Lebergott, *The American Economy*, (Princeton, NJ: Princeton University Press, 1976) p. 164

14 Ezra Benson, United States Secretary of Agriculture from January 21, 1953 to January 20, 1961

15 Calculated with Social Security Administration's online benefit calculator at www.SSA.gov

16

FREE ENTERPRISE RETIREMENT (Low Income)				
Year	Earnings	12.4% Saving	Interest at 7%	Total in Retirement Account
1	$18,000	$2,232	$156	$2,388
2	$18,000	$2,232	$323	$4,944
3	$18,000	$2,232	$502	$7,678
4	$18,000	$2,232	$694	$10,604
5	$18,000	$2,232	$898	$13,734
6	$18,000	$2,232	$1,118	$17,084
7	$18,000	$2,232	$1,352	$20,668
8	$18,000	$2,232	$1,603	$24,503

Free Enterprise Retirement (Low Income)				
Year	Earnings	12.4% Saving	Interest at 7%	Total in Retirement Account
9	$18,000	$2,232	$1,871	$28,606
10	$18,000	$2,232	$2,159	$32,997
11	$18,000	$2,232	$2,466	$37,695
12	$18,000	$2,232	$2,795	$42,722
13	$18,000	$2,232	$3,147	$48,101
14	$18,000	$2,232	$3,523	$53,856
15	$18,000	$2,232	$3,926	$60,014
16	$18,000	$2,232	$4,357	$66,603
17	$18,000	$2,232	$4,818	$73,654
18	$18,000	$2,232	$5,312	$81,198
19	$18,000	$2,232	$5,840	$89,270
20	$18,000	$2,232	$6,405	$97,907
21	$18,000	$2,232	$7,010	$107,149
22	$18,000	$2,232	$7,657	$117,037
23	$18,000	$2,232	$8,349	$127,618
24	$18,000	$2,232	$9,090	$138,940
25	$18,000	$2,232	$9,882	$151,054
26	$18,000	$2,232	$10,730	$164,016
27	$18,000	$2,232	$11,637	$177,885
28	$18,000	$2,232	$12,608	$192,725
29	$18,000	$2,232	$13,647	$208,604
30	$18,000	$2,232	$14,759	$225,595
31	$18,000	$2,232	$15,948	$243,775
32	$18,000	$2,232	$17,220	$263,227
33	$18,000	$2,232	$18,582	$284,042
34	$18,000	$2,232	$20,039	$306,313
35	$18,000	$2,232	$21,598	$330,143
36	$18,000	$2,232	$23,266	$355,641
37	$18,000	$2,232	$25,051	$382,924
38	$18,000	$2,232	$26,961	$412,117

FREE ENTERPRISE RETIREMENT (Low Income)				
Year	Earnings	12.4% Saving	Interest at 7%	Total in Retirement Account
39	$18,000	$2,232	$29,004	$443,354
40	$18,000	$2,232	$31,191	$476,777
41	$18,000	$2,232	$33,531	$512,539
42	$18,000	$2,232	$36,034	$550,805
43	$18,000	$2,232	$38,713	$591,750
44	$18,000	$2,232	$41,579	$635,560
45	$18,000	$2,232	$44,645	$682,438
Total	$810,000	$100,440	$581,998	$682,438

FREE ENTERPRISE RETIREMENT (Middle Class)				
Year	Earnings	12.4% Saving	Interest at 7%	Total in Retirement Account
1	$48,000	$5,952	$417	$6,369
2	$48,000	$5,952	$862	$13,183
3	$48,000	$5,952	$1,339	$20,475
4	$48,000	$5,952	$1,850	$28,276
5	$48,000	$5,952	$2,396	$36,624
6	$48,000	$5,952	$2,980	$45,557
7	$48,000	$5,952	$3,606	$55,114
8	$48,000	$5,952	$4,275	$65,341
9	$48,000	$5,952	$4,991	$76,283
10	$48,000	$5,952	$5,756	$87,992
11	$48,000	$5,952	$6,576	$100,520
12	$48,000	$5,952	$7,453	$113,925
13	$48,000	$5,952	$8,391	$128,269
14	$48,000	$5,952	$9,395	$143,616
15	$48,000	$5,952	$10,470	$160,038
16	$48,000	$5,952	$11,619	$177,609
17	$48,000	$5,952	$12,849	$196,410
18	$48,000	$5,952	$14,165	$216,528

FREE ENTERPRISE RETIREMENT (Middle Class)				
Year	Earnings	12.4% Saving	Interest at 7%	Total in Retirement Account
19	$48,000	$5,952	$15,574	$238,053
20	$48,000	$5,952	$17,080	$261,086
21	$48,000	$5,952	$18,693	$285,730
22	$48,000	$5,952	$20,418	$312,100
23	$48,000	$5,952	$22,264	$340,316
24	$48,000	$5,952	$24,239	$370,506
25	$48,000	$5,952	$26,352	$402,810
26	$48,000	$5,952	$28,613	$437,376
27	$48,000	$5,952	$31,033	$474,361
28	$48,000	$5,952	$33,622	$513,935
29	$48,000	$5,952	$36,392	$556,279
30	$48,000	$5,952	$39,356	$601,587
31	$48,000	$5,952	$42,528	$650,066
32	$48,000	$5,952	$45,921	$701,940
33	$48,000	$5,952	$49,552	$757,444
34	$48,000	$5,952	$53,438	$816,834
35	$48,000	$5,952	$57,595	$880,381
36	$48,000	$5,952	$62,043	$948,376
37	$48,000	$5,952	$66,803	$1,021,131
38	$48,000	$5,952	$71,896	$1,098,979
39	$48,000	$5,952	$77,345	$1,182,276
40	$48,000	$5,952	$83,176	$1,271,404
41	$48,000	$5,952	$89,415	$1,366,771
42	$48,000	$5,952	$96,091	$1,468,814
43	$48,000	$5,952	$103,234	$1,577,999
44	$48,000	$5,952	$110,877	$1,694,828
45	$48,000	$5,952	$119,055	$1,819,834
Total	$2,160,000	$267,840	$1,551,994	$1,819,834

[17] Ezra Benson, United States Secretary of Agriculture from January 21, 1953 to January 20, 1961

[18] Oliver J. Thatcher, *The Library of Original Sources, Volume X*, (New York: University Research Extension, 1907) p. 29

[19] 2002 Federal Income Tax Rates

[20] Ayn Rand, *The Virtue of Selfishness*, (New York: Signet, 1961) p. 116

[21] Based on 2002 numbers from report produced by the Congressional Budget Office, "Historical Effective Federal Tax Rates:1979 to 2002", March 2005

[22] PBS, "American Porn," Originally Aired on February 7, 2002

[23] Mathew 16:26, King James Version

[24] Malachi 3:5, New King James Version

[25] 1 Timothy 3; 3, 8, Titus 1; 7,11, 1 Peter 5:2, King James Version

[26] Jay Van Andel, *An Enterprising Life*, (New York: Harper Collins, 1998) p. 162

[27] Henry S. Randall, *The Life of Thomas Jefferson, Volume III*, (New York: Derb & Jackson, 1858) p. 648; S.E. Forman, *The Life and Writings of Thomas Jefferson*, (Indianapolis: Bowen–Merrill Company, 1900) p. 159

[28] Abraham Lincoln, *Life and Works of Abraham Lincoln, Volume V*, (New York: The Current Literature Publishing Co., 1907) p. 67–68, 186

MYTH 11

[1] Cecil Selig

[2] Genesis 3:11, New King James Version

[3] Genesis 3:12, New King James Version

[4] Genesis 3:13, New King James Version

[5] Genesis 3:13, New King James Version

[6] Matthew 26:21, King James Version

[7] Matthew 26:22, King James Version

[8] Bernard Shaw, *Plays: Pleasant and Unpleasant, Volume 1*, (Chicago: Herbert S. Stone and Company, 1898) p. 201, Act II in *Mrs. Warren's Profession*

[9] Steve Young, *Steve Young's Hall of Fame Send Off*, July 30, 2005

[10] Saundra Davis Westervelt, *Shifting the Blame*, (New Brunswick, NJ: Rutgers University Press, 1998) p. 4,7

[11] Thomas S. Monson, "In Search of an Abundant Life," Tambuli, Aug. 1988, p. 3

[12] Viktor E. Frankl, *Man's Search for Meaning*, (New York: Pocket Books, 1984) p. 178

[13] Viktor E. Frankl, *Man's Search for Meaning*, (New York: Pocket Books, 1984) p. 178

[14] Stephen R. Covey, *The Seven Habits of Highly Effective People*, (New York: Simon & Schuster, 1989) p. 69–70

[15] George G. Ritchie with Elizabeth Sherrill, *Return from Tomorrow*, (Grand Rapids, MI: Fleming H. Revell, 1978) p. 114–116

[16] Luke 23:34, King James Version

[17] Luke 23:46, New International Version

[18] Matthew 5:33–34, King James Version

[19] Matthew 7:12, Contemporary English Version

[20] H. Burke Peterson, "Removing the Poison of an Unforgiving Spirit," *Ensign*, Nov. 1983, p. 59

[21] Jeffrie G. Murphy, *Getting Even: Forgiveness and Its Limits*, (New York: Oxford University Press, 2003) p. 18–19

[22] Ephesians 4:26, King James Version

[23] II Kings 5:10, New King James Version

[24] II Kings 5:11, New King James Version

[25] II Kings 5:12, New King James Version

[26] II Kings 5:13, New King James Version

[27] Don Soderquist, *Live Learn Lead to Make a Difference*, (Nashville, TN: J. Countryman, 2006) p. 9

MYTH 12

[1] Ayn Rand, *Capitalism*, (New York: Signet, 1967) p. 325

[2] Fred G. Gosman, *Spoiled Rotten*, (New York: Villard, 1992) p. 32

[3] Thomas J. Stanley, William D. Danko, *The Millionaire Next Door*, (New York: Simon & Schuster, 1996) p. 142–143

[4] "What was the Coast Guard's role in the world's first heavier than air flight made by the Wright Brothers on 17 December 1903?" *United States Coast Guard*. Retrieved December 8, 2006, from http://www.uscg.mil/history/faqs/Wright_ Brothers.html

[5] Charles Ludwig, *The Wright Brothers*, (Milford, MI: Mott Media, 1985) p. 172

[6] Fred Howard, *Wilbur and Orville*, (New York: Alfred A. Knopf, 1987) p. 118

[7] Judith A. Dempsey, A *Tale of Two Brothers*, (Victoria, BC, Canada: Trafford Publishing, 2003) p. 26

[8] Fred C. Kelly, *The Wright Brothers*, (Mineola, NY: Dover Publications) p. 8

[9] "The Unlikely Inventors", *Public Broadcasting Service (PBS)*. Retrieved December, 11, 2006, from http://www.pbs.org/wgbh/nova/wright/inventors.html

[10] *Academic American Encyclopedia*, (Princeton, NJ: Arete Publishing Co., 1980) p. 212

[11] "Wright Brothers", *Wikipedia*. Retrieved December 7, 2006, from http:// en.wikipedia.org/wiki/Wright_brothers

[12] Tom D. Crouch, *The Bishop's Boys*, (New York: W. W. Norton & Company, 1989) p. 273–274

[13] Tom D. Crouch, *The Bishop's Boys*, (New York: W. W. Norton & Company, 1989) p. 429

[14] Tom D. Crouch, *The Bishop's Boys*, (New York: W. W. Norton & Company, 1989) p. 429

[15] Fred Howard, *Wilbur and Orville,* (New York: Alfred A. Knopf, 1987) p. 16

[16] Judith A. Dempsey, A *Tale of Two Brothers*, (Victoria, BC, Canada: Trafford Publishing, 2003) p. 26

[17] Tom D. Crouch, *The Bishop's Boys*, (New York: W. W. Norton & Company, 1989) p. 12

[18] Louise Borden and Trish Marx, *Touching the Sky*, (New York: Margaret K. McElderry Books, 2003)

[19] Tom D. Crouch, *The Bishop's Boys*, (New York: W. W. Norton & Company, 1989) p. 465–466

[20] Attributed to Abraham Lincoln but not found in his works.

[21] Elbert Hubbard, *Love, Life & Work*, (The Roycrofters, 1906) p. 84

MYTH 13

[1] Statistic Source: Tiburon; *Entrepreneur*, July 2006, p. 24

[2] U.S. Department of Health and Human Services, retrieved June 20, 2006, from http://www.newstepsolutions.com/debt-statistics.htm

[3] Complied by Rev. Frederick S. Sill, *A Year Book of Colonial Times*, (New York: E.P. Dutton and Company, 1906) p. 15

[4] Thomas J. Stanley, William D. Danko, *The Millionaire Next Door*, (New York: Simon & Schuster, 1996) p. 48, 71

[5] Joseph Addison, *The Works of Joseph Addison, Volume III*, (New York: Harper & Brothers Publishers, 1864) p. 42

[6] Burke Hedges, *Read & Grow Rich*, (Tampa, FL, INTI Publishing, 2000) p. 3

[7] Socrates. *Wikiquote*. Retrieved January 1, 2007, from http://en.wikiquote.org/wiki/Socrates

[8] *Publisher Weekly*, September 18, 2006, p. 4

[9] Mark Twain. *Wikiquote*. Retrieved January 1, 2007, from http://en.wikiquote.org/wiki/Mark_Twain

[10] Robert Kiyosaki, *Rich Dad, Poor Dad*, (Paradise Valley, AZ: TechPress, Inc., 1998) p. 152

[11] Alvin Toffler cited in Jarvis Finger, Neil Flanagan, *The Management Bible*, (London: New Holland Publishers, 2006) p. xv

[12] Revelation 3:17, King James Version

[13] Revelation 3:17, New International Version

[14] Revelation 3:16, English Standard Version

[15] Mark 11:13, New King James Version

[16] Don Soderquist, *Live Learn Lead to Make a Difference*, (Nashville, TN: J. Countryman, 2006) p. 92–93

[17] Isaiah 28:13, King James Version

[18] Matthew 13:12, Inspired Version

[19] Jeremiah 8:13, New International Version

[20] Matthew 5:48, King James Version

[21] David Noel Freedman, *The Anchor Bible Dictionary, Volume 6*, (New York: Double Day, 1992) p. 907
Walter A. Elwell, *Baker Encyclopedia of the Bible, Volume 1*, (Grand Rapids, MI: Baker Book House, 1988) p. 491 During the time of the New Testament, a talent was approximately 750 ounces of silver. A pence was approximately 1/8 of an ounce of silver. Thus, one talent equaled 6,000 pence (750 divided by 1/8). One pence was the day wage of a laborer. To calculate the 2006 dollar value equivalents, I estimated the wage of a 2006 laborer at $50 per day ($6.25/hour for 8 hours) and multiplied that by the number of pence. Thus, one talents in the New Testament is equal to $300,000 in 2006 US currency (6,000 multiplied by $50).

[22] Mathew 25:21, King James Version

[23] Matthew 25:26–27,30, New International Version

24 Matthew 19:30, King James Version
25 Edwin A. Locke, *The Essence of Leadership*, (New York: Lexington Book, 1991) p. 79

MYTH 14

1 Luke 18:10–14, New King James
2 Mathew 6:5, New International Version
3 Blaine Lee, *The Power Principle*, (New York: Simon & Schuster, 1997) p. 132
4 Jeremiah 9:23–24, Contemporary English Version
5 Philippians 2:3, New Century Version
6 Edited by Robert L. Herrmann, *God, Science, and Humility*, (Philadelphia: Templeton Foundation Press, 2000) p. 174
7 C.S. Lewis, *Mere Christianity*, (New York: Simon & Schuster, 1996) p. 110
8 John 12:43, King James Version
9 Haggai 1:6, New International Version
10 Thomas J. Stanley, William D. Danko, *The Millionaire Next Door*, (New York: Simon & Schuster, 1996) p. 88
11 Sam Walton, *Sam Walton*, (New York: Doubleday, 1992) p. 234
12 Matthew 6:20
13 C.S. Lewis, *Mere Christianity*, (New York: Simon & Schuster, 1996) p. 111
14 C.S. Lewis, *Mere Christianity*, (New York: Simon & Schuster, 1996) p. 110
15 Abraham Lincoln
16 Alan L. Chisholm, "Coping With Envy," *Psychotherapy & Spirituality Institute*, retrieved January 11, 2007 from http://www.mindspirit.org/psiqa04.htm
17 Genesis 37:3–4, King James Version
18 Acts 7:9, King James Version
19 *Wal-Mart*, retrieved January 8, 2007, from http://www.walmartfacts.com/content/default.aspx?id=3
20 In 1985, Sam Walton became the wealthiest man in America with a net worth of $2.8 billion ($5.1 billion in 2006 dollars). At his death in 1992, Sam net worth was estimated at $28 billion. He left his ownership in Wal-Mart to his wife and four children whose combined net worth in 2005 was approximately $80 billion.
21 Vance H. Trimble, *Sam Walton*, (New York: Dutton, 1990) p. 6–8
22 Don Soderquist, *Live Learn Lead to Make a Difference*, (Nashville, TN: J. Countryman, 2006) p. 121
23 Bentonville, AK had a population of 11,257 at the 1990 census.
24 Michael Bergdahl, *What I Learned From Sam Walton*, (New York: John Wiley & Sons, 2004) p. 114
25 Daniel Gross, *Forbes Greatest Business Stories of All Times*, (New York: John Wiley & Sons, 1996) p. 274
26 Michael Bergdahl, *What I Learned From Sam Walton*, (New York: John Wiley & Sons, 2004) p. 132

[27] Daniel Gross, *Forbes Greatest Business Stories of All Times*, (New York: John Wiley & Sons, Inc.) p. 280

[28] Don Soderquist, *Live Learn Lead to Make a Difference*, (Nashville, TN: J. Countryman, 2006) p. 44–45

[29] Daniel Gross, *Forbes Greatest Business Stories of All Times*, (New York: John Wiley & Sons, 1996) p. 283

[30] Daniel Gross, *Forbes Greatest Business Stories of All Times*, (New York: John Wiley & Sons, 1996) p. 270

[31] C.S. Lewis, *Mere Christianity*, (New York: Simon & Schuster, 1996) p. 114

[32] Rabindranath Togare

[33] Proverbs 16:18, King James Version

[34] Psalms 131:1, Good News Translation

[35] Matthew 23:11, King James Version

MYTH 15

[1] William S. Sahakian, Mabel Lewis Sahakian, *Ideas of the Great Philosophers*, (New York: Barnes & Noble Books, 1993) p. 28

[2] John 13:17, King James Version

[3] The National Commission on Terrorist Attacks Upon the United States, The 9/11 Commission Repot, (Washington, D.C.: Government Printing Office, 2004) p. xv

[4] David Hench, "Ticket Agent Haunted by Brush with 9/11 Hijackers," *The Portland Press Herald*, March 6, 2005

[5] David Hench, "Ticket Agent Haunted by Brush with 9/11 Hijackers," *The Portland Press Herald*, March 6, 2005

[6] David Hench, "Ticket Agent Haunted by Brush with 9/11 Hijackers," *The Portland Press Herald*, March 6, 2005

[7] September 11, 2005, "I Was the One," The Oprah Winfrey Show, Harpo Productions, Inc.

[8] David Hench, "Ticket Agent Haunted by Brush with 9/11 Hijackers," *The Portland Press Herald*, March 6, 2005

[9] David Hench, "Ticket Agent Haunted by Brush with 9/11 Hijackers," *The Portland Press Herald*, March 6, 2005

[10] September 11, 2005, "I Was the One," The Oprah Winfrey Show, Harpo Productions, Inc.

[11] Drew Griffin (CNN Correspondent), March 3, 2006, "Airline Worker Remembers Gut Feelings of 9/11," CNN

[12] The National Commission on Terrorist Attacks Upon the United States, *The 9/11 Commission Report*, (Washington, D.C.: Government Printing Office, 2004) p. 1–6

[13] The National Commission on Terrorist Attacks Upon the United States, *The 9/11 Commission Report, Executive Summary*, (Washington, D.C.: Government Printing Office, 2004) p. 1

[14] David Hench, "Ticket Agent Haunted by Brush with 9/11 Hijackers," *The Portland Press Herald*, March 6, 2005

15 September 11, 2005, "I Was the One," The Oprah Winfrey Show, Harpo Productions, Inc.

16 David Hench, "Ticket Agent Haunted by Brush with 9/11 Hijackers," *The Portland Press Herald*, March 6, 2005

17 Drew Griffin (CNN Correspondent), March 3, 2006, "Airline Worker Remembers Gut Feelings of 9/11," CNN

18 Drew Griffin (CNN Correspondent), March 3, 2006, "Airline Worker Remembers Gut Feelings of 9/11," CNN

19 Michael Dorman, "An Untold Story of 9/11," *Newsday*, April 17, 2006

20 David Hench, "Ticket Agent Haunted by Brush with 9/11 Hijackers," *The Portland Press Herald*, March 6, 2005

21 Galileo Galilei

22 Hyrum W. Smith, *The Ten Natural Laws of Successful Time and Life Management*, (New York: Warner Books, 1994) p. 147

23 Romans 12:2, New Living Translation

24 Henry David Thoreau, *Thoreau's Thoughts*, (Boston: Houghton, Mifflin and Company, 1890) p. 11

25 Daniel 3:4–6, English Standard Version

26 Daniel 3:15–16,18, English Standard Version

27 Daniel 6

28 Job 27:5, Contemporary English Version

29 Job 27:5–6, New International Version

30 Acts 5:19–21, New International Version

31 Acts 5:28–29, New International Version

32 Henri-Frédéric Amiel, *Amiel's Journal*, (London, Macmillan and Co., 1893) p. 44

33 1 Corinthians 2:14, New King James

34 James 4:4, New American Standard Bible

35 1 Timothy 4:1, New International Version

36 1 Timothy 1:19, Contemporary English Version

37 Stephen R. Covey, A. Roger Merrill, Rebecca R. Merrill, *First Things First*, (New York: Simon & Schuster, 1994) p. 175, 178

38 Exodus 20:15, King James Version

39 Psalm 37:21, New American Standard

40 Griffin (CNN Correspondent), March 3, 2006, "Airline Worker Remembers Gut Feelings of 9/11," CNN

41 Proverbs 20:7, New Living Translation

Мүтн 16

1 Quinn McKay, *The Bottom Line on Integrity*, (Salt Lake City, UT: Gibbs Smith, 2004) p.71–72

2 Quinn McKay, *The Bottom Line on Integrity*, (Salt Lake City, UT: Gibbs Smith, 2004) p. 72–73

3 Exodus 20:16, King James Version

4 Exodus 20:15, King James Version

5 Matthew 16:26, New Century Version

[6] PBS, "American Porn," Originally Aired on February 7, 2002

[7] W. Steve Albrecht, *Business with Integrity*, (Provo, UT: Brigham Young University Press, 2005) p. 5–6

[8] James Allanson Picton, *Spinoza: A Handbook to the Ethics*, (Archibald Constable and Company, 1907) p. 236

[9] 1 Timothy 1:19, New Century Version

[10] John Breen, Mark Teeuwen, *Shinto in History*, (Honolulu: University of Hawaii Press, 2000) p. 169

[11] David Green, *More Than a Hobby*, (Nashville, TN: Thomas Nelson, 2005) p. 122

[12] Jay Van Andel, *An Enterprising Life*, (New York: Harper Collins, 1998) p. 53–54

[13] Kevin Rollins, Former President/CEO of Dell

[14] Donald Trump, "The Bottom Line—Your Guideline," *Inside Trump Tower Newsletter*, Issue 14: It's Not Personal, It's Business, August 30, 2005

[15] CBS, "Porn in the U.S.A.," Originally Aired on September 5, 2004

[16] American Family Association, "Omni Hotels Drop In-Room Porn," *AFA Journal*, January 2000: Volume 24, Issue 1

[17] *The Big Book of Business Quotations*, (New York: Basic Books, 2003) p. 37

[18] *The Big Book of Business Quotations*, (New York: Basic Books, 2003) p. 106

[19] James E. Faust, "Integrity, the Mother of Many Virtues," *Ensign*, May 1982

[20] Malachi 3:5, New King James Version

[21] Quinn McKay, *The Bottom Line on Integrity*, (Salt Lake City, UT: Gibbs Smith, 2004) p. 46

[22] Daniel Yankelovich, *Profit with Honor*, (New Haven, CT: Yale University Press, 2006) p. 63

[23] William H. Child, *Business with Integrity*, (Provo, UT: Brigham Young University Press, 2005) p. 21

[24] Exodus 20:15, King James Version

[25] Ephesians 4:28, New King James Version

[26] Quinn McKay, *The Bottom Line on Integrity*, (Salt Lake City, UT: Gibbs Smith, 2004) p. 147

[27] Quinn McKay, *The Bottom Line on Integrity*, (Salt Lake City, UT: Gibbs Smith, 2004) p. 146

[28] Acts 5:29, King James Version

[29] Jon M. Huntsman, *Winners Never Cheat*, Upper Saddle River, NJ: Wharton School Publishing, 2005, p. 8

[30] Robert C. Gay, *Business with Integrity*, (Provo, UT: Brigham Young University Press, 2005) p. 49

[31] Jon M. Huntsman, *Winners Never Cheat*, Upper Saddle River, NJ: Wharton School Publishing, 2005, p. 9–11

[32] Jon M. Huntsman, Sr., *Business with Integrity*, (Provo, UT: Brigham Young University Press, 2005) p. 91–92

[33] Jon M. Huntsman, *Winners Never Cheat*, Upper Saddle River, NJ: Wharton School Publishing, 2005, p. 40–41

[34] Ned C. Hill, *Business with Integrity*, (Provo, UT: Brigham Young University Press, 2005) p. 79–80

35 Mission and Values, *Huntsman International*, Retrieved January 18, 2007, from http://www.huntsman.com/index.cfm?PageID=831

36 Jon M. Huntsman, *Winners Never Cheat*, Upper Saddle River, NJ: Wharton School Publishing, 2005, p. 9

37 1 King 3:5, Contemporary English Version
1 Kings 3:9, New International Version

39 1 King 3:11, Contemporary English Version

40 Jared Sparks, *The Writings of George Washington, Volume IX*, (Boston, Little, Brown and Company, 1855) p. 421

MYTH 17

1 Vice Admiral James B. Stockdale, *A Vietnam Experience*, (Stanford, CA, Hoover Press, 1984) p. 28

2 Jim Collin, *Good to Great*, (New York: Harper Collins, 2001) p. 84–85

3 Viktor E. Frankl, *Man's Search for Meaning*, (New York: Pocket Books, 1984) p. 96

4 William Chambers, *The Moral Class-Book*, (London: W. and R. Chambers, 1856) p. 126–128

5 Shad Helmstetter, *What to Say When You Talk to Your Self*, (New York: Pocket Books, 1986) p. 20

6 Lou Tice, *Personal Coaching for Results*, (Nashville, TN: Nelson, 1997) p. 93

7 Mark Victor Hansen, Future Diary, (Newport Beach, CA: Mark Victor Hansen Publishing, 1997) p. 43

8 Vishnu Karmaker and Thomas Whitney, *Mental Mechanics of Archery*, (Littleton, CO: Center Vision, Inc., 2006) p. 7

9 Philippians 4:13, New King James Version

MYTH 18

1 Jon M. Huntsman, Sr., *Business with Integrity*, (Provo, UT: Brigham Young University Press, 2005) p. 94

2 David J. Schwartz, *The Magic of Thinking Big*, New York: Simon and Schuster, 1959, p. 204

3 2 Corinthians 9:6, King James Version

4 Anthony Robbins, *Unlimited Power*, (New York: Fireside, 1997) p. 113–114

5 Matthew 5:48, Contemporary English Version

6 Mathew 7:24

7 Matthew 7:26–27

8 Matthew 15:14, King James Version

9 1 Corinthians 11:1, New International Version

MYTH 19

1 Warren G. Bennis, Burt Nanus, *Leaders: Strategies for Taking Charge*, (New York: HarperCollins, 2003) p. 70

2 Michael Pearn, Chris Mulrooney, and Tim Payne, *Ending the Blame Culture*, (Brookfield, VT, Gower Publishing, 1998) p. 11–12

[3] Sylvester Stallone, *The Official Rocky Scrapbook*, (New York: Grosset & Dunlap, 1977)

Chris Nashawaty, "The Right Hook," *Entertainment Weekly*, February 18, 2002; Anthony Robbins, "An Oscar-Winning Strategy," *Unleash the Power Within: Personal Coaching from Anthony Robbins That Will Transform Your Life!* (Audio CD), (Nile, IL: Nightingale-Conant, 2005)

[4] Jacob Wassermann, *Columbus, Don Quixote of the Seas*, (Boston: Little, Brown and Co., 1930) p. 19–20

[5] Words written by Columbus in his ship log, October 11, 1492; Bill Halamandaris, *The Heart of America: Ten Core Values That Make Our Country Great*, Deerfield Beach, FL: Health Communications, Inc., 2004) p. 30

[6] William D. Phillips, Jr. and Carla Rahn Phillips, *The Worlds of Christopher Columbus*, (New York: Cambridge University Press, 1992) p. 152–153

MYTH 20

[1] Charles A. Coonradt, *The Game of Work*, (Salt Lake City: Shadow Mountain, 1991) p. 16

[2] Charles A. Coonradt, *The Game of Work*, (Salt Lake City: Shadow Mountain, 1991) p. xx

[3] Simon Firth, "Nearly 40 Years Later, A Bing Study Is Still Going," *The Bing Times*, November 2005, p. 7

[4] Genesis 25:29–34, New International Version

[5] Nate Chapnick, "Top 10 Vehicles Owned by Billionaires," *Forbes*, Retrieved January 9, 2007 from http://www.forbesautos.com/advice/toptens/billionaire2006/01-billionaires.html

[6] Calculated at 6 percent interest

[7] Genesis 41

[8] Matthew 24:6–8

[9] Mathew 25:8–9, King James Version

[10] Matthew 25:11–12, New International Version

[11] Matthew 25:13, King James Version

[12] J. Reuben Clark, *Conference Report*, April 1938, p. 103

[13] Calculated at 10 percent return

PAY YOURSELF FIRST				
Year	Earnings	10% Saving	Interest at 10%	Total in Account
1	$45,000	$4,500	$450	$4,950
2	$45,000	$4,500	$945	$10,395
3	$45,000	$4,500	$1,490	$16,385
4	$45,000	$4,500	$2,088	$22,973
5	$45,000	$4,500	$2,747	$30,220
6	$45,000	$4,500	$3,472	$38,192
7	$45,000	$4,500	$4,269	$46,961
8	$45,000	$4,500	$5,146	$56,608
9	$45,000	$4,500	$6,111	$67,218
10	$45,000	$4,500	$7,172	$78,890
11	$45,000	$4,500	$8,339	$91,729
12	$45,000	$4,500	$9,623	$105,852
13	$45,000	$4,500	$11,035	$121,387
14	$45,000	$4,500	$12,589	$138,476
15	$45,000	$4,500	$14,298	$157,274
16	$45,000	$4,500	$16,177	$177,951
17	$45,000	$4,500	$18,245	$200,696
18	$45,000	$4,500	$20,520	$225,716
19	$45,000	$4,500	$23,022	$253,237
20	$45,000	$4,500	$25,774	$283,511
21	$45,000	$4,500	$28,801	$316,812
22	$45,000	$4,500	$32,131	$353,444
23	$45,000	$4,500	$35,794	$393,738
24	$45,000	$4,500	$39,824	$438,062
25	$45,000	$4,500	$44,256	$486,818
26	$45,000	$4,500	$49,132	$540,450
27	$45,000	$4,500	$54,495	$599,445
28	$45,000	$4,500	$60,394	$664,339
29	$45,000	$4,500	$66,884	$735,723
30	$45,000	$4,500	$74,022	$814,245
31	$45,000	$4,500	$81,875	$900,620
32	$45,000	$4,500	$90,512	$995,632
33	$45,000	$4,500	$100,013	$1,100,145
34	$45,000	$4,500	$110,465	$1,215,110
35	$45,000	$4,500	$121,961	$1,341,571
36	$45,000	$4,500	$134,607	$1,480,678
37	$45,000	$4,500	$148,518	$1,633,695
38	$45,000	$4,500	$163,820	$1,802,015
39	$45,000	$4,500	$180,652	$1,987,167
40	$45,000	$4,500	$199,167	$2,190,833
Total	$1,800,000	$180,000	$2,010,833	$2,190,833

SECURITY GUARD TO MILLIONAIRE				
Year	Income	Saving	Account Value	Return
1978	$15,195	$152	N/A	N/A
1979	$16,924	$390	N/A	N/A
1980	$22,003	$1,100	N/A	N/A
1981	$33,429	$1,413	N/A	N/A
1982	$33,878	$1,665	$11,655	N/A
1983	$36,419	$1,813	$19,478	51.6%
1984	$36,640	$2,732	$28,192	30.7%
1985	$37,008	$3,200	$45,558	50.2%
1986	$38,783	$3,363	$72,550	51.9%
1987	$41,153	$3,577	N/A	N/A
1988	$43,374	$4,098	$95,412	N/A
1989	$47,168	$3,923	$153,579	56.9%
1990	$45,125	$4,042	$163,536	3.9%
1991	$46,335	$4,029	$192,803	15.4%
1992	$45,243	$4,395	$231,258	17.7%
1993	$52,574	$5,234	$204,229	-14.0%
1994	$59,071	$4,693	$230,079	10.4%
1995	$56,016	$5,415	$333,022	42.4%
1996	$62,917	$5,162	$385,178	14.1%
1997	$57,736	$5,356	$514,779	32.3%
1998	$59,510	$5,296	$667,571	28.7%
1999	$61,413	$6,242	$680,672	1.0%
2000	$73,202	$6,022	$667,992	-2.7%
2001	$68,663	$6,643	$570,213	-15.6%
2002	$74,557	$6,643	$615,475	6.8%
2003	$78,039	$6,958	$668,837	7.5%
2004	$80,693	$7,048	$751,467	11.3%
2005	$88,152	$7,712	$777,515	2.4%
2006	$96,382	$8,213	$880,010	12.1%
2007 estimate*	$102,568	$8,739	$1,054,631	18.9%
Totals	**$1,610,170**	**$135,268**	**$1,054,631**	**18.9%**

*Estimate based on average annual raise, average percent savings and average annual return.

16 Dwight Edwards Marvin, *The Antiquity of Proverbs*, (New York: G.P. Putnam's Sons, 1922) p. 188

17 Patricia Sullivan, "William 'Bud' Post III; Unhappy Lottery Winner," *Washington Post*, January 20, 2006, page B08

18 Clark DeLeon, "Divvying up Ben: Let's Try for 200 More," *Philadelphia Inquirer*, February 7, 1993, page B02

19 Benjamin Franklin, *Essays and Letters, Volume 1*, (New York: R. & W.A. Barton & Co., 1821) p. 91

[20] Romans 13:8, New International Version

[21] 2 Kings 4:7, King James Version

[22] Proverbs 22:7, English Standard Version

[23] Napoleon Hill, *The Laws of Success, Volume 1*, (Los Angeles: Renaissance Books, 2001) p. 253

[24] Luke 16:13, New International Version

[25] Benjamin Franklin, *Essays and Letters, Volume 1*, (New York: R. & W.A. Barton & Co., 1821) p. 92–94

MYTH 21

[1] Mark Henricks, "Failure to Launch?" *Entrepreneur Magazine*, February 2007

[2] Bureau of Labor Statistics, May 2005 Monthly Labor Review

[3] Michael E. Gerber, *The E-Myth Revisited*, (New York: HarperCollins, 1995) p. 82

[4] Jay Van Andel, *An Enterprising Life*, (New York: Harper Collins, 1998) p. 53

[5] David Noel Freedman, *The Anchor Bible Dictionary, Volume 6*, (New York: Double Day, 1992) p. 907
Walter A. Elwell, *Baker Encyclopedia of the Bible, Volume 1*, (Grand Rapids, MI: Baker Book House, 1988) p. 491 During the time of the New Testament, a talent was approximately 750 ounces of silver. A pence was approximately 1/8 of an ounce of silver. Thus, one talent equaled 6,000 pence (750 divided by 1/8). One pence was the day wage of a laborer. To calculate the 2006 dollar value equivalents, I estimated the wage of a 2006 laborer at $50 per day ($6.25/hour for 8 hours) and multiplied that by the number of pence. Thus, one talents in the New Testament is equal to $300,000 in 2006 US currency (6,000 multiplied by $50).

[6] Matthew 25:25, King James Version

[7] Exodus 15

[8] Exodus 16:3, Contemporary English Version

[9] Exodus 16:3, Contemporary English Version

[10] Ayn Rand, *Atlas Shrugged*, (New York: Dutton, 1992) p. 1064

[11] Henry Ford, *My Philosophy of Industry*, (New York: Coward-McCan, Inc., 1929) p. 25

[12] Retrieved March 12, 2007, from http://www.1800contacts.com/ ExternalRelations/TheCompanyHistory.htm

[13] Retrieved March 12, 2007, from http://en.wikipedia.org/wiki/Post-it_note

[14] Harold C. Livesay, *American Made*, (New York : Pearson-Longman, 2007) p. 121

[15] Ray Kroc, *Grinding it Out*, (New York: St. Martin's Paperback, 1987) p. 86

[16] Michael E. Gerber, *The E-Myth Revisited*, (New York: HarperCollins, 1995) p. 92

[17] Siri Schubert, "Bound to Succeed," *Business 2.0*, March 16, 2005; Karen E. Spaeder, "Designed to Sell, *Entrepreneur*, May 2006 p. 50

[18] Vance H. Trimble, *Sam Walton*, (New York: Dutton, 1990) p. 138

[19] *Wal-Mart*, Retrieved March 14, 2007 from http://walmartstores.com/ GlobalWMStoresWeb/navigate.do?catg=6

20 *McDonald's Corporation*, Retrieved March 14, 2007, from http://mcdonalds.com/ corp/about/mcd_history_pg1/mcd_history_pg3.html

21 Thomas J. Stanley, *The Millionaire Mind*, (Kansas City: Andrews McMeel Publishing, 2000) p. 184

22 U.S. Census Bureau, Current Population Survey, 2006 Annual Social and Economic Supplement

23 *Entrepreneur Magazine*, March 2007, p. 70

24 David Rockefeller, Sr., grandson of John D. Rockefeller, Sr. (1839–1937). John D. Rockefeller, Sr. is the founder of Standard Oil, and in 1916 he became the world's first billionaire ($18 billion in 2006 dollars). The world's largest company ExxonMobil with $378 billion in revenue in 2006 is the descendant of Standard Oil.

25 Luke 14:28, King James Version

MYTH 22
None

MYTH 23

1 C.S Lewis, *Mere Christianity*, (New York: Simon & Schuster, 1996) p.166

2 Matthew 18:18–25, King James Version

3 Luke 18:26, King James Version

4 Mark 10:24, King James Version, bold added

5 Luke 6:20, King James Version

6 1Timothy 6:17, King James Version

7 Deuteronomy 8:18, King James Version

8 Genesis 13:2, King James Version

9 Genesis 26:13–14, English Standard Version

10 Mathew 27:57, King James Version

11 Matthew 6:33, King James Version

12 Luke 14:26, King James Version

13 Herb Miller, *Money Is Everything*, Nashville: Discipleship Resources, 1994, p. 23

14 1 Timothy 6:10, King James Version, bold added

15 David Van Biema, Jeff Chu, "Does God Want You To Be Rich?" *Time Magazine*, September 10, 2006

16 Ephesians 4:6, New Century Version

17 Genesis 3:19, New King James Version

18 1 Timothy 5:8, King James Version

19 *Brother Lawrence*, (New York: Fleming H. Revell, 1895) p. 11, 19

20 *Brother Lawrence*, (New York: Fleming H. Revell, 1895) p. 13, 20

21 Sam Walton, *Sam Walton*, (New York: Doubleday, 1992) p. 252–253

22 Rick Warren, *The Purpose Driven Life*, (Grand Rapids, MI: Zondervan, 2002) p. 88

23 Colossians 3:23, New American Standard Bible

24 Luke 12:15, New International Version

25 Isaiah 56:11, King James Version

26 Ecclesiastes 5:10, New International Version

27 Luke 12:16–20, New International Version

28 Luke 16:19–23, New International Version

29 Malachi 3:5, New King James Version

30 1 Timothy 3:3,8; Titus 1:7,11; 1 Peter 5:2, King James Version

31 Mathew 16:26, King James Version

32 Joshua 1:8, New International Version

33 Jan D. Andersen, "Financial Freedom on Any Income," Assistant Professor of Family and Consumer Sciences, California State University, Sacramento

34 Matthew 6:19

35 Herb Miller, *Money Is Everything*, (Nashville: Discipleship Resources, 1994) p. 19

36 John Wanamaker (1838–1922), U.S. Business Man

37 Thomas J. Stanley, William D. Danko, *The Millionaire Next Door*, (New York: Simon & Schuster, 1996) p. 46

38 Luke 16:10–11, New Life Version

MYTH 24

1 Juan Williams, *Eyes on the Prize: America's Civil Rights Years, 1954–1965* (New York: Viking Penguin Inc., 1987) p. 57

2 Matthew 25:32–45, King James Version

3 "Smallpox," *Wikipedia*. Retrieved April 16, 2007, from http://en.wikipedia.org/wiki/Smallpox

4 David R. Henderson, "Income Mobility: Alive and Well," Retrieved April 10, 2007, from http://www.hoover.org/publications/digest/2905081.html

5 Andrew Carnegie

6 Andrew Carnegie, *The Gospel of Wealth and Other Timely Essays*, (New York: The Century Co., 1901) p. 15

7 Thomas Jefferson, *The Writings of Thomas Jefferson, Volume XI*, (Washington, D.C.: Thomas Jefferson Memorial Association, 1903) p. 92–93

8 Lady Katie Magnus, *Jewish Portraits*, (London: T. Fisher Unwin, 1888) p. 151

9 Jon M. Huntsman, Sr., *Business with Integrity*, (Provo, UT: Brigham Young University Press, 2005) p. 98, 101–102

10 James 1:27, New International Version

11 Jon M. Huntsman, *Winners Never Cheat*, (Upper Saddle River, NJ: Wharton School Publishing, 2005) p. 167

12 C.S. Lewis, *Mere Christianity*, (New York: Simon & Schuster, 1996) p. 82

13 Luke 12:15–21, English Standard Version

14 Jon M. Huntsman, *Winners Never Cheat*, (Upper Saddle River, NJ: Wharton School Publishing, 2005) p. 159

15 David Green, *More Than a Hobby*, (Nashville, TN: Thomas Nelson, 2005) p. 195–196

16 Acts 4:32, 34, New International Version

17 Mark Victor Hansen, *The Miracle of Tithing*, p. 49

18 1 Kings 17:13–16, English Standard Version

19 Matthew 19:29, Contemporary English Version

[20] Hyrum Smith, *The 10 Natural Laws of Successful Time and Life Management,* (New York: Warner Books, 1994) p. 203

[21] Mark Victor Hansen, *The Miracle of Tithing,* p. 9

[22] Luke 6:38, Contemporary English Version

[23] Genesis 14:20, Contemporary English Version

[24] Genesis 28:22, New International Version

[25] Leviticus 27:30, New International Version; Deuteronomy 14:22, King James Version

[26] Malachi 3:10–11, New International Version

[27] Matthew 25:21, King James Version; Psalms 95:11, King James Version

[28] 2 Corinthians 9:7, New King James Version

CONCLUSION

[1] John F. Kennedy

[2] John 8:32, New King James Version

[3] Matthew 23:11, King James Version

[4] Proverbs 20:7, New Living Translation

[5] Philippians 4:13, New King James Version

[6] 2 Corinthians 9:7, New King James Version

[7] Philippians 4:13, New King James Version

[8] Samuel W. Bailey, *Homage of Eminent Persons to THE BOOK,* (New York: 1871) p.12

ILLUSTRATION CREDITS

ABOUT THE AUTHOR

Cameron began writing books and learning to speed read while in college. By his senior year, Cameron was a published author and was reading at a rate of over 3,000 words a minute. Upon graduating with honors in business, he began his entrepreneurial career and founded several companies. He took one of his companies from an idea to over $1 million in revenue in its second year and then grew the business to over $10 million in revenue its fifth year. He is currently the president of three organizations: The Ladder to Success Corporation—a for-profit marketing consulting company; the Claim Your Victory Corporation, a for-profit company involved in the exploration for oil and natural gas resources; and the Does Your Bag Have Holes? Foundation, an educational charity. In addition to his business successes, Cameron has served in an overseas missionary ministry and is currently a volunteer pastor. He is a recipient of the Circle of Honor Award for being an "exceptional example of honor, integrity, and commitment." Cameron grew up in Oregon and is married to the former Paula Brackett of Indiana. They are the parents of two children, Mitchell and Kennedy.

ABOUT THE DOES YOUR BAG HAVE HOLES? FOUNDATION™

The Foundation's mission is to inspire the world to learn and live the principles of prosperity. The Foundation teaches these principles through real-life stories and powerful parables. These learning tools demonstrate ways that people can infuse spirituality into everyday living. Through engaging books and seminars, the Foundation provides a clear vision of financial and spiritual freedom within everyone's reach. All revenue are used to further the Foundation's mission and for other humanitarian efforts.

The author of this book, Cameron C. Taylor, as well as other experts affiliated with the Foundation are available to present to businesses, associations, schools, and churches on a wide range of topics. To schedule a speaker, contact the Foundation.

428 E. Thunderbird Road #504, Phoenix, AZ 85022
Phone: 1-877-No-Holes (664-6537)
Fax: 1-480-393-4432
Email: Speaker@DoesYourBagHaveHoles.org

GIFTS FROM THE
DOES YOUR BAG HAVE HOLES? FOUNDATION

The Does Your Bag Have Holes? Newsletter contains exclusive articles, inspiring stories, practical advice, and biblical insights to help you live a prosperous life.

To receive a FREE subscription, go to www.DoesYourBagHaveHoles.org and click on the Newsletter link

~~$12/Year Retail~~

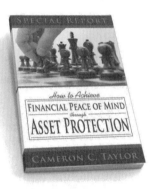

*Special Report:
How to Achieve Financial
Peace of Mind through Asset Protection*

From this special report, you will learn strategies most advisors are unaware of including:

~~$19.95 Retail~~

- How to legally save up to 40% in income taxes each year.
- How to protect 100% of your professional and personal assets from a lawsuit.
- Legal strategies that eliminate 100% of capital gains tax on the sale of real estate, a business, or other assets.
- Tools you can use to pass assets to your heirs tax-free.
- How to use asset protection entities (C-Corporations, S-Corporations, LLCs, Trusts, Limited Partnerships) to achieve your financial goals.

**To receive a FREE copy, go to
www.DoesYourBagHaveHoles.org
and click on the Special Reports link**

The 10 Habits of the Prosperous Software System™

Join the Ranks of the Prosperous and Financially Independent by Using This Proven, Easy-to-Use, Step-by-Step System

DESCRIPTION

This system will help you to live the 10 habits of the prosperous. This program will make it easy for you to set and monitor your financial goals, live below your income, build up savings and investments, and create financial independence. As a result, you will become the master of your finances and achieve financial peace of mind.

Price: **$19.95**
Retail Price: ~~$49.95~~
You Save: $30.00 (60%)

30-Day Money Back Guarantee

To order this software, go to www.DoesYourBagHaveHoles.org and click on Software or call 1-877-No-Holes (664-6537)

E-Books

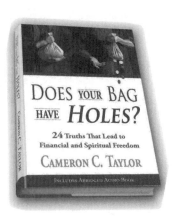

Does Your Bag Have Holes?
E-Book (PDF)

- Easily search the book for reference and research
- Cut and paste the text for presentations and lessons
- Easy to take anywhere
- Full color images

Price: $4.95
Retail Price: ~~$17.95~~
You Save: $13.00 (73%)

Statement of Excellence Workbook
E-Book (PDF)

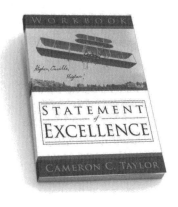

Designed to help you discover, write down, and achieve your inspired goals and mission. This mind-enlarging, life-improving, and entertaining workbook takes you step-by-step through the process. Completing and implementing the exercises in the Statement of Excellence Workbook will put you in the top 3 percent of achievers in the world.

Price: $2.95
Retail Price: ~~$14.95~~
You Save: $12.00 (80%)

SHARE THE BOOK WITH OTHERS

As an exclusive offer to purchasers of the book, the Does Your Bag Have Holes? Foundation is offering a highly discounted price to allow you to share this book with family, friends, employees, congregation members, co-workers, etc.

"I recommend sharing this message with all your loved ones."
–Lee Gillie, High School Science Teacher

"It is a must-read for all Christians!"
–Finn Laursen, Executive Director,
Christian Educators Association International

- Only $6 per book—you save $11.95 (67%) off retail price
- FREE abridged audio book included with each book
- FREE shipping

ORDER FORM

Product Description	Retail Price	Discount Price	# of Cases	Total
Case of 22 Books	~~$395~~	$132		
Shipping				Free
Total Order Amount				

We accept checks, Visa, MC, AE, and Discover

Name_____

Shipping Address_____

City/State/Zip_____

Phone Number_____

Email _____

Credit Card #_____

Exp. Date:_____CSC:_____(3 digit number on back of card)

To order, mail this form to:
Does Your Bag Have Holes? Foundation
428 E. Thunderbird Road #504, Phoenix, AZ 85002
Or call 1-877-No-Holes (664-6537)

Share The Book With Others

As an exclusive offer to purchasers of the book, the Does Your Bag Have Holes? Foundation is offering a highly discounted price to allow you to share this book with family, friends, employees, congregation members, co-workers, etc.

"I recommend sharing this message with all your loved ones."
–Lee Gillie, High School Science Teacher

"It is a must-read for all Christians!"
–Finn Laursen, Executive Director,
Christian Educators Association International

- Only $6 per book—you save $11.95 (67%) off retail price
- FREE abridged audio book included with each book
- FREE shipping

Order Form

Product Description	Retail Price	Discount Price	# of Cases	Total
Case of 22 Books	~~$395~~	$132		
Shipping				Free
Total Order Amount				

We accept checks, Visa, MC, AE, and Discover

Name_____

Shipping Address_____

City/State/Zip_____

Phone Number_____

Email _____

Credit Card #_____

Exp. Date:_____CSC:_____(3 digit number on back of card)

To order, mail this form to:
Does Your Bag Have Holes? Foundation
428 E. Thunderbird Road #504, Phoenix, AZ 85002
Or call 1-877-No-Holes (664-6537)